Ireland's Revolutionary Diplomat

BARRY WHELAN

Ireland's Revolutionary Diplomat

A Biography of Leopold Kerney

UNIVERSITY OF NOTRE DAME PRESS
NOTRE DAME, INDIANA

University of Notre Dame Press
Notre Dame, Indiana 46556
undpress.nd.edu

Copyright © 2019 by the University of Notre Dame

Published in the United States of America

Library of Congress Cataloging-in-Publication Data

Names: Whelan, Barry, 1984– author.
Title: Ireland's revolutionary diplomat : a biography of Leopold Kerney /
    Barry Whelan.
Description: Notre Dame, Indiana : University of Notre Dame Press, [2019] |
    Includes bibliographical references and index. |
Identifiers: LCCN 2019002014 (print) | LCCN 2019005070 (ebook) |
    ISBN 9780268105075 (pdf) | ISBN 9780268105082 (epub) | ISBN
    9780268105051 (hardback : alk. paper) | ISBN 0268105057 (hardback :
    alk. paper) | ISBN 9780268105068 (pbk. : alk. paper) | ISBN 0268105065
    (pbk. : alk. paper)
Subjects: LCSH: Kerney, Leopold, 1881–1962. | Kerney, Leopold,
    1881–1962—Political and social views. | Ambassadors—Ireland—
    Biography. | Revolutionaries—Ireland—Biography. | Ireland—Foreign
    relations—1922– | Ireland—Foreign relations—Europe. | Europe—
    Foreign relations—Ireland. | Europe—Politics and government—
    1918–1945. | Europe—History, Military—20th century.
Classification: LCC DA965.K47 (ebook) | LCC DA965.K47 W54 2019
    (print) | DDC 327.4170092 [B]—dc23
LC record available at https://lccn.loc.gov/2019002014

♾ *This paper meets the requirements of ANSI/NISO Z39.48-1992
(Permanence of Paper).*

CONTENTS

AGA   Archivo General de Administración
AMAE   Archivo del Ministerio de Asuntos Exteriores
BMH   Bureau of Military History
BNAK   British National Archives, Kew
CID   Criminal Investigation Department
CPIA   Communist Party of Ireland Archive
CPGB   Communist Party of Great Britain
C3   Garda crime and security branch
DCLA   Dublin City Public Library and Archives
DÉD   Dáil Éireann Debates
DFA   Department of Foreign Affairs
DGS   Dirección General de Seguridad
DT   Department of the Taoiseach
FF   Fianna Fáil
FS   Free State
GAA   Gaelic Athletic Association
G2   Irish army intelligence
IAC   International Agricultural Confederation
IBA   International Brigade Association
IPP   Irish Parliamentary Party
IRA   Irish Republican Army
IRB   Irish Republican Brotherhood
IRCS   Irish Red Cross Society
KO   Kriegsorganisationen
LKPA   Leopold Kerney Private Archive
MAI   Military Archives of Ireland
MI5   British Security Service
MI6   also known as SIS (Secret Intelligence Service)

NAI   National Archives of Ireland
NCO   noncommissioned officer
NLI   National Library of Ireland
RDS   Royal Dublin Society
RUC   Royal Ulster Constabulary
SOE   Special Operations Executive
TCD   Trinity College Dublin
UCD   University College Dublin
UCDA   University College Dublin Archives

INTRODUCTION

The primary aim of this book is to provide, for the first time, a complete biography of the life and times of Leopold Kerney. The study begins with Kerney's childhood and charts the early influences on his life that shaped his political creed and republicanism. His ideology as a republican and economic nationalist is followed throughout the course of the investigation of his career in various overseas missions in France, Spain, and Argentina in the 1920s, 1930s, and 1940s. By the time Kerney became an adult, and shaped by his republican philosophy, he was committed to the cause of Irish independence despite a background, education, and social class that had tied him to an Anglicized identity. The reasons behind his rejection of a privileged education at Trinity College Dublin (TCD), his conversion from Protestantism to Catholicism, and his acceptance into the republican movement are all examined. Kerney, like many of the revolutionary generation, came to define himself as anti-British, and this theme is traced throughout the book. Kerney maintained this characteristic through most of his career, but by the end of World War II his hostility toward Britain had mellowed considerably. By the time he led a mission to South America it is clear that he was embarrassed by the anti-British attitude of the Irish diaspora in Argentina, a trait he had rejected by then.

Kerney's early adolescent interest in economics was formed by observation and readings, particularly from works by the nationalist writer John Mitchel. When Kerney joined the nascent diplomatic service in 1919, he found in Arthur Griffith a shared viewpoint on how economics formed a key tenet of Irish foreign policy—that establishing direct trade with other countries fosters stronger bilateral ties while asserting national independence from Britain. In France Kerney set about implementing this economic vision. Initiating trade deals and agreements was undoubtedly his strongest skill set. This core element of his philosophy is followed from his time in Paris during the War of Independence, on the continent during the Anglo-Irish Economic War, and in Spain from prior to the outbreak of the Spanish Civil War up to the mission to South America in 1947.

A major research finding and central theme that runs throughout this investigation is the close and friendly lifelong relationship that Kerney maintained with Éamon de Valera (called "Dev" or the "Chief" by his political followers). The book traces the origins of their comradeship during the fallout from the Anglo-Irish Treaty. De Valera's republican and constitutional vision for Ireland came to encapsulate for Kerney the true national path, and he stayed loyal to de Valera throughout the Irish Civil War, during the Sinn Féin split, after the creation of Fianna Fáil in 1926, and during the wilderness years when Kerney found himself in the cold politically. Letters and correspondence between the men throughout the 1920s help illustrate their closeness. After de Valera was elected to government office in 1932 as president of the executive council, he moved to reinstate Kerney into the service. The book traces the multiple times de Valera intervened personally in Kerney's favor and how, despite reproaches from within the civil service, from serving ministers and the director of Irish army intelligence (G2), de Valera maintained his confidence in Kerney's ability as a loyal, trustworthy, and competent official and colleague throughout his lifetime. Although Kerney's time in Spain created a natural distance between the men, the study goes on to highlight de Valera's continued faith in his republican stalwart, which is demonstrated by his request for Kerney to stay on in the service beyond retirement and the Taoiseach's recommendation that Kerney leave retirement to head the political, diplomatic, and economic mission to Argentina in 1947. Through analyzing this close friendship, this book aims to rebut contentions that Kerney was incompetent and unsuited to heading a diplomatic mission.

It is clear from the decade-long research undertaken for this book in Irish, Spanish, French, German, and British public repositories, as well as through unprecedented access to the Kerney private papers, that the study of Irish foreign policy and how it was framed has been neglected in many respects. A picture emerges from this research of the Department of External Affairs that is far from the glowing one it is often identified with under the stewardship of Joseph Walshe. In fact, this book calls into question Walshe's handling of Irish foreign policy in the 1930s and 1940s, as well as his obsession with Catholicism in defining Ireland's place in the world and in its external relations. Kerney's fraught relationship with Walshe can be sourced to their opposing views on Irish foreign policy. While the former embraced economics as a key component of external relations, the latter saw in Catholicism the element driving national independence. This book contends that Kerney was an early pioneer of the seminal role of trade in external relations and that his vision, not Walshe's, has stood the test of time, as evidenced in the current title of the state body, the Department of Foreign Affairs and Trade.

Throughout this book the hostile relationship between Kerney and Walshe is studied, from their split over the treaty to Kerney's libel action against the historian Professor Desmond Williams, which forms a core element of the investigation. This theme is evident from Kerney's different educational background, his return to the service through political intervention, his past anti-treaty sympathies, and his conversion to Catholicism, which are all shown to be underlying factors that influenced the secretary's dislike of the diplomat. Moreover, this book investigates at length the efforts made by the secretary to frustrate Kerney's career in France and in Spain through a practice of deliberate administrative and financial obstruction, pettymindedness, and deception. The level of deceit practiced by Walshe against a serving colleague, often behind the back of Kerney's benefactor de Valera, is shown in this study to have involved the support of Colonel

Dan Bryan of G2. The book traces the wartime and postwar efforts of both Walshe and Bryan to discredit and blacken Kerney's reputation. The research on which it is based proves conclusively that they aided Professor Williams in putting forth his spurious allegations that Kerney actively negotiated with Nazi Germany to alter Ireland's neutral policy during World War II in return for a united island.

There have been several explorations of Kerney by historians, most of whom have examined the perceived contentious moments in his career. The first significant publication came out in 1953, when Professor Thomas Desmond Williams of University College Dublin (UCD) published several articles in a series titled "A Study in Neutrality" in the journal *Leader* and then in the daily newspaper *Irish Press* that analyzed Irish neutrality during World War II.[1] Williams built on his postgraduate research as well as his service in the British Foreign Office and the British intelligence service to publish this ground-breaking work, which revealed to the Irish public how its government and civil service had charted an independent foreign policy that was not as neutral as previously thought. Williams examined the diplomats who were the eyes and ears of the country abroad, and he critically studied Leopold Kerney during the war, though without naming him.[2] Williams charged Kerney with endangering Irish neutrality after the diplomat met a senior official in Hitler's SS (a paramilitary organization of the Nazi regime) and an agent of the Abwehr (the German military intelligence agency) to apparently open up a secret line between Nazi Germany and the Irish government, with Kerney acting as a go-between in this proposed channel with the support of the Irish Republican Army (IRA). While Williams's series was, overall, commendable, his sources for the damning charges against Kerney were flimsy. He used no references and based his claims on off-the-record discussions with former colleagues of the diplomat. Kerney sued Williams in a famous libel case as a result of these false charges. The former diplomat won his action, forcing a public apology by Williams. The case had a disastrous impact on Williams's career; the historian was reluctant to publish much material thereafter in the area of diplomatic history. Despite this court rebuttal, several historians since have maintained that Williams's contentions about Kerney were sound.

Chief among those who agreed with Williams's argument was Eunan O'Halpin.[3] He focused on the role G2 played after independence in safeguarding the state from enemies both internal and external, many of whom posed a real threat to security. O'Halpin drew strongly on the career of G2 director Colonel Dan Bryan, whom the historian interviewed extensively and whom, in his book, he judged to have played a critical role, particularly during World War II, in capturing Abwehr agents, breaking German ciphers, and liaising closely with British intelligence, most notably with Guy Liddell, director of counterespionage for MI5, and his brother Cecil Liddell, head of the Irish section of MI5. O'Halpin's research detailed how G2 came to view Kerney suspiciously and as a menace to Irish interests. The historian traced Kerney's reappointment to the diplomatic service in 1932 and was scathing in his criticism of the diplomat, labeling him a "monumental fool," a "man of hopeless judgement" who was an unsuitable choice to head an overseas mission in wartime—or any time, in fact.[4] In his analysis of Kerney, O'Halpin took up much of the criticism begun previously by Desmond Williams in 1953. Yet although Williams had relied on fragmentary evidence, innuendo, and private conversations to build up his case against Kerney, O'Halpin had access to public files and used them to support his contention. However, many important files were not produced in his book. Also absent were the records of the Williams-Kerney libel case and the acceptance that Williams's public apology had cleared Kerney's name of any wrongdoing or dereliction of duty.

Other historians also supported Williams and O'Halpin in their assessment of Kerney without offering any new insights. A rather selective analysis has been the general trend from the 1990s to examine these events, now termed "controversial," in Kerney's career when the diplomat was apparently at the center of a couple of conflicts. John Duggan analyzed the Kerney-Veesenmayer meeting during World War II, at which the diplomat met a senior SS official to discuss Ireland's neutrality, and broached the libel action but still contended that Kerney was wrong in meeting this senior Nazi without prior approval from Dublin.[5] Mark Hull examined Kerney's handling of the case of Frank Ryan, a former IRA leader who was imprisoned in fascist Spain, and the Veesenmayer meeting.[6] His analysis also disapproved of Kerney's handling of both of these important events in his career. Andrew Roberts likewise supported this viewpoint without providing any material from Kerney's side.[7] Several of the conclusions drawn from these historians will be shown to be unsustainable in light of the archival material produced in this book.

Other historians who have examined these prominent events in Kerney's career have drawn different conclusions and have been more balanced in their assessment. Chief among them has been Dermot Keogh, whose work on Irish diplomacy, particularly its relationship with the most important overseas mission, the Vatican, confirms many of the findings of this book in regard to Catholicism and Irish foreign policy, as well as the poor leadership and management of the Department of External Affairs under Walshe's leadership.[8] Keogh's book challenged many preconceived ideas about this relationship. Moreover, Keogh's argument that Kerney, like his colleagues at the time, were diplomats "by accident" helped account for any shortcomings in the collective performance of Ireland's diplomatic service, and Keogh contended that the diplomat had given Veesenmayer no quarter at their meeting.[9] Donal Ó Drisceoil, who examined state censorship during the war, detailed how the diplomat was placed on a blacklist by the censorship authorities because he was suspected of being in correspondence with dissidents deemed prejudicial to safeguarding the state.[10] The historian's analysis provided insights into another aspect of Kerney's career, his misuse of the diplomatic bag. Ó Drisceoil's overall examination of Kerney, like Keogh's, was balanced and fair.

Tim Pat Coogan examined the Kerney-Williams libel case in considerable detail and judged the former diplomat to have acted correctly in his meetings with the Germans.[11] However, Coogan makes a rather sensationalist claim that the evidence Williams acquired for his allegations came mainly from de Valera, who acted as his principal source, something this book shows to be inaccurate. Barry McLoughlin investigated the issues surrounding Ryan's release and argued that Kerney did all he could for Ryan given the reality on the ground.[12] As a result of his analysis, McLoughlin believed that Kerney acted as a normal head of mission would in such difficult circumstances and should not be pilloried for his honest efforts. This book supports this viewpoint with new archival material found during research in the private collection of Kerney as well as public repositories.

Interest in Kerney's most celebrated episodes continued to draw historical interest, but new material was not produced. A change in this pattern occurred in 1997 with the launch by the Royal Irish Academy, in association with the Department of Foreign Affairs, of a project intended to bring the history of Irish diplomacy from a selective readership into the mainstream public arena. Since its inception this project has published a series titled *Documents on Irish Foreign Policy*, which consists of volumes on diplomatic material since 1919 for public dissemination.[13] Edited by a team of historians, archivists, and researchers under the stewardship of Executive Editor Michael Kennedy, the project has provided valuable material that chronologically outlines the development of Ireland as a nation and its place in international affairs. Many of Leopold Kerney's reports have been reproduced in the series. These reports cover broader aspects of Kerney's career. Yet the publications are not without flaws. Given the selectiveness that underpins the series, many documents that readers might find interesting and significant have not been produced, while the "official" history it disseminates has left a void in the anti-treaty diplomatic reports produced during the Irish Civil War. For this reason many important reports that Kerney and his anti-treaty diplomatic colleagues wrote for the "republican" government under Éamon de Valera are not included, and Kerney's time as de Valera's de facto diplomatic representative in France is largely ignored. Kennedy expanded public awareness into another aspect of Kerney's career, his appointment to a mission to Spain.[14] This brief examination of Kerney's accreditation to the Spanish Second Republic was, overall, fair and balanced. More significantly, Kennedy compiled the biographical entry for Kerney in the *Dictionary of Irish Biography*.[15] While Kennedy is to be commended for providing a brief biographical sketch of the diplomat's life, the biographical entry is lacking in detailed archival referencing. Important documents from accessible repositories containing such items as Kerney's reports on the Frank Ryan case and on the Veesenmayer meeting, for instance, are not quoted. Coupled with this imbalance, Kennedy's entry contains several elementary errors in relation to Kerney's life and events, including in his place of birth, that render it an unreliable source on the diplomat. Moreover, the questionable imputations made in the entry are at variance with many of the findings of this study.

Beyond the historical domain, Kerney has become a source of interest to his family, as well as to filmmakers and fiction writers. His last surviving child, Eamon, created a website on his late father that referenced many of his diplomatic reports and countered the charges made against him by historians with opposing views.[16] As an eyewitness to his father's life and custodian of his private papers, Eamon Kerney produced a website that is an invaluable reference point, though its critics may question its impartiality given the familial ties to the subject. *The Enigma of Frank Ryan* was a film directed by Des Bell with Fearghal McGarry as historical consultant that featured Kerney's role in Frank Ryan's release from Burgos Prison. In it the character Kerney is portrayed as a conniving figure who willingly hands Ryan over to the Germans and acts without sanction from Dublin. The film hypothesizes many aspects of Ryan's imprisonment in Spain that this book will challenge by providing the full historical picture of the Frank Ryan case and Kerney's role in it. Interest in Kerney has also extended to fiction writers. He features in the novel *The City in Darkness* by Michael Russell, which dramatizes the role of Kerney, Ryan, and German military intelligence during the war.[17] The novel does not set out to portray Kerney in a positive or a negative light, and it is, on the whole, an engaging read.

Restoring the reputation of any historical figure is no easy task, especially in this case, as Kerney's credibility has been called into question by successive leading historians, many of whom have passed damning judgments on Kerney. Yet through unhindered access to the Kerney private collection as well as through archival research across Europe, it has become clear that the supposed controversies surrounding Kerney do not reflect the truth or the historical reality. This book aims to show that at all times Kerney acted in his nation's best interest and that, if there were doubts about his competence at the time the events described took place, they were often raised by individuals with a personal vendetta against him or were formed through the lack of full information at the time. Moreover, this book will show that at no stage during any of the controversies, from Kerney's handling of the Ryan case to the meeting with Veesenmayer in August 1942—and even the misuse of the diplomatic bag—did de Valera, as Taoiseach (the Irish prime minister) and minister for external affairs, ever feel the need to recall, demote, reassign, or sack Kerney. On the contrary, de Valera, the man whose opinion ultimately mattered most at the time, defended his loyal colleague despite the scheming of civil servants, and Kerney remained, throughout his life, Dev's republican diplomat.

FROM AFFLUENT SANDYMOUNT TO WAR-TORN PARIS, 1881–1918

Number 22 Sandymount Road, Dublin, a prosperous coastal suburb, was the unlikely birthplace of a man whose future life and career would be defined as much by its modesty as by his staunch republican beliefs.[1] Leopold Harding Kerney was born into a world of prosperity and Anglo-Irish respectability.[2] His father, Philip Kerney, was a journalist who rose through the profession to become subeditor of the *Daily Express* in Ireland, where he served for over forty years, and editor of the *Weekly Irish Times*.[3] Philip was an active member of the Institute of Journalists and was elected the association's auditor in 1902.[4] On 10 December 1863 he married Anne Knight in the Church of Saint Mary, Donnybrook. Her family protested against their courtship on religious grounds. The Knights were a Church of Ireland family, while the Kerneys were Catholics. In the interests of all concerned, Philip agreed to convert to Protestantism, and the marriage went ahead. In time the couple would have nine children together, six boys and three girls.

Their first child, Mario, was born on 17 October 1864 at 13 Albert Place. He was "feable [*sic*] minded," could not read, and, as a result of his disability, required constant care throughout his life.[5] The second child, Henry, was born on 25 April 1866 at 7 Bath Avenue. A healthy boy, Henry was the first son to be sent by his parents for an Anglicized education in the Erasmus Smith's Intermediate Trust School on Great Brunswick Street. The trust had been established by Royal Charter in 1669 after its founder, Erasmus Smith, petitioned King Charles II.[6] Smith, a merchant and adventurer, had supplied Oliver Cromwell's forces with provisions during the Cromwellian conquest of Ireland in 1649–53. Smith had also invested in the conquest and received over 49,000 acres of land in different counties in Ireland.[7] He proposed using the revenue from these estates to establish a trust that would educate young boys in the English language and in the Protestant religious ethos.

By the late nineteenth century the trust had evolved its curriculum to instruct and inculcate young boys for careers in the British Civil Service administration and the British Army. It also provided scholarships for higher education at TCD, a university generally perceived as being for the Protestant Ascendancy at this time. The rapid expansion of the British Empire at the close of the century increased job opportunities for young Protestant graduates of high social class. Professional schools in law, medicine, science, engineering, mathematics, and the humanities were all available to these new graduates in TCD to fill the myriad posts and positions created by Britain's dynamic expansion and global reach, particularly following the acquisition of territory in southern Africa. Moreover, TCD's associations and club societies offered these young Protestant graduates a network through which to meet and exchange ideas among their fellows in a city whose population beyond the high iron railings of the campus was predominantly Catholic.[8] Henry fulfilled his parents' ambition for his education, and he became a senior British civil servant working in the Ottoman Bank in Constantinople, which had been set up after the Crimean War, when Turkey was bankrupt and British and

French investors administered the bank to recover their investments. Henry subsequently worked for the Reparations Commission in Berlin after World War I. By all accounts he was an "Empire man," with an entirely Anglocentric outlook throughout his life.

The Kerneys' first girl, Agnes, was born on 27 July 1868 at 71 Blessington Street but died from pneumonia a few months later, on 11 February 1869. Another boy, Nicholas, was born on 16 November 1869. He showed considerable academic ability and followed his father's career path by becoming a journalist and later editor of the South African newspaper *Argus*. The couple welcomed the arrival of another baby girl into the family home on 27 June 1872, but Florence, as she was called, died a few months later. The first child born at 22 Sandymount Road, on 29 December 1874, was Maurice. He, like all the other brothers, would emigrate from Ireland. Maurice became a language teacher in Germany. Another son, Arnold, was born on 1 April 1877 and worked for American Express for several years before managing an estate in Brittany, France. Annie Henrietta Louise, known fondly by the family as "Dot," was born on 3 May 1879. A handwritten note in the family Bible, dedicated to "our darling Dot," records her death a few years later, on 10 June 1895, from tuberculosis. The last child, Leopold—or "Poley" as he was affectionately known—was born on 11 December 1881.

Leopold's earliest childhood recollections were of himself, his sister Dot, and his mother playing on the main green in Sandymount Village and enjoying walks together along the strand on sunny days. These recollections were perhaps the only happy memories of a childhood that was otherwise characterized by profound sadness. In 1895 his mother died unexpectedly when he was fourteen, and, soon after, Dot died, turning his world upside down. He had been particularly close to his last surviving sister. After their deaths Leopold was raised by servants and a niece of the family, Christabella Knight, who moved into the home shortly afterward to help Philip take care of the children. She was a Brethren whose strong religious beliefs and domineering personality irked Leopold and instilled in him a stubbornness and cautious attitude toward religion from a young age.

As the twentieth century dawned, major changes had been occurring in the balance of education in Ireland. No longer was attending elite Protestant schools for the well-to-do the privilege of the few. Instead, a system of national education had been developed and pioneered by the Catholic hierarchy to provide the majority of young Irish boys with free schooling by the Irish Christian Brothers. The Christian Brothers imbued education with a cultural nationalism, hyper-Catholicism, and a yearning for the Irish language.[9] This education shaped the outlook and philosophy of the future leaders and activists of the Irish revolutionary generation. As Tim Pat Coogan has acknowledged, "The [Irish Christian] Brothers were not trying to foment revolution or the spread of Wolfe Tone's doctrines, but they were consciously trying to inculcate in them a love of Irish culture, its language, its history, and its songs in an era when official textbooks encouraged Irish schoolchildren to thank God for being born 'a happy English child.'"[10] Ireland was changing rapidly, and this was reflected profoundly in education as the Catholic hierarchy sought to control the new generations and instill in them Catholic doctrine and a nationalist philosophy. The minority of Church of Ireland educationalists continued to promote an elitist Anglican and pro-British ethos, but the winds of change were there for all to feel.

Education was the crucible that shaped Leopold's life principles, his philosophy, and how he acquired knowledge and formed opinions and points of view. Despite his many commitments at the *Irish Times*, Philip Kerney recognized not only the value of education as a career path for his youngest son but also the dichotomy within the education system prevailing at the time, and this was reflected in his desire for Leopold to acquire knowledge. On the one hand, he wanted him to continue an exclusive Protestant education like the one provided for Henry, yet he was aware of the changes taking root in Ireland, and for this reason he adopted a blended learning environment for Leopold. The boy attended the same Protestant school as Henry, where he excelled in mathematics, but young Leopold was also taught at home by his father, thanks to his own "intimate knowledge" of several European languages, and, importantly, Philip encouraged Leopold to learn independently and develop his own thoughts and understandings on subjects as diverse as politics, history, and languages.[11] Philip's educational approach for his son mirrored his own fused political outlook in an Ireland that was politically pulling toward Home Rule. He believed in a semiautonomous Ireland in control of domestic affairs but still tied to Britain and its empire for finance, foreign policy, and defense. Philip also guided the young Leopold's sporting pursuits, preferring that the boy take up English rather than native Irish games such as Gaelic football or hurley, and so, encouraged by his father, Leopold captained the local cricket team.[12] He also played school rugby in Ballsbridge with the Bective Rangers seconds team.[13] The absence of the Gaelic Athletic Association (GAA), an ardently nationalist organization at the time, was another distinguishing feature of Kerney's life compared to those of his later compatriots. In adulthood he would continue to play English rather than Irish sports.

Leopold was aware of his father's former acquaintance with John Devoy—the famous Fenian—when they were learning Irish together in their teens, and their friendship endured throughout Devoy's exile to America.[14] This fostered in Leopold an interest in reading up on Irish politics and the armed resistance to British governance all over the island, particularly from enemies of the crown. Leopold was now determining his own attitude toward politics and history, but perhaps the most significant book that left a lasting indelible impression on him came from the writings of Irish nationalist John Mitchel. In his book *The Last Conquest of Ireland (Perhaps)*, Mitchel argued that British maladministration had caused the Great Famine. For the first time, and contrary to what Leopold was taught in school, not everything British was positive or glowing; in fact, Britain seemed incompetent, especially in its response to an economic crisis in its own realm. The book also served to identify Britain in Leopold's mind in an exclusively English context. Mitchel's contention raised economic questions of national significance. Leopold linked independence with economics, not politics. If Ireland was to stand as a free and sovereign nation, the best measure of such an aspiration was economic independence: break England's stranglehold on the island's economic life, and Ireland could be free. His private studies of works by Irish nationalist writers made Leopold very skeptical about what others were trying to teach him at school. Years later he recalled his boyhood schooling and questioned why he was taught "one hour of English history five days a week and one half-hour of Irish history every Saturday—the Irish history being a narrative of English military victories in Ireland and Irish crimes, and written by an Englishman of course."[15]

Economics continued to influence the teenage mind of Leopold as he grew older. Together with his best friend, Jack Larchet,[16] he frequently enjoyed fishing for crabs off Poolbeg Lighthouse at the mouth of the River Liffey. In a letter to one of his brothers, written when he was Ireland's minister to Spain in the 1930s, Leopold recalled an important moment in his life during one of these fishing adventures. He remembered ships of all sizes sailing up the mouth of the Liffey but noticed that none of them had Irish names. All of them were English ships carrying the English ensign. Immediately he asked himself why there were no indigenous Irish ships and why Ireland did not have its own merchant fleet or any control over its maritime trade. Mitchel's argument had stuck in his mind. Surely if another famine was to occur, it was best not to rely on outside assistance for humanitarian relief but instead to have a native fishing fleet to ensure adequate supplies of food, he thought. The event also sparked his awareness of Ireland's vulnerable geographic position. The island was largely isolated from continental Europe and tied completely to Britain. He began to understand the importance of economic independence. The economy he began to favor was one that traded freely with Europe, not Britain, one that was open and not protectionist or isolationist.

These doubts encouraged Leopold to read further into Ireland's maritime history. He studied the Navigation Act passed by Westminster in 1651 and came to realize that Britain had deliberately disconnected Ireland from the continent. Kerney became convinced from this point on that, to prevent another famine and to ensure Ireland's independence, an indigenous maritime fleet needed to be constructed and that Ireland's near-total dependence on the British market had to be broken. The nation's future lay not with its nearest neighbor, which Ireland supplied with cheap food, but with trading openly and directly with continental Europe. It was not the Gaelic language, politics, or culture that was moving him down the path to the concept of

Irish independence. It was his education that was decisive in shaping his political principles and nationalist philosophy.

Following his father's wishes, the boy studied at TCD but never graduated, much to his father's displeasure. Public schooling had failed to influence Leopold to follow in Henry's footsteps. On the contrary, his private readings of works by Irish nationalists had done far more to raise his awareness of historical and contemporary injustices, to question the role Britain played in Ireland, and to be skeptical of official or authoritative viewpoints on matters. This skepticism was certainly a key factor in his decision to drop out of university education and quit a promising career in the British Empire. His consciousness was more aligned now with a nationalist orientation. It would still take him several years to crystallize his philosophy into a republican definition, but his conscience was clear. He had turned his back on his Anglicized roots even if this decision narrowed his career prospects. In the 1901 census, when he was aged nineteen, Leopold's profession is listed as "civil servant (census clerk)" but it is doubtful that he was then a functioning civil servant.[17] More likely he declared this as his profession because his schooling had prepared him for a career in the British Civil Service. This is confirmed by his decision to emigrate from Ireland that year and leave the family home—never to return. The uncertainty of his career was reflected in his travel movements. He moved like a wanderer unsure of a final destination. Leopold went to Britain to join his older brothers Henry and Nicholas, but he did not settle down, perhaps impeded professionally by his failure to graduate with a university degree. He decided to leave Britain and spent the next ten years traveling around Europe. This travel was itself another form of education, as he experienced and encountered new cultures that broadened his horizons beyond those of the parochial Protestant enclave he had been reared in.

For two years Leopold worked in Germany with his brother Maurice in Plauen, Saxony. Travel records from the Hamburg-to-London line record his profession as "Lehrer" or teacher.[18] During these two years, living with Maurice, he taught English to German students before moving to Zwickau in the same district. His time there would have been an exciting one given the rise of Germany as an international military power under Kaiser Wilhelm II and the escalating tensions between the imperial camps across Europe. From Zwickau he traveled around Italy, France, and Belgium and then back to England, where the 1911 census shows him, aged twenty-nine, living with his brother Maurice in Middlesex and described as a "forwarding agent."[19] This commercial experience may have ultimately helped him secure a position in Paris, where he joined Lady Duff Gordon's international fashion firm, Lucile Ltd., in 1912. The firm had global outlets in Chicago, New York, and London, selling elegant clothes, lingerie, and cloaks. His new office was 11 Rue de Pentièvre. Despite not having any formal qualifications, Kerney had a head for figures, which may have helped in his appointment as cashier and chief accountant with a starting salary of £260 per annum. Accounting suited him given its overlap and interaction with the field of economics, something he had had an innate interest in since boyhood. Kerney remained with the firm for the next seven years until he voluntarily resigned on 4 September 1919 to join the nascent Irish consular service. During his time there he performed his tasks with diligence and professionalism. A letter from the managing director on his resignation states: "We found him thoroughly trustworthy and very efficient in any duties undertaken by him."[20]

In Paris Leopold soon met his future wife, Raymonde Jeanne Marie Élie, twelve years his junior. She was from the village of Saint Caprais-de-Bordeaux near Créon. They shared sad childhoods. She remembered the day her cousin had walked her to a convent, where she was placed in the care of nuns at the age of four. Her mother, Julie Élie, had been forced to leave France due to financial difficulties and worked for a Lady Elizabeth Peabody from Massachusetts, described in the 1911 census as a woman of "private means."[21] The records note Julie's age at the time as forty, that she was a widow, the mother of three children, who worked as a "lady's maid."[22] By 1911 Raymonde had been reunited with her mother, and she stayed with her in Market Harborough Leicestershire in a sixteen-room house while on holiday from a two-year stay in a Mill Hill convent. The following year she returned to France and worked as a secretary in Paris. It was there that she met Leopold. The couple courted for two years, and in 1914 they agreed to marry.

Unfortunately, Raymonde's mother would not entertain any ideas of a marriage unless Kerney converted to Catholicism and promised to raise any future children in the Catholic faith. Leopold was faced with the same situation that his father had confronted. After the formative years of his education, Leopold's conversion to Catholicism became the second key event in shaping his nationalist outlook. As Owen Chadwick states, for many young Irish nationalists, Catholicism marked not only one's faith but also one's "cultural and political difference from Protestant Britain."[23] Kerney came to this realization too. He was not drawn to Catholicism as a faith, and he would remain throughout his life quite detached from any religious commitment or devotion. Instead his decision to convert was largely a personal choice made for political reasons. He viewed Protestantism by this time as an English entity and a nefarious import that had undermined and quelled a native culture and heritage that were overwhelmingly Catholic in their identity. By changing his religion he was showing his political commitment to Irish nationhood. As Patricia Craig has observed, the "yoking together of Irishness and Catholicism" was a visible characteristic of the nationalist movement.[24] Kerney's conversion moved in tandem with this broader confluence of Catholicism and nationalism, although for him his journey had been longer. His conversion was the clearest expression yet of his rejection and repudiation of his Anglicized youth and schooling. He was now like his Catholic brethren—"psychologically" committed to an independent Ireland but unsure yet of how this was to be achieved "in practice," a point Craig noted for most of that revolutionary generation.[25]

The young couple arranged their wedding venue in Saint Gregory's Catholic Church London, a half-way point for both families. As international events proved, the timing for the wedding could not have been more ill fated. On 4 August the German Army invaded Belgium, prompting Britain and France to declare war on Germany. All across the country, France was engulfed by patriotic fervor and passionate cries for national unity, encapsulated in President Raymond

Poincaré's emotive phrase *union sacrée*. In spite of the first mobilization of millions of men into the French Army, which paralyzed the transport network, Kerney was determined to wed his bride at the appointed time and venue. He secured places on a river boat traveling down the Seine toward Le Havre, and there he purchased two tickets to travel on a boat destined for Southampton. The couple were duly married on 14 August 1914 at Saint Gregory's Catholic Church on the day that the first French offensive in the West began.[26] After a brief honeymoon in London, the newlyweds returned to Paris to news that more than forty thousand French soldiers had been killed in just three days of fighting during the Battle of the Frontiers.[27] It was the first indication that the war was of unparalleled scale in death, destruction, and suffering. In early September the German Army stood just forty kilometers outside the besieged capital. Thousands of the city's wealthiest inhabitants fled. On 2 September the government also evacuated the city and headed for Bordeaux, bringing with them the entire gold reserves of the Bank of France. Luckily, the French Army and the British Expeditionary Force, including thousands of Irishmen in regular regiments, managed, at the Battle of the Marne, to drive the Germans back between 6 and 9 September.[28] Unable to make any headway, the Germans raced to the sea, hoping to outflank the Allied armies, but to no avail. Both sides dug in for a defensive war that was to last for over four years.

Although the Third Republic had carved out its own colonial empire in North Africa and Southeast Asia, Kerney admired and believed in the French revolutionary principles of freedom, liberty, and equality and church-state separation. His nationalist hero and inspiration, John Mitchel, had lived in Paris, and Irish republicanism drew much influence from the French republican tradition. Kerney's time in Germany had given him a good understanding of its society, culture, and politics, but his assimilation into French life also helped him see the war from France's perspective. He distinguished between the French model of government and the German one, which was characterized by autocratic rule and militant imperialism. By now his attitude toward France's ally, Britain, another country where he had lived for some time, and its empire was also firmly established, and he saw little difference between it and the German Empire. Kerney had never shared his father's political support for the Home Rule movement and had hitherto refused to join the thousands of other Irishmen in the British Army.

Although Paris had been saved from immediate occupation thanks to the "Miracle of the Marne," Kerney witnessed the most beautiful capital in Europe transformed into a wartime city under military control. All the terraces of fashionable cafés were deserted. Instead the city was a hive of military activity as garrisons, troop camps, pillboxes, military impediments, and hospitals for the wounded sprang up under the orders of the new city governor, General Joseph Gallieni, who also directed the hundred thousand–strong city garrison.[29] No one could leave Paris without a permit.[30] Once again the French capital became the city of barricades as hundreds of trees were felled to make street barriers, while at night searchlights beamed through the darkness probing the skies for enemy aircraft. Goods were rationed, and many commodities were extremely difficult to buy. News was also in short supply and came mainly from communiqués issued by the war ministry.

Every family in Paris was in some way affected by the war, especially by the Battle of Verdun, a major military campaign that dragged on for over ten months, exhausting both sides and leaving hundreds of thousands dead. Rod Kedward summed up the battle as simply "pitiless, brutalising slaughter."[31] Raymonde's two brothers were serving at the front, but this horrific wartime experience was not shared by Kerney. Inside Paris he lived a rather settled, happy, and leisurely life far from the trenches and harm. His absence from the fighting was not lost on local Parisians. At Lucile, where he worked, he frequently carried out the duties of other male colleagues who had been drafted into the French Army and frequently found himself explaining his absence from the front to clients. Thousands of foreigners had already volunteered for service in the French Army, including Irishman and future colleague Michael MacWhite, who enlisted in the French Foreign Legion and was awarded the Croix de Guerre and the Médaille Militaire for brave combat service. But Kerney avoided making any voluntary commitments to enlist, even though he supported

France and the ideals of its republicanism. Fear of trench warfare in a modern industrial conflict, combined with the enormous death rates, was an obvious factor, but so was Kerney's dislike of any form of military struggle or armed violence. Throughout his life he would avoid taking up any weapon for any cause. Besides, his portly physique did not make him suited to armed combat.

The year 1916 was also the year in which seminal events occurred in Ireland. A major military uprising was brutally suppressed and the leaders executed. Yet another act of armed revolutionary violence failed to dislodge British hegemony over the island, or so it seemed. The initial public backlash to the destruction gave way to support for the rebels and emboldened the nationalist cause back home, as well as reawakening the nationalist zeal of expatriates like Kerney with a belief that only total independence could secure the national destiny of Ireland. Also, for the first time Kerney came across the name Éamon de Valera in the French newspapers. He could not have known at that time the central role de Valera was to play in his life in the coming years. Despite this, such historic events in Ireland were too far away for Kerney to take an active part in, and the rising was viewed negatively by the French people, even as a betrayal by some. This struggle to account for his commitment to France and its republican principles in its hour of need or to explain the rationale behind the rising back home was compounded by the fact that he was a British subject in possession of a British passport, and any attempts to explain his political views to French people unfamiliar with Irish politics were always frustrating. Most believed Ireland was an integral part of the British Empire, and they viewed the presence of thousands of Irish soldiers at the front alongside British troops as a testament of their loyalty to the crown and the Allied struggle. For that very reason, Kerney, in their eyes, should have been fighting at the front.

Despite these frustrations, the war years in Paris proved a happy period for Kerney and Raymonde, including the birth of their first child. If Kerney was unwilling to take up arms to defend France and its republican principles, he symbolically showed his loyalty to his adopted country by recording the child's name on the birth certificate in French—Jean Michel. The name was also a clear indication of the importance of John Mitchel's writing in awakening Kerney's consciousness as a young boy to the failures of British rule in Ireland and to the cause of an independent, sovereign Irish state. By naming his son after a prominent nationalist activist, Kerney was ensuring that, if his generation failed to achieve the republic, the cause would pass down to the next.

By 1917 the war was entering a more brutal and destructive phase. On 22 July the Third Battle of Ypres or Passchendaele began with an enormous artillery bombardment that lasted for ten days. The French sacrifices at Verdun the previous year had exhausted their efforts, and the onus passed to the British to break down the German defenses on the Western Front, this time along the Belgian coast. The involvement of so many Commonwealth troops—Australians, New Zealanders, and Canadians—highlighted just how enormous the operation was and, moreover, the drastic manpower shortages, which were at "bedrock" level.[32] The battle finally ended on 4 November 1917 with the village captured but little else gained for the great effort expended. The Official History of the war recorded 238,000 casualties for the campaign, but some argue that the true figure was closer to 350,000.[33] The October Revolution in Russia further underscored the dire situation facing the Allies in 1917.

During that winter it seemed that the French military authorities had finally caught up with Kerney, and he was ordered to join a British unit or else be detained for draft evasion. The ongoing mass slaughter on the Western Front and fears of leaving his young family without a father were obvious inducements to avoid enlistment, yet Kerney chose to draft letters to the French authorities and to the Irish Parliamentary Party (IPP) leader, John Redmond, outlining his fears about being conscripted into the war. The letters stressed that for political rather than personal reasons he could never serve in the British Army or swear allegiance to the British king, but he had no problem joining a French unit, although he had avoided doing so up until then.[34] His political philosophy would not be swayed. He had finally set his republican principles to paper. Redmond took up the issue, and in the end neither the French nor the British seemed particularly interested in pursuing the matter further.

With the threat of possible conscription lifted from his shoulders, Kerney spent the remainder of the war in relative comfort. He was promoted at Lucile and was earning a good income of £600 per annum. This allowed him to raise his young family in Bougival, where they lived in comfortable accommodations, something unthinkable for the average French soldier in the frontline trenches. When the war finally ended, on 11 November 1918, it brought Parisians back onto the streets singing "La Marseillaise" and celebrating the triumph of the republic. It was the ideals of the republic and the sacrifices made to defend the republic that Kerney identified with and hoped might someday be realized in Ireland. Little did he know at the time, but political events across the sea were about to change his life forever.

CHAPTER 2

THE FIRST IRISH CONSUL IN PARIS, 1919–1921

On 14 December 1918 voters turned out in Ireland for a general election that would have a momentous effect on the course of Irish politics in the twentieth century. Hitherto, the Irish Parliamentary Party (IPP) had had the "unchallenged support and unquestioned allegiance of the great majority of nationalist Ireland," but its firm grip over the electorate was wiped out in 1918 as a result of controversial attempts by the British government to introduce conscription in Ireland and the vocal opposition of the Catholic Church to any such coercive measures.[1] An angry public transferred its support to Sinn Féin (We Ourselves), which canvassed on a platform of national independence. The failure of the IPP to implement the 1914 Home Rule Act, which had been suspended because of the Great War, alienated younger voters from the party. Perhaps more importantly, as Diarmaid Ferriter has shown, the extension of the franchise by the 1918 Representation of the People Act and the eligibility of more female voters caused a threefold increase in the number of those able to vote and thus accounted for the landslide victory Sinn Féin received.[2] The party won seventy-three seats compared to six seats for the IPP and 46.9 percent of the votes cast. The decisiveness of the victory encouraged the Sinn Féin leadership to supplant British administration in Ireland by refusing to take their seats in Westminster and convening a shadow parliamentary assembly, known as Dáil Éireann, in Dublin to declare Irish independence.

The first meeting of Dáil Éireann (now the lower house and principal chamber of the Irish legislature but then the only house) took place on 21 January 1919, the same day that the War of Independence began. The Dáil declared Irish independence from the British Empire and spelled out the democratic program for the new republic. During the following meetings the language of the deputies became more belligerent in tone and strikingly anti-British, a characteristic of the revolutionary generation and something Kerney would also display in time when he joined the cause. Dr. Richard Hayes favored war rather than negotiation with the British government: "Men who set out to overthrow such tyrannies are no criminals—on the contrary, the real criminals are the representatives in this country of that foreign government which has no fundamental right or title here. And not only are they the real criminals—they are mean, unprincipled criminals as well."[3] Another deputy, Pádraig Ó Máille, longed for the "day of retribution" to come, when God would strike down the British, whom he referred to as "black-coated rascals."[4] Although the language was fiery and militant, the deputies knew that the independence struggle needed a broad base to win public and international support for Ireland's struggle. The Dáil hoped that US president Woodrow Wilson would stand by his "Fourteen Points" commitment to the principle of self-determination for ethnic minorities by supporting Ireland's case for admission into the Paris Peace Conference as a sovereign nation and thus accord the republic international recognition.

RECRUITMENT

The political challenges facing the leaders of the Irish revolution over the next few months were enormous. A new government, departments, civil service, local government, army, judicial court system, and propaganda agency all had to be set up, manned, and financed. Another challenge was that many of the deputies were frequently absent from duty due to arrest or were on the run. The leader of Sinn Féin—Éamon de Valera—was himself imprisoned in Lincoln Jail—before he escaped. It was de Valera who understood more than most the importance of establishing a consular service abroad for the cause of Irish independence. De Valera was also president of Dáil Éireann, and he outlined the role he envisioned the new consular service playing in the struggle for independence and international recognition:

> We shall send also to other countries a number of duly accredited ambassadors and consuls to see that the position of Ireland is understood as it truly is, and not as English propaganda would represent it, and in general to see that the interests of Ireland in these countries are in no way neglected. We shall thus resume that intercourse with other peoples which befits us as a separate nation, that intercourse which it has been the chief aim of English statescraft to cut off.[5]

On 18 June the Dáil established a "national civil service" and a "consular service" to carry out the functions of the republic at home and abroad.[6] The Dáil had approved the appointments of Seán T. O'Kelly and George Gavan Duffy as republican envoys to the Paris Peace Conference. Of all the diplomatic missions in operation abroad, Paris would become the epicenter of Irish activities. The mission's objective was to gain Irish admission into the crucial Versailles peace talks and thereby attain international recognition for the republic. Kerney had just returned from a private trip to Ireland where he had sold French goods to friends from his boyhood days who by now were, in his eyes, "anglicised most of them beyond redemption."[7] The business venture served as an experiment for him to see if his economic philosophy of free trade between the countries was feasible: "I had long entertained the idea of developing direct trade between France and Ireland, and I decided on this occasion to make an experiment in that direction."[8] Although he lacked any previous experience as a commercial traveler and had no business connections in Ireland, he packed a large trunk with French goods and sold them easily in Dublin: "I succeeded in booking orders from business firms and in thereby proving to my own satisfaction that certain classes of French goods could compete successfully with English ones in Ireland; on various occasions I earned £5 as the result of half an hour's congenial work and I easily covered the expenses of my holiday."[9]

When he learned of the presence of the Irish delegation in Paris, Kerney and a friend of his, Michael O'Carroll from Borrisoleigh, County Tipperary—who owned a tailoring business in the French capital—visited the mission delegates to wish them luck. Kerney made a good impression on the delegates, who were impressed with his recent business deals. O'Kelly in particular was impressed with the idea of establishing direct trade between Ireland and France, and he approached Kerney to ask if he would be willing to provide "advice and assistance to Irish firms desirous of trading with France."[10] Kerney agreed, and the start of his official connection with the Irish republic began, as well as lifelong friendships with O'Kelly and Duffy.

At another meeting, O'Kelly called on O'Carroll's tailoring business on Boulevard Haussmann and there asked Kerney if he would be willing to assist the cause by dealing "with any enquiries of a commercial nature."[11] The Dáil wanted the newly established consular service to perform political, administrative, propaganda, and commercial activities on its behalf overseas. The commercial aspect of the service was particularly urgent, as the Dáil needed to secure funding and direct trade with overseas countries to finance the war and all other expenses. The focus on trade and commercial activities for overseas diplomats appealed to Kerney given his interest in economics, and it tied in with his economic philosophy of linking Ireland's economy more closely with the continent and not Britain. The minister for industries, Eoin MacNeill, shared this viewpoint: "Ireland had hardly any export or import [trade] except what passed between Ireland and England under English control."[12] To fulfil this specific role, the Sinn Féin leadership wanted to recruit men with a proven track record in commerce, who had good business connections at home and abroad, and who were bilingual. O'Kelly saw that Kerney had a business background, albeit as an accountant, and that he spoke fluent French and had a keen interest in promoting direct trade. Kerney enthusiastically agreed to help in any volunteer capacity he could, and he decided to take advantage of another trip to Ireland to meet members of the republican government. He had now entered the ranks of the republican movement and was being encouraged to work with trade matters, an area he had a keen interest in.

In July 1919 Kerney traveled to Dublin to see the republican leadership: "It was my earnest desire to meet prominent Irish Republicans during my visit to Dublin," he wrote,[13] and he called on 6 Harcourt Street, the headquarters of Sinn Féin, to meet Robert Brennan, the director of national elections and publicity: "There I met Bob Brennan, who had played an important part in connection with the general election for all Ireland held in December 1918, and out of which the Republic had come triumphant."[14] He also met Desmond FitzGerald, the substitute director of propaganda. Kerney recalled FitzGerald's English accent "grating on my ears," and although the two men seemed on the surface to get on well, it would not be the last time either man would pass comment on the other.[15] FitzGerald escorted Kerney to a house on Pembroke Road where Ernest Blythe, director of trade and commerce, was in hiding but was very eager to meet Kerney about promoting direct trade with Europe. Kerney noted Blythe's "very unkempt condition."[16] The strain of life on the run was etched into the director's face.

Despite his unkempt appearance, Blythe impressed Kerney: "He greeted me in the northern Irish accent, he being a native of the province of Ulster; I was told later that he was a Protestant, of English stock, and one of the proofs that the Republican movement was a non-sectarian one."[17] A few days after this meeting, the British raided the house. Blythe escaped capture by hiding on the roof for several hours in his pajamas. Kerney recorded his concern that suspicion might fall on him as a possible spy: "I wondered at the time whether I, an unknown man, might be suspected of having been in collusion with the British, but, apparently, none of my new friends entertained so unjust a thought."[18]

FitzGerald also arranged for Kerney to meet Art Ó Briain, a member of the secretive Irish Republican Brotherhood (IRB) and organizer of the Irish Self-Determination League in Great Britain. As with most of the people he was meeting, Kerney got on well with Ó Briain, and the two men became good friends. One key difference, however, was that Kerney had never joined and never did join any secret-oath-bound organization, nor would he take up a gun for the cause of Irish freedom, unlike most of the republican colleagues he met. On Thursday, 31 July he met for the first time Arthur Griffith, then the minister for home affairs and acting president of the Dáil due to de Valera's absence in America, in Thomas Loughlin's outfitting shop on Parliament Street to be formally appointed trade representative of the Dáil in France, upon Blythe's recommendation. Kerney noted that Griffith was "rather reserved in his attitude at first, but soon expanded, and we had quite a long chat together."[19]

Agnès Maillot identified Arthur Griffith as a leading figure in formulating Irish foreign policy in this period: "Griffith was convinced that political autonomy would have little weight if it was not supported by economic independence."[20] Maillot's contention is supported by Gerard Keown, whose examination of Irish foreign policy in its early years likewise identified Griffith as an instrumental figure in defining the roles overseas diplomats were to undertake: "Griffith envisaged an Irish consular service supplying commercial intelligence and support for Irish business and the establishment of a mercantile marine that would enable Ireland to emulate the commercial success of Norway."[21] Kerney and Griffith were of the same mind that the true test of Irish independence was economic freedom.

Although Griffith was an economic nationalist who espoused self-sufficiency, he was also cognizant of the need for Ireland to reorientate its economy away from Britain and to trade directly with the continent in order to demonstrate to the world that Ireland was a sovereign European nation charting its own course on the international stage. Political support at home and abroad would then follow naturally. It is noteworthy that Kerney supported the juxtaposition of foreign affairs and trade: "I was convinced of the soundness of

Arthur Griffith's policy of direct trade between Ireland and other countries and of the desirability of eliminating the control exercised by English intermediaries over all trade between Ireland and countries other than England."[22]

The Dáil by now had approved the sum of £10,000 for a consular service, and Griffith asked Kerney if he would accept a part-time position on £200 per annum. That salary was quite small in comparison to what he was earning at Lucile, and Raymonde was expecting another baby in a few months. Financial remuneration did not seem to have interested Kerney. Rather, like most of his contemporaries, he was moved by patriotic idealism for the struggle. Griffith's aspirations for Ireland's economy and the role he envisioned overseas diplomats undertaking in this regard were the final confirmations Kerney needed to officially join the republican movement, as it confirmed his own economic philosophy on free trade. He enthusiastically accepted the position as trade representative (later renamed Irish consul): "Arthur Griffith produced from one of his pockets £50, representing the first quarter's payment in advance, in £1 notes, the dirty appearance of which struck me very much; he also handed me my Credentials as Trade Representative to France from the elected Government of the Irish Republic."[23]

The ad hoc nature of Kerney's appointment, without any formal interview or examination process, may seem strange, but in fact this was the norm for how the Dáil's political representatives recruited officials for the service of Dáil Éireann. In his research into the civil service during the revolutionary period, Martin Maguire found that most appointments were made after personal conversations: "The reality for the departments of the Dáil government was that it was more important that staff be discreet, loyal to the republic and willing to face the danger that loyalty entailed. The departments could not be too fussy about procedures of recruitment and officials were recruited by any and every means."[24] While departments of the Dáil recruited in a rather informal and nonhierarchical way, Maguire also made another striking observation: "What bound the civil service to the Dáil was a shared and intense commitment to achieving an independent Ireland."[25] In this also, Kerney's experience mirrored that of other servants. His republican ideology was passionate, and his willingness to serve the cause was equally unwavering.

Before returning to France, Kerney accompanied Griffith to his friend Thomas Loughlin's home at 164 Botanic Road that day to meet Michael Collins, the minister for finance. Kerney noted that Collins was in good humor because "not even half-a-crown had been found in a raid which had just taken place at his offices."[26] Kerney also recalled Collins "refusing to have anything to drink that evening," obviously conscious that he was a man wanted by the British authorities and had to be ever alert should the house be raided by the enemy.[27] That was another reminder of the dangerous nature of his new employment. At any time Kerney could be shadowed and imprisoned for his new activities. Yet this stark reality did not frighten him. He relished the chance to fulfil a life's ambition to undermine and break England's stranglehold over Ireland through economic means.

Back in France, the mood among the delegates who were working on gaining Irish entrance into the international peace conference was optimistic. As George Gavan Duffy wrote: "Things have changed; the wheels of God grind slowly, but they grind exceedingly sure. Today the Republic!"[28] Duffy's optimism was misjudged. The staffing levels were too small for the Paris delegation—a lamentably defining characteristic of Irish overseas missions for decades to come. Duffy and O'Kelly were supported by Victor Collins (a former journalist), Annie Vivanti (an Italian writer), Margaret Gavan Duffy (unpaid), and a Mr. Caulfield (an activist). Despite the enthusiasm and zeal that these people put into their work, none of them had any experience in the art of diplomacy and politics. Such shortcomings severely limited the scope and efficiency of their mission. The delegation operated from its headquarters in the Grand Hotel, where the delegates entertained guests, churned out propaganda material, and tried to build up Ireland's case for admission into the Paris Peace Conference. The Dáil had high hopes for success at the conference, but the French authorities were unwilling to alienate their wartime ally Britain, and attempts by the delegation to gain entry into the recently constituted League of Nations proved fruitless. Clearly, in the eyes of the French authorities

Ireland did not matter much in the greater scheme of postwar international relations. The diplomatic delegation was largely ignored and even disapproved of in some quarters, where the war in Ireland was seen as a domestic British concern. The delegates, moreover, had few important connections outside journalistic circles, and, even then, efforts to get French reporters to come to Ireland and write on the war foundered. Worryingly for the Dáil, the two republican envoys became ill, especially O'Kelly, who complained of kidney trouble and possibly suffered from rheumatic fever.

The difficulties that the delegation was experiencing contrasted sharply with Kerney's enthusiastic drive to secure trade deals. He operated alone most of the time and away from the confines of the Grand Hotel. This independence of action was a common feature of Irish representatives abroad in the initial years, until Joseph Walshe's centralization measures stymied such behavior by the late 1920s. As Gerard Keown noted: "Circumstances were such that central control was frequently an aspiration with individuals largely left to their own devices."[29] Kerney relished this freedom of action and the opportunity to fulfil a childhood dream—to break English dominance over Irish economic life. On his own initiative he traveled around France, Belgium, the Netherlands, and Spain, filing no claims for expenses, and built up a network of clients, businessmen, and investors who were willing to deal directly with Irish companies rather than through the intermediaries of the British. Privately, things were also going well for the Kerney family. Raymonde gave birth to a baby girl, Micheline, on 21 October 1919, and the family lived at a charming villa named Marie Thérèse in La Celle Saint-Cloud, outside of Paris. In early spring of 1920 Kerney returned to Dublin to brief the Department of Trade and Commerce on his work. Although he had gotten on well with Ernest Blythe at their first meeting, on this occasion their relations soured somewhat. Kerney's blunt and matter-of-fact approach irked people at times, and at this meeting he requested that his position be made a full-time appointment. From his perspective the request was a declaration of his commitment to the consular service, but he also hoped that permanency would reflect the complete confidence of the republican government in him. Blythe, who was notoriously stingy with the dispersal of public funds, felt the salary Kerney asked for was "too high."[30] He agreed to raise the matter with the Dáil.

On 27 April, Duffy, by now in charge of the Paris mission owing to O'Kelly's illness, received notification from Dublin that Kerney was to be promoted to the position of full-time trade consul on a salary of £600 per annum.[31] It appeared that the Sinn Féin government was happy with Kerney's role, but minor controversies were never far from the surface throughout Kerney's career. The next one occurred shortly after his return to Paris. Dublin saw Duffy as the leader of the diplomatic mission in Paris in O'Kelly's absence and expected him to monitor and report back on Kerney's trade activities, something Duffy was unwilling to do given the sizeable number of duties he was already carrying out. The Dáil sanctioned £700 for the lease of premises for the consular work, a paltry sum given the cost of renting in the capital. The minister for finance, Michael Collins, and Ernest Blythe wanted to pay the amount into the delegation's account. Kerney argued that his new full-time position made him separate from the delegation and that he alone should be in charge of the dispersal of this money. Blythe, clearly annoyed, was prepared to "wash my hands of him [Kerney]."[32] Duffy stood by his colleague, with whom he was on "excellent terms," and argued that Kerney had performed his duties admirably and was very trustworthy.[33] On 13 July the minister for finance apologized for causing any friction and agreed to separate the work of the consul and the delegation from then on. Collins also agreed with Kerney's suggestion that his consular account be independently audited every financial year. His new home and office was a flat on Rue de la Terrasse.

VICTORY IN SIGHT

Throughout 1920 the War of Independence intensified and Sinn Féin's resolve stiffened in the face of British reprisals, according to Martin Gilbert: "It [Sinn Féin] wanted to govern the whole of Ireland, freed completely from British rule. Full independence, not limited autonomy, was the goal."[34] Fired up by this militancy, the Sinn Féin leadership understood the importance of foreign policy to make Ireland's case as internationalist as possible. More men were recruited to the consular service in Paris to work on propaganda activities and augment the work being undertaken by other consular representatives in Europe and abroad. Michael MacWhite was one new recruit. He was a former soldier from the French Foreign Legion who had been awarded the Croix de Guerre and Médaille Militaire for his distinguished service during the Great War. Duffy was delighted to have MacWhite on his staff as secretary to the mission to replace his wife, who had returned to Dublin to look after their children.[35] MacWhite spoke fluent French, and his service in the French Foreign Legion was useful in winning influence in and connection to Parisian society. Kerney worked with MacWhite to establish an Irish-French society, and they worked jointly on propaganda material.

In November the mission was augmented by another member, Joseph Walshe. Like all the other recruits to the service, Walshe was a diplomat by accident. He was an ex-Jesuit seminarian, a devout Catholic, and a rather peculiar character, as Dermot Keogh noted: "He was secretive and mistrustful. Walshe also had a reputation for deviousness. . . . He was inclined to interpret his role rather narrowly looking askance at such 'plebeian' areas as trade and commerce, which had to be 'tolerated.'"[36] Walshe's disdain for trade matters as key components of Irish foreign policy clashed with Kerney's economic viewpoint. It was natural that Kerney, who saw the essential link between foreign policy and the promotion of trade as an expression of political independence, would cross swords with Walshe on this important issue. In any small organization, conflicts and interpersonal rivalries are common, yet Walshe had a knack for stirring up resentment. In his first meeting with Kerney he made a passing remark about his French wife, Raymonde, and asked whether she could be trusted with "confidential" information. This comment and their quarrel over what constituted the essential dynamics of Irish foreign policy sowed the seeds of a bitter personal feud between the two men that would rumble on for years.

One of the first measures the Dáil had approved to undermine Britain's ability to fight the war in Ireland was to encourage a boycott of British goods coming into the country. Not only would this, it was hoped, reduce the crown's revenue, but it would also reinforce psychologically the notion that Ireland was a separate national and economic entity. While this was a lofty idea in theory, in practice it was extremely difficult to implement. To begin with, French public opinion was still strongly pro-British on account of the Great War. In addition, Kerney had no facilities, no car, and no staff to assist him with this boycott policy. Despite these difficulties, he undertook the challenge with gusto: "Nothing gave me greater pleasure than to translate and circulate as widely as possible the successive Boycott Orders which reached me from Mr Blythe, Minister for Commerce."[37] On 11 August Kerney managed to persuade the French commercial directory *Bottin* to put Ireland under a separate heading. Armed with the boycott orders and a copy of the directory, he traveled around France and Belgium. Again his good interpersonal skills and language fluency helped open doors. The Office National du Commerce Exterieur passed on to him contact details of leading firms and manufacturers, a significant achievement given the fact that the whole Irish diplomatic mission in Paris was not officially recognized by the French government. As Kerney later recorded:

> Many French firms availed themselves of the opportunity thus presented to them. My work attracted the attention of the French authorities, and I received notable assistance from the Office National du Commerce Exterieur. I received many visits from Irish exporters and importers. I remember having Irish toilet soap put on sale in Paris, and, at the same time, French household soap imported into Ireland. I helped to establish a trade in rabbit skins with France. I met with some success in having "jambon de York" retailed to the public as "Irish ham."[38]

Before long Irish and French importers and exporters were exchanging goods with each other rather than with Britain. Kerney's travels across the country also opened his eyes to the creation of potential new industries back home. One in particular caught his attention, and he wrote detailed reports recommending the establishment of an indigenous sugar beet industry in Ireland once the war was won.

He wrote: "I visited sugar factories in the north of France and made reports on that industry with a view to its introduction into Ireland."[39] More and more the presence of Ireland became better known to the French public and to state authorities. Kerney was given a prominent position as a distinguished guest—consul general of the Irish Republic—by the mayor of Lyons, Edouard Herriot, at the inauguration of the Lyons Fair, and after the banquet he gave interviews to newspapers promoting Ireland.

Over time, Kerney's commercial activities grew increasingly effective in the political sphere, as Griffith had imagined they would. The more companies that decided to trade with Ireland directly rather than through London, the more the island's political independence was asserted thanks to economics. Of all Ireland's industries, agriculture was undoubtedly its strongest, and, owing to the territorial devastation and enormous decline in animal numbers caused by the Great War, the Irish consul focused his attention on the agri-food sector and future markets for such products on the continent. In one of the few areas of postwar international economic collaboration, France set up the International Agricultural Confederation (IAC) made up of twelve countries to encourage interstate trade and cooperation. On 12 July 1921 in Paris, the IAC held its annual meeting, which was attended by the Irish Farmers' Union.

The Irish were in a strong position to market their goods and were helped by the "woefully inadequate" international efforts to coordinate and promote postwar recovery and reconstruction.[40] The Irish delegation marketed their produce to French, Italian, Belgian, Dutch, and Eastern European delegates. Kerney used this international trade event not only to foster trade but also to psychologically assert the real presence of an independent Irish delegation to his European counterparts; this was economic self-reliance in practice. The conference proved a major success for trade and publicity purposes, and Kerney, as head of the Irish delegation, drafted a proposal to hold the next annual meeting in Dublin to coincide with the RDS (Royal Dublin Society) Horse Show.[41] This was an inventive idea, as the war had drastically reduced the numbers of draft horses on the continent. The Irish horse breed was of excellent stock, and other related equestrian goods, such as oats, could also be showcased to potential buyers. If the next conference was held in Ireland, it would again showcase Ireland as a distinct entity from Britain to an international audience. The French had approached Kerney about the possibility of allowing Britain to join the IAC. Still conscious that Ireland was at war with France's former wartime ally and never one to miss a chance to put one over on the "old enemy," Kerney said that such a move would require a reciprocal invitation to Germany, to which the French naturally rejected.

Although most of Kerney's time was taken up with consular business, he usually called on the Paris mission every week to help out with some political or propaganda work. Every year Kerney organized the most important event on the calendar, the Saint Patrick's Day celebration, where normally a hundred guests drawn from the Irish colony in Paris and "foreign sympathisers" of the national struggle attended to enjoy some Irish music and dance and a poetry recital.[42] The occasion always provided a good media story as well as a morale boost for the overseas diplomats. The amateurishness of the whole event was brought home one year when Kerney organized a banquet in the Palais d'Orsay restaurant. For the occasion Raymonde had made an Irish flag with the colors green, white, and gold. When she unveiled it to her husband and to Seán T. O'Kelly, the men departed for a private chat to discuss whether Raymonde had gotten the colors correct: "At that early stage in our struggle, I think there was some uncertainty as to whether the third colour should be gold or orange," Kerney recorded.[43] Not wishing to offend his wife, knowing the care, time, and effort she had put into making the flag, Kerney told her it was wonderful. He made it the official flag of the celebration, and he used it on every diplomatic mission he served in throughout his life.

PEACE BECKONS

In the general election of May 1921, Sinn Féin candidates had again returned unopposed to a second Dáil, and six republican women were also elected, highlighting the party's popular appeal. The majority of the Irish people had registered their support for the nationalist struggle. The presence of forty thousand British troops and ten thousand armed police and the hard-line military tactics employed to defeat the IRA were not winning the war for Prime Minister David Lloyd George. The guerrilla tactics adopted by the IRA and the excellent propaganda work carried out by the consular service abroad gradually brought a realization in Whitehall that peace talks should be tabled.[44] Kerney realized that the collective unity of the Sinn Féin movement had finally forced the British government to a truce in mid-July and also to the negotiation table, marking a watershed moment in Irish history and for this revolutionary generation.

It is clear that Kerney's view of the struggle mirrored that of most of his colleagues. Little is known about his attitude toward the darker side of the war, particularly the sectarianism that had become a feature of the fighting in Cork and Belfast. Throughout the conflict Kerney never joined the IRB, unlike his colleagues Arthur Griffith, Seán T. O'Kelly, and Art Ó Briain. He likewise never joined the IRA and had no association with that organization. Similarly, he was not inclined to involve himself in politics. He never joined the Sinn Féin party. He was not a romantic either, as he never spoke Irish or showed an appreciation for the revival of Gaelic culture, unlike many of his contemporaries, particularly de Valera. He was at heart a nationalist, but one who saw open direct trade with the continent rather than with Britain as the highest expression of independence. He reveled in working to achieve this independence. With this "broad internationalist vision" he epitomized a cornerstone of Irish foreign policy at this time, as Gerard Keown has observed.[45] Both personally and professionally, the years 1919–21 marked a very happy time in Kerney's life. He now knew who he was as a person, and he identified himself completely as a republican who had turned his back on his childhood roots, which he characterized by their "anglicised atmosphere of contented provincialism."[46]

CHAPTER 3

THE TREATY AND THE IRISH CIVIL WAR, 1921–1922

With the political leadership of Sinn Féin and the British government respecting the ceasefire enacted on 11 July 1921 and the start of preliminary negotiations underway, the work of the consular service continued in the background. Most of Kerney's direct contact with Dublin was made through his superior, Minister for Trade and Commerce Ernest Blythe, or through the various men who served as ministers for foreign affairs.[1] Every few months Kerney traveled to Dublin from Paris to confer with Blythe and bring him up to date on his activities. During the War of Independence he had often taken circuitous routes around the capital to avoid being detected or betraying a safe house. He still exercised such caution with the truce in operation. These trips kept him abreast of political events inside the country and the general mood of the people.

A political agreement was finally reached in London on 6 December with the signing of the Anglo-Irish Treaty. The Dáil vote on the treaty resulted in its passing by 64 votes to 57, and although Kerney acknowledged that it created a "new situation" politically, in his mind it did not in any way alter his function as consular representative: "[The treaty] did not interfere with my activities on behalf of closer economic relations between France and Ireland. I remained a servant of the Republic, and, on the invitation of the Republican Minister for Trade and Commerce, Mr Blythe, I visited Dublin in February 1922 for the special purpose of giving information to Irish exporters and importers."[2] He was aware that Éamon de Valera and other anti-treaty delegates had refused to accept the majority vote or be bound by its decision. Kerney also knew that when de Valera sought reelection as president of the parliament and lost, the Sinn Féin movement was split decisively on the treaty. Whether he knew about the deep divisions within the IRA is uncertain, as events were moving rapidly. He was finally given an outline of the political situation as it affected him through a letter from Blythe on 18 January 1922. The timing of the letter is quite significant. It reached him just before the Irish Race Congress opened in Paris.

THE IRISH RACE CONGRESS

In the letter Blythe spelled out the official position that the consul now found himself in. He outlined three facts that he wanted Kerney to bear in mind. First, that the republican government "remains in being" and that he should continue with his duties uninterrupted.[3] Second, that the Dáil, as the sovereign national assembly, had approved the treaty and the establishment of a provisional government of the "Irish Free State."[4] And finally, that the majority of the Irish people were "beyond doubt" in favor of the treaty.[5] Blythe specifically reminded Kerney that as a consular official he was to abstain from any involvement in the political controversy. He was not to express any opinion on the treaty or to do anything likely to cause difficulty for the new Irish Free State once it was constituted. He was simply to carry on his duties as before, to which Kerney agreed: "You may rely upon my fulfilling my duties in accordance with the letter and spirit of your instructions."[6]

Equally stressed by Blythe in the letter is a clear indication that the entity known as the Irish Free State would in time take over the consular service. This would become a critical bone of contention with Kerney months later. This rather anomalous situation at the time understandably caused confusion for all serving officials, as Gerard Keown has opined: "Envoys were confronted with the ill-defined nature of their status; they could not claim to represent the Free State, which did not yet exist, while they remained representatives of a republic that did not exist either."[7]

In the run-up to the Irish Race Congress in Paris, Kerney obeyed Blythe's instructions. There is nothing in Blythe's communication to suggest he questioned Kerney's allegiance, but the minister did suspect that some of the traveling Sinn Féin delegates to the congress might use the occasion to sound out officials. Behind the scenes, supporters of the treaty were secretly dispatching their own men to watch over the event. Michael MacWhite was requested to attend the congress by the minister for foreign affairs, George Gavan Duffy, and to keep an eye on the anti-treatyites.[8] In the course of MacWhite's mission he came to believe that Kerney was already sympathetic to the anti-treaty side: "At the time of the Race Congress in Paris last year he [Kerney] was a supporter of de V[alera]."[9]

As early as August 1919, the Dáil had approved a suggestion from the Irish Republican Association of South Africa to hold a world conference to unite the distant diaspora in support of the republic. The congress opened in Paris on 20 January 1922 and lasted for a week. Almost from the start, disagreements surfaced over the composition of a new umbrella organization called Fine Gaedhael (Gaelic Tribe), which was to absorb and coordinate all other international bodies affiliated with the cause.[10] Robert Brennan, the subsecretary of the Ministry of Foreign Affairs, had organized much of the congress, and he was proposed for nomination as secretary of Fine Gaedhael. This proposal was challenged by Eoin MacNeill, the chairman of Dáil Éireann, who saw this as a "partisan" selection; he suspected that the anti-treaty faction was deliberately filling positions with its supporters to gain control of the organization.[11] MacNeill instead proposed that two secretaries be appointed, but Brennan believed MacNeill simply did not trust him to carry out the functions impartially and so resigned. The president of Sinn Féin, Éamon de Valera, and Harry Boland were also accused of using the congress to gain support against the treaty. The gathering was a public relations disaster and a very costly expense (£5,963).[12] Not as many delegates from abroad traveled as had been anticipated, and those who did witnessed the disunity of the Irish political movement. The whole event was overshadowed by an atmosphere of distrust and recrimination. It did little to further the image of Ireland internationally and undermined efforts to utilize "diasporic nationalism."[13]

Kerney's main input at the congress was a speech he delivered on the importance of establishing direct trade, particularly of manufactured goods, with the continent. His speech was notably caustic in tone, perhaps because he was aware of the more extreme-minded republican delegates in attendance. The consul saw England as Ireland's only "enemy," and he blamed England for all of Ireland's woes.[14] He wanted to wrest control of trade out of British hands and put it back in the hands of Irish manufacturers and merchants. He argued that there should be no letup in making the republic open to direct trade and as internationalist as possible in case the terms of the treaty were breached by the British: "The English middleman . . . has got to disappear, and I hope it may soon be possible to squeeze him out completely. When we strike England in her trade, we strike her in her stomach, and when we do that she begins to find peace a desirable thing."[15]

Kerney's fiery public speech, with its republican undertones and anti-British outlook, was a new departure for him, but it impressed de Valera, and in the first meeting between the two men they struck up an instant rapport. The consul noted how polite and courteous the Sinn Féin president was to him. Seen from one viewpoint, de Valera could have been showing a degree of flattery to win over future allies. It was, after all, the anti-treaty attendees at the conference who went out of their way to praise Kerney's work for the republic thus far. As Kerney wrote: "Art Ó Briain introduced me to him [de Valera]; his first remarks were in praise of the work which I was doing; having a poor enough opinion of it myself, I demurred somewhat, but he brushed aside my protest saying that his information came from those who were in a position to know."[16]

DIVISIONS APPEAR

On 21 February the Dáil deputies tried to smooth over their differences at the Sinn Féin Ard Fheis (high assembly), but as the weeks passed it was clear that attitudes on both sides had hardened, especially within the military, as Meda Ryan has demonstrated.[17] Although the anti-treaty faction continued to attend Dáil proceedings, they refused to recognize any ministerial posts, acts, or communications emanating from the Provisional Government that had been set up after the Dáil ratified the treaty. The Dáil and the Provisional Government coexisted until the public voted in a general election on a constitution for an Irish Free State. Until that happened, this transitional period created a complex legal position from both an Irish and a British perspective. The anti-treaty deputies repeatedly questioned the authority of the Provisional Government to represent the nation. From their viewpoint, the Dáil was the only legal government of the country. This is a line Kerney would adopt in the months to come.

The differences of opinion over the treaty were also being reflected in the civil service, which was in a state of total confusion. The Provisional Government was preoccupied with transferring its authority from the departing British departments of government during this transitional period. The British Civil Service, known as the Dublin Castle service, was being subsumed by the Provisional Government under its authority as the British rescinded control of the country to the Provisional Government in accordance with the treaty agreement. In the meantime there was the difficult issue of the Dáil departments and its civil service to add to the constitutional ambiguity. To keep the country functioning, notepaper was issued bearing the heading Dáil Éireann, and Dáil civil servants continued to act on its behalf until the general election. This was done for legal and practical reasons in the hope of preventing a civil war. It succeeded in assuaging Kerney's anxieties for several months: "My letters of appointment as Consul of the Republic had never been revoked. I was never advised, officially or otherwise, of any modifications in the Republican regime. I was never requested to abandon my allegiance to the Republic or to give allegiance to any other regime set up in its place. All official communications which I received either from the Republican Minister for Trade and Commerce, Mr Blythe, or from the Republican Minister for Foreign Affairs, Mr Gavan Duffy, were written on the usual Republican letter paper with the heading 'Dáil Éireann.'"[18] With measures like this in place, Irish foreign policy still functioned, albeit rather cautiously. In February Kerney traveled to Dublin to liaise with Ernest Blythe over trade matters and to meet Irish exporters and importers to discuss matters with them. The consul recorded that he was the "first to turn up in the morning and the last to go at night."[19] He noted with regret that the "volunteer spirit" that had previously been a hallmark of everyone involved in the independence struggle was "on the wane."[20] Kerney could see before his eyes that the national debate over the treaty was splitting the entire republican movement in two, and it also affected him: "The realisation of the change caused me regret when I first became aware of it," he wrote.[21] To distance himself from either faction, he attended meals and engagements with both sides during this time in Dublin.

In March de Valera spoke of Sinn Féin's unity in the past tense, writing of "when we were all one organisation," and his supporters became known as the dissenting minority.[22] They formed their own party on 15 March called Cumann na Poblachta (League of the Republic). However, de Valera's attitude reflected only one political viewpoint on what were myriad complex opinions on the anti-treaty side, a point stressed by Meda Ryan.[23] Within the military, senior commanders like Liam Lynch saw the treaty as a denial of the republic proclaimed in 1916 and a breach of the republican oath. The anti-treaty IRA began raiding, looking for "arms, money and transport" to continue fighting for the elusive "republic."[24] Pro- and anti-treaty military units occupied former British barracks. The country seemed to be rudderless and lawless, with no central authority capable of commanding the situation. Every national organization—the IRB, the IRA, Sinn Féin, and Cumann na mBan (The Women's Council, an Irish republican women's organization)—was divided over the treaty. Attempts to form military and political pacts failed, and civil war moved one step closer when anti-treaty forces occupied the Four Courts on 14 April. The fabric of authority was fading.

On 16 June a general election finally was held, in accordance with part of the treaty, for the formation of a constituent assembly that would pave the way for the establishment of the Irish Free State. The public voted overwhelmingly for pro-treaty candidates, who won a huge overall majority of 486,277 votes to 132,161 for the anti-treaty side. The ordinary citizen was simply tired of war.[25] This healthy show of majority support accorded the Provisional Government a clear public mandate to put the treaty into effect. Despite arguing that the treaty was flawed, de Valera's anti-treaty faction had campaigned in the election and suffered a major defeat. When the anti-treaty side was faced with an uphill struggle to achieve a republic by constitutional means, the balance of power on the anti-treaty side shifted to the anti-treaty IRA, which was not prepared to accept anything less than a united and independent Ireland by force of arms and pledged no allegiance to any parliament or political authority. The Provisional Government, under pressure from Whitehall following the assassination of Field Marshall Sir Henry Wilson by Irish republicans, decided to act against the garrison occupying the Four Courts. When an ultimatum was issued and rejected, the building was bombarded, and the civil war began on 28 June.

After the outbreak of the civil war the Provisional Government treated the Dáil and the civil service as under its control, and an oath of fidelity was imposed across all services. However, as Martin Maguire has shown, this oath was directed not at expressions of anti-government opinions but rather "against activities incompatible with public service," such as armed rebellion.[26] Throughout these tumultuous events, Kerney and his activities appear to have been overlooked by his superiors, who were understandably preoccupied with more pressing concerns. Besides, he had not made any public statements or taken any actions that were in any way deemed unlawful or that had given rise to any suspicions about his loyalty. He was seen simply as a dutiful official: "All my communications respecting trade matters continued to be addressed to the Minister for Trade and Commerce or to the Minister for Foreign Affairs of the Republic," he wrote.[27]

Nevertheless, while politicians and military commanders fell out over the treaty, Kerney's commercial activities were achieving notable successes: "I was in the happy position that my work was still confined to trade activities and was unaffected by the serious differences which had arisen in the political field at home."[28] A major success for Kerney came when he finally realized his boyhood dream, inspired by John Mitchel's writings and encouraged by Griffith's vision for Irish foreign policy, to establish a direct shipping link between Ireland and the continent. The consul had founded a company with French investors for an ambitious trade project although the tragedy of the civil war was unfolding back home.

The consul had long believed that politics alone would not guarantee Ireland's sovereignty; economics would play a vital role. A loan of 500,000 francs was floated for a shipping company to launch direct services between Brest and Cork. After months of negotiations, Kerney had also secured the backing of the Cork Chamber of Commerce and Shipping and the Cork Industrial Development Authority for the venture. The French investors purchased a boat, the SS *Banba*, which was to carry passengers and goods on a weekly basis. The decision to operate from Brest was a sensible one. It was the closest continental port at the time, and Ireland was viewed favorably by the people of Breton, who themselves had long felt oppressed under French control. Kerney hoped Irish tourists would be enticed to holiday in sunny Brittany now that it could be reached in less than a day by sea. When the *Banba* pulled into Cork harbor on its maiden voyage, Kerney noted a line of British soldiers standing along the pier.[29] Given the fierce fighting that had taken place in Cork between the IRA and British forces, it is perhaps not surprising that the British troops feared that the ship might be carrying arms. As Kerney recorded: "There was some suspicion as to the nature of the cargo we carried in those troublous [*sic*] times; we ran the gauntlet, as we berthed, of numerous loaded rifles carried, as it seemed to us, somewhat nonchalantly at disquieting angles."[30]

Kerney gave interviews to journalists from various newspapers while passengers disembarked and goods were unloaded from the ship and loaded onto it before it continued its voyage on to Dublin. The consul was honored with a banquet by the Cork Chamber.[31] The ship's captain, Poilvet, was presented with a traditional Irish black-thorn bouquet. The magnitude of this new trade route was significant above and beyond the fact that it was established in the middle of a civil war. Although both countries had traded for centuries, it had been trade of a sporadic and limited nature. Now, for the first time, the foundations of large-scale direct trade between Ireland and France had been laid. The *Banba* project marked a significant break in Ireland's historic link as a colony because it challenged Britain's monopoly and total dominance on all maritime traffic around the Irish seas. Psychologically it also demonstrated that Ireland could manage its own external trade affairs, symbolically shown by the Irish tricolor on the ship's mast. For Kerney personally, this proud moment fulfilled a lifetime's dream and a key principle of his republican philosophy, which valued economic freedom for Ireland and a reorientation of its economy toward the continent. He had achieved all this largely on his own, with no resources or staff support. The *Banba* project stands as tangible evidence of his skill and ability as a consular official. The service ran for several months and marked the culmination of Kerney's efforts as consul for the Irish republic in France.

CROSSING THE RUBICON

The outbreak of the Irish Civil War had severely impeded the sweeping changes that the Provisional Government had planned for the civil service since January by merging the Castle and Dáil administrations into one unified civil service. While the overall situation in this regard was chaotic, the government took steps to bring about conformity by insisting that civil servants acknowledge its authority following the general election mandate. As mentioned earlier, an oath of fidelity was imposed on all functionaries, and anyone who refused to take the oath could be suspended or dismissed. This practice was hampered, however, by the fact that the Irish Free State would not legally come into existence until 6 December 1922. As Martin Maguire has shown, confusion over what legitimately was the state during this period caused widespread "organisational confusion."[32] All notepaper still bore the heading of Dáil Éireann, and correspondence with overseas officials was still done through Dáil Éireann and its authority. As far as Kerney was concerned, he had been appointed by the Dáil, and he addressed all his reports to that body until told to do so otherwise: "Throughout that tragic year I remained faithful to the Republic," he wrote.[33] Moreover, as Maguire suggests, the overriding concern of the Provisional Government was to defeat the anti-treaty IRA rather than to confirm the absolute loyalty of the civil service: "The immediate task facing the fledgling State was waging war, the most State-defining activity of all."[34]

Kerney maintained later that when the civil war began he was instructed by his superior, Ernest Blythe, to not concern himself with events in Ireland as they had no bearing on Kerney's status: "On 29th June, 1922, the day after the bombardment of the Four Courts which let loose civil war in the country, the Minister for Trade wrote to me, in his official capacity as Minister of the Republic, a letter in which he said, 'The present is not a conflict between two opposing political parties. . . . The action of the Government is quite independent of any pronouncements made in the British House of Commons.' This letter was interpreted by me as meaning that, in spite of appearances, there was no political question at issue in the disturbances which had broken out."[35] This response can be interpreted several ways: that Kerney strictly followed Blythe's instruction from that moment onward and abstained from any viewpoint on political developments, that he chose to deliberately ignore the obvious state of civil war in the country in anticipation of a republican administration being formed, or that he maintained silence in the hope that the British would somehow break their agreement and reignite a united Irish effort for total independence.

On 9 September, Desmond FitzGerald took over as minister for external affairs of the Provisional Government. On his desk was a detailed analysis of the consular service compiled by his predecessor,

George Gavan Duffy. In Duffy's report he stated that the consular service found itself in a very "anomalous" position owing to the treaty.[36] In the report Duffy argued that it was important to keep the overseas missions alive should the ceasefire with Britain break down. He relegated to fourth place the overall importance of the French mission to overseas operations, a comedown from its high standing during the War of Independence and his own time in Paris. FitzGerald took up his post hoping to expand the activities of the ministry abroad, but during his tenure Kerney recorded that he had never once known about FitzGerald's appointment, nor had he received a single communication directly from the minister: "When Mr Gavan Duffy resigned his position and was succeeded by Mr Desmond FitzGerald, I was not advised of the change. I never had a single communication from Mr Desmond FitzGerald. I continued to address my letters to the Minister for Foreign Affairs and I received letters from that department of Dáil Éireann (i.e. the Government of the Republic) signed by a gentleman who described himself as Secretary."[37]

Kerney's saying this is rather strange, as he did have a face-to-face meeting, however short, with FitzGerald, Blythe, and Joseph McGrath, the minister for industry and commerce, of the Provisional Government on 30 September, when the *Banba* pulled into Dublin Port.[38] By this date the civil war had raged for three months, and Kerney's conscience was already weighing heavily on his mind: "For my part, I hoped against hope that the British Parliament would never pass that Act [Irish Free State Constitution ratifying the 1921 Anglo-Irish Treaty], and I knew that, once it was passed, I should have to decide without delay whether my conscience would let me enter into the service of this 'Free State,' for up to that date I had continued to remain a representative of the Republic of Ireland."[39]

If any of the ministers suspected that Kerney was an opponent of the treaty, they had every opportunity to raise the matter with him and sever his employment during his frequent trips to Dublin. That they did not do so suggests that they trusted him to be a faithful employee who was aware of the constitutional position of the Provisional Government and would remain loyal to it once the Irish Free State formally came into existence on 6 December 1922. Kerney's continued service and his restraint in not involving himself in the political upheaval caused by the treaty stood in marked contrast to the actions of other republican diplomats with whom he had worked, who had already made their views and positions on the treaty very clear, most notably Seán T. O'Kelly, Art Ó Briain, and Robert Brennan.

If Kerney in anyway doubted the authority or legitimacy of his superiors or the offices they led during this transitional period, he, too, could have voiced his views and resigned. His silence perhaps reveals that he was biding his time either until the Irish Free State was formally enacted or, more likely, that he hoped the British would break the truce and that the republican movement would be united again. His decision not to declare himself for the anti-treaty side after the civil war broke out shows that he was not prepared to support the anti-treaty IRA in keeping with his abhorrence of violence generally and specifically that of unaccountable oath-bound secret organizations. Furthermore, the lack of any political oversight of the anti-treaty IRA, which saw itself as the de facto republican government, was not something Kerney agreed with. He always felt that any military body needed to be under the control of and answerable to a civilian body. When Éamon de Valera moved to create such an entity in October, Kerney immediately acted.

For months de Valera had been sidelined by the anti-treaty IRA, which held supremacy over the republican movement in the civil war. The Sinn Féin president had gradually reemerged from the shadows following unsuccessful peace talks with General Richard Mulcahy, the minister for defense, on 6 September. The discussions broke down because de Valera simply rejected any peace terms: "What we are fighting for is the right of the people of this nation to determine, without foreign dictation, what shall be the government institutions under which they shall live."[40] It was this belief articulated by de Valera— that Britain both during and after the treaty was operating in the shadows and manipulating events in Ireland—that found a receptive ear in Kerney. The oath of allegiance to the British monarch was another critical point of contention with the treaty that Kerney could never agree to. His views are worth quoting at length:

To my mind, the Republican regime was the only legal one, because it rested on the clearly-expressed will of the Irish people, in direct opposition to the will of England. I could not, in my heart and conscience, accept the theory that the government of Ireland by England was legal in any degree. It appeared to me that the proposed "Free State" had no legal basis, seeing that it accepted its powers and constitution from a British Act of Parliament, that, consequently, it recignised [*sic*] the pretended legality of England's claim to ownership of Ireland, and that it tacitly admitted England's contention that the Republic of Ireland was an illegal regime because it had been set up without England's consent.[41]

On 17 October de Valera finally won over the IRA executive to support a republican government, and a twelve-body council of state was formed under his leadership to mobilize the civil population for the cause of the republic, albeit under the aegis of the IRA. The government was announced on 25 October, as much to counter the action of the bishops who were opposed to the anti-treatyites as to win popular support. Kerney saw this political development as "welcome news."[42] For him the republic now had a reconstituted and legitimate political authority, and he decided to make contact with this government while still in the pay and service of the Provisional Government: "I wrote to President de Valera and asked for instructions. I pointed out that I could not, under any circumstances, work for a Government which gave allegiance to England, that I was ready to resign my position on the spot if the Republican Government so wished but that I could not hand any such resignation to any usurping government which I did not recignise [*sic*], and I likewise expressed my willingness to continue to work for the Republic if that should be the Government's wish."[43] The following timeline of events indicates Kerney's behavior during this period. On 2 October he received a letter from the secretary of external affairs, Joseph Walshe (pro-treaty), that informed the consul that he was now answerable only to External Affairs. A few days later, Kerney received another letter from Walshe advising him to discontinue using the term "République Irlandaise" in letter headings. Incredibly, Kerney maintained that he did not know the identity of this man or who the minister of the department was, three days after he had had a face-to-face meeting with FitzGerald in Dublin. While this was unfolding, Kerney wrote to Robert Brennan (anti-treaty), Walshe's predecessor, on 9 November offering his services to or resignation from de Valera's newly formed republican and anti-treaty government if it so wished. This correspondence was obviously unknown to both FitzGerald and Walshe, who had no inkling that Kerney was already committing himself to the anti-treaty side even before the Irish Free State was formally enacted. This is borne out a few weeks later by a communiqué from External Affairs to Kerney enclosing a £300 check, a request for inventory letters, and a quarterly estimate for next year's consular activities from the Irish Free State.

Years later Kerney would argue the familiar republican line that the treaty had been enforced on Ireland by British coercion, that the Four Courts had been bombarded using British guns, that the Irish Free State was a betrayal of the republic, and that those who supported the treaty broke their solemn oath to the republic: "I did not suspect that Mr Blythe, who had induced me to become Consul of the Republic, would be capable of affirming one day that the Republic had never existed. . . . The Provisional Government, which had been set up under Michael Collins at England's request, and which had been tolerated by the Republican Government of which Arthur Griffith had become President, had pocketed the faithless Republican Government immediately after the outbreak of civil war on 28th June 1922. It had therefore become necessary to answer that coup d'état by the reconstitution of the Republican Government."[44]

Kerney was not the only consular official who saw things in a similar light, but it was the tardiness of his decision that is quite striking, as is his correspondence with the shadow republican government behind the backs of his colleagues. It appears that the arrival of de Valera onto the political scene, combined with the obvious good impression he had made on Kerney at the Irish Race Congress, had finally convinced him to choose sides. Yet all this was still taking place in relative secrecy and totally unbeknownst to the Provisional

Government. On 11 December Kerney received a delayed letter from de Valera, himself in hiding, dated 22 November, that acknowledged Kerney's offer of service. De Valera requested estimates of expenditures and a report on his recent activities: "It is our intention to renew all our old activities <u>as soon as possible</u>; and it would be a source of particular pleasure to us, should our finances permit it, to retain our Consulate in Paris. If that is decided on, I shall propose that the Consul be at the same time our Diplomatic and Publicity Agent there, so that both services may be combined."[45] After reviewing Kerney's report, the shadow republican government confirmed him in his position as consul and extended his powers as diplomatic representative of the "Irish Republic," but this letter did not reach him until 16 January 1923. When he received it, he immediately accepted the position. Not until 22 January did he do the sensible thing, which perhaps should have been done weeks if not months before: reveal where his allegiance really stood. In a letter styled and addressed to the "Minister for Foreign Affairs of Dáil Éireann" he advised that "any correspondence which they might have to send to me should reach me through the medium of the legal Government of the Irish Republic."[46] The wording of the letter shows how Jesuitical Kerney could be at times. His departure deprived FitzGerald and his department of an experienced trade agent and linguist at a time when such skills were in short supply. Moreover, his occupancy of the consulate denied the Free State an important overseas base. Walshe's views on Kerney's actions are noteworthy:

> Mr Kerney has written the following letter dated the 22nd January to this Department:
>
> "I have to inform you that my appointment as Irish Consul in Paris has been confirmed by the Government of the Irish Republic and that consequently all further communications which you may wish to send to this Consulate should reach me through the medium of my Government."
>
> The Minister [FitzGerald] wishes you to ask Kerney to hand over the finances he has on hand as well as the office furniture. A list of the furniture is enclosed. His money on hand at the end of December was:

22,558 francs. The best attitude to adopt is that you take the handing over as a matter of course.

The property and money belong to the Irish Government and to refuse your request would be patent dishonesty.

I attach, a formal letter giving you power to take over from him.

If he refuses to hand over perhaps you could convey to him that a notice will of course be issued to the Irish press warning all traders etc, to have nothing to do with him. Naturally the Irish Government can only treat him as a common thief and must arrest him as such when he arrives here.[47]

Kerney denied any misappropriation of public funds under his control: "I duly accounted to the reconstituted Government of the Republic for such funds and property of the Republic as were in my possession or under my control on 31st December 1922."[48] If Walshe's views on Kerney were stinging, the minister's were even more forthright. FitzGerald stood up in the Dáil chamber and accused Kerney of "treachery" to the Irish state and to the Irish people.[49] Kerney looked to posterity to decide who had been the traitor:

> Mr Desmond FitzGerald, of whose official existence as Minister for Foreign Affairs of the Republic I had been left in complete ignorance, and who now blossomed forth as Minister for External Affairs of the "Free State", got up in the lower house of the "Free State" parliament (which now usurps the Republican title "Dáil Éireann") and declared that the Consul in Paris had acted treacherously and gone over to the Republicans. When the facts are known, I am prepared to accept the judgement of the Irish people as to whether it is Desmond FitzGerald or I who have acted the traitor's part.[50]

Years later, as he looked back over these events and how they impacted his career and family life, Kerney believed that he had done nothing wrong and had never resigned his services. He had stood by the republic from beginning to end. The acrimony of the treaty fallout and the subsequent civil war forced former friends and allies, for a variety of reasons, to pick sides and accuse each other of betrayal. FitzGerald's personal slight was indicative of the bitterness that marked this period of Irish history and would last for decades. Kerney hoped that in the fullness of time other generations would pass impartial judgment on who was right and who was wrong:

> It will therefore be clear to all unprejudiced minds that from 31st July 1919, up to this date [31st July 1925], I have remained steadfast in my allegiance to the cause of Irish independence. Men whom I once trusted have chosen to abandon that allegiance. Now, as of six years ago, I obey the dictates of my conscience. If I was right then, I am right now. If I am wrong now, I must have been wrong then. I cannot expect my attitude to be the subject of impartial judgement on the part of men who once thought as I did and do, but who have since changed their allegiance. I, at least, have not changed and do not propose to do so.[51]

CHAPTER 4

THE CONSULAR AND DIPLOMATIC ENVOY OF THE IRISH REPUBLIC, 1922–1926

De Valera's shadow government was in reality a clandestine and nominal government. It had no popular support or effective national administration. The republican funds that had financed the War of Independence had been frozen by the Provisional Government. The members of the republican cabinet were all on the run. Meetings were infrequent, and it could project its authority only through decrees. In one such proclamation it revoked the Dáil majority vote on the treaty taken on 7 January 1922 and declared it null and void. The cabinet authorized legal and extralegal measures to secure funding. Envoys were dispatched to the United States to raise funds, and another decree issued on 5 January 1923 threatened reprisals against anyone who paid taxes, rent, or duties to the Irish Free State. Such persons were declared to be "enemies of the republic" and liable to punishment.[1]

Despite costly military setbacks, the anti-treatyites vowed to fight on until the republic was established, declaring: "Victory for the Republic, or utter defeat and extermination, are now the alternatives."[2]

Austin Stack, the republican minister for finance, believed that £2,000 needed to be raised every month to finance all overseas operations, but this target was never achieved. As a consequence, the diplomatic wing operated on a shoestring and relied heavily on voluntary assistance. The operation of an overseas diplomatic mission was in truth beyond the resources of the organization. After Kerney took a voluntary pay reduction, his salary totalled £700 per annum, which Stack argued was still too high, although, as minister for foreign affairs, de Valera defended it. Communications between Kerney and de Valera were handled via Britain. Reports were sent to covering addresses and couriered to Art Ó Briain, the anti-treaty representative in Britain, who then sent them to another covering address in Ireland. To prevent detection, reports needed to be small and appear innocuous in the post. Frequently couriers were arrested in transit with documents and reports in their possession, which hindered communications. House raids and other searches also disrupted communications. To speed things up, Kerney often used telegram messages, but this was costly, and he always had to pay for them initially out of his own pocket. Nevertheless, the composition and wording of his reports and correspondence to the republican government reflect a man whose mind was at ease once more. He had won the confidence of de Valera and had found his place again as "Diplomatic Envoy of the Irish Government."[3]

DEV'S MAN IN PARIS

No Irish diplomatic mission in France had ever been officially recognized by the French government, and this continued for several more years. The Irish Free State was precluded from external representation by the treaty, and the republican mission was not acknowledged. Although this hindered both sides, it did not stop them from carrying out spying activities against each other. The Free State ran a bureau in Paris and used the intermediary of the British ambassador to contact the French authorities. Neither Desmond FitzGerald nor Joseph Walshe had forgiven Kerney's "treachery," as they saw it, and both employed their bureau officials, Seán Murphy and Vaughan Dempsey, to monitor his movements.[4] Right from the start, they also liaised closely with the Directorate of Intelligence to break the republic's communications with its overseas agents and to find the covering addresses. If they could break this network, they could also stop the flow of funds being paid to finance the overseas operations in Britain, Genoa, and the United States.[5] Paris was seen as the linchpin holding the various overseas republican operations together. Break it, and the others would fail. Gerard Keown has acknowledged Kerney's importance at this time in sustaining the anti-treaty cause abroad: "The activities of anti-treaty representatives after the civil war had ended in Ireland were a thorn in the government's side. . . . The situation was particularly acute in Paris."[6]

Kerney's main priority had shifted dramatically from commercial activities to political affairs. His overriding interest was in raising the political profile of the republic abroad through propaganda work and in countering any efforts by the Free State to portray itself as the lawful representative entity of Ireland in France. He did this by circulating new editions of the *Irish Bulletin*, the gazette of the republic during the War of Independence, in kiosks and shops throughout Paris. He contacted several societies, such as the Cercle Celtique and the Société d'Economie Sociale, which invited him to give political speeches attacking the validity of the Free State to audiences usually numbering a hundred guests. He used his own former acquaintances, as well as friends and colleagues of Seán T. O'Kelly in journalist circles, to get articles published in leading newspapers. His own contacts, particularly with prominent female republicans like Hanna Sheehy Skeffington and Dr. Catherine Lynch, helped him obtain information from Ireland that he used to publish propaganda abroad. Many of the articles he wrote in France were republished in influential American journals, such as the *Irish World*. Valuable assistance was also provided by the small Irish colony, some of whose members were remarkably eccentric figures such as William Gibson, 2nd Baron Ashbourne, a wealthy cultural nationalist who wore traditional Gaelic dress wherever he went in Paris. Undoubtedly the fact that both the Department of External Affairs and its Paris bureau were far from fully established aided Kerney. As Patrick Keatinge commented, the "administrative vacuum" caused by the departure of experienced republican envoys from the diplomatic service inhibited the smooth functioning of External Affairs for some time.[7] This period of reconstruction allowed Kerney to stay one step ahead of the Free State for several months.

The person most involved in overseeing the administrative rebuilding of External Affairs was Joseph Walshe, a man who was quickly to become Kerney's most formidable adversary. Walshe's biographer, Aengus Nolan, explained how the secretary "had his own ideas on how best to organise the department" while ensuring its survival from the prying eyes of the Department of Finance.[8] Dermot Keogh likewise highlighted how, after the civil war ended, Walshe was instrumental in forging a hyper-Catholic image for Irish foreign policy. The secretary, himself a former Jesuit seminarian and "devout Catholic," used every opportunity to replace some of the republicans with former clerical students, like Vaughan Dempsey, thereby ensuring that the next generation of diplomats would be model Catholic representatives to the world.[9] Men like Kerney, converts and non-religious, were relics of a bygone age. Former friends, like Michael MacWhite, derided their former colleague in this new era of Walshe's administrative reforms and Catholic branding of Irish foreign policy. MacWhite poked fun at the thought of Kerney even running a mission on his own: "The acting Trade Agent there [in Paris] knows no more about trade than my boots."[10]

Walshe saw the key function of Irish foreign policy as being active in the political arena, and he devoted most of his department's attention to Anglo-Irish relations, as well as Commonwealth and League of Nations matters, yet all that would be in the future. In the meantime, External Affairs struggled to counter the political and propaganda activities of the republican diplomatic service overseas. In his communications to Walshe, Vaughan Dempsey's reports reflected both the growing frustration Free State officials felt throughout 1923 at the success of anti-treaty propaganda in France and a deep-rooted bitterness toward Kerney from his former colleagues for his perceived betrayal: "If we give opportunity to Kerney to enter into controversy with us, there is the possibility of his turning the whole affair into something like a political dogfight, and if there are any public incidents I am informed by people in administerial circles that the French Government would probably expel the whole circus bag and baggage, Free State and Irregulars and let us fight out our differences elsewhere."[11] Dempsey's solution as to how to deal with Kerney was to request the British embassy in Paris to put pressure on the Quai d'Orsay, headquarters of the French Ministry of Foreign Affairs, to have him expelled from the country: "A word would suffice for the expulsion from France of the ex-Trade Agent," he wrote.[12] Dempsey's colleague Seán Murphy pushed for the precedent of George Gavan Duffy's expulsion to be honored and pressed the French authorities to "expel" Kerney as a troublemaker.[13]

However, getting Kerney out would prove rather trickier, as he was married to a Frenchwoman and had children born in the country. Such a public incident, moreover, might prove counterproductive. Nevertheless, Murphy felt it was worth considering: "As the Quai d'Orsay moves slowly I shall be very glad to have your instructions as soon as possible so that I may ask to have K [Kerney] expelled, if you desire."[14] The other matter of concern for the Free State was that Kerney occupied the former consulate and had accepted £300 prior to his defection. FitzGerald and Walshe consulted George McGrath, the comptroller and auditor general, to see whether Kerney could be evicted by a bailiff or prosecuted in a French court. This, however, was judged a rather undignified method and was swiftly dropped. The department preferred to gain official recognition from the French government first and then pursue these matters legally.

The importance of Kerney's role was also recognized by the republican government even as the Irish Civil War drew to an end. On 23 May, the day before de Valera issued a statement calling on republican forces to cease fighting, he wrote to Kerney stressing his invaluable service to the republic. The Sinn Féin president informed Kerney that the political situation was now "critical," that the war was lost but that the civil administration would remain in operation and that the republic would be achieved by political and nonviolent means: "You realise how much, owing to the difficulties of communication and enemy pressure, we have to rely on the wise personal initiative of our representatives abroad."[15] The communication reflected de Valera's personal attachment to Kerney, his belief in the envoy's abilities as well as his understanding that Irish foreign policy, albeit from the anti-treaty side, needed to remain as internationalist as possible. The note is also important for later consideration in this book, as it highlights the degree of freedom and emphasis on personal initiative that de Valera encouraged Kerney to exercise in discharging his duties.

Throughout 1923 de Valera wrote to Kerney more often than at any time previously, and their correspondence reflected a growing friendship between the men as well as a loyal trust that was to last for decades. The military defeat of the anti-treaty side marked one of the lowest points in de Valera's political career, yet Kerney's continued service and commitment to the cause in this period were not forgotten by the republican leader. On 20 June de Valera advised Kerney that from September's end the republic could probably set aside only £100 for a diplomatic mission on the continent. Despite this unfortunate news, the envoy remained undaunted in his commitment to the cause and personally to de Valera, who he believed personified the republic. In another letter to Kerney, de Valera praised his continued sacrifices for the republican struggle and assured him that soon they would be "on the high road once more."[16] As always, Kerney blindly followed his "Chief," as he called him, on the road to God-knows-where despite the obvious financial sacrifice and emotional strain this rocky path placed on his young family.

In July Kerney carried out two important tasks for de Valera. The first involved a trip to Vienna to attend a meeting connected with the League of Nations. A core focus of the Free State was gaining admission into the League of Nations because, as Gerard Keown has demonstrated, international diplomacy remained "the best guarantee of the rights" of small countries in the interwar years.[17] De Valera wanted the republic's cause to be promoted at the conference to counter the Free State's work, but he had no funds to give to his envoy to carry out the mission. Unperturbed, Kerney secured funding from an Irish American, Thomas Hughes Kelly, and both men traveled to the conference, where they handed out pamphlets and met many of the conference delegates to let the republic's case be known. The envoy was becoming increasingly adept at handling political matters, and he used these gatherings to link the republican cause with the causes of other oppressed minorities, particularly those opposed to the British Empire. This transition from a trade agent to a diplomat is illustrated by the bulk of his correspondence from this time, which was concerned with foreign affairs and not economic affairs. In one speech Kerney advocated nonviolent resistance to British rule by highlighting the career of anti-militarist and socialist Jean Jaurès at a Parisian political demonstration. These first tentative steps in analyzing political affairs would prove very useful over a decade later, when he began compiling detailed political reports. De Valera was pleased with his political activities, and he remembered to send a note to Kelly to thank him for assisting Kerney. The note reveals the softer side of the republican leader: "I cannot tell you what anguish of heart I have suffered during the past year. I thank God that the killing of brothers is ended."[18]

The second political task the envoy carried out concerned the detention of republican prisoners in Irish jails. The anti-treatyites tried to highlight the poor conditions and brutal treatment meted out to their prisoners by Free State authorities as a breach of the Geneva Conventions. Some of the witness statements were shocking. One detainee, Joseph Clark, claimed that after his arrest by the Criminal Investigation Department (CID) he had been detained in Portobello Barracks and beaten about the body with a "45 Webley [a revolver] by Intel [Intelligence] off [Officer]," that his moustache had been "tore off" and his ears "twisted" with pliers.[19] Eunan O'Halpin has documented at length the brutal role of the CID, whose officers "sometimes killed prisoners."[20] The republicans sent female delegates to the League of Nations to protest these abuses. Kerney liaised with them in order to garner international support for their plight: "Mr Kerney has given us valuable assistance up to date," the republican delegates noted.[21] Kerney took on the task of refuting the findings of the League's investigative team, and on 12 July he sent a detailed report to de Valera challenging the report of the International Committee of the Red Cross on its inspection of Mountjoy Prison, Newbridge, Tintown, and Gormanstown camps. He also wrote articles on the state of these facilities for republican papers.[22] The republican government had long argued that these male and female detainees were held in poor sanitary conditions with little medical treatment and inadequate food, a perception that has been challenged by recent historical research.[23] In his report Kerney identified several flaws in the committee's investigation, including the facts that no prisoners had been interviewed and other major facilities, such as Kilmainham and North Dublin Union, had not been inspected. He also questioned the figure given for the total prisoner population, arguing that it was in fact 11,750, not 7,369. The issue of prisoners was another avenue de Valera was eager to exploit, as their continued detention won over moderate public opinion for Sinn Féin against the Free State, and in this instance again, Kerney's work was seen as valuable. On the same day he wrote this report, which de Valera marked as "very good," Kerney received a photograph from his superior.[24] It delighted the republican consul: "I am glad to have it for the Office and shall moreover always treasure it as a precious souvenir of the present struggle for the independence of our Country."[25]

SOLDIERING ON

In a blaze of publicity, de Valera was arrested on the election platform in his constituency of Ennis. The media frenzy gave the republicans the publicity boost they desperately needed. De Valera was unique amongst Irish political figures as the one man whose personality and prominence could secure front-page international coverage. Kerney delighted in reading the French press reports and seeing images of the arrest. With the "Chief" in prison, Patrick Ruttledge took over the leadership of Sinn Féin and enjoyed a good working relationship with Kerney at an important time. In November hunger strikes by republicans began in Mountjoy seeking unconditional release, and Ruttledge wanted these strikes publicized in international newspapers. There was no letup in Kerney's workload. He was churning out 600 copies of the *Irish Bulletin* a week and sending them to 369 French deputies and senators as well as subscribers in Spain, Belgium, Switzerland, Sweden, Denmark, and Norway. He continued his work uninterrupted even after an attack of severe rheumatism. The strain of the past year took its toll on other republican figures. Robert Brennan, the republican director of publicity, collapsed from mental exhaustion while in Paris, and Kerney had to care for him over the next few months. Brennan's successor, Mary MacSwiney, was amazed at Kerney's tireless endeavors: "LHK [Leopold Harding Kerney] seems such a topper to work. I am convinced that all the help given him will be the best expenditure possible."[26] Clearly his usefulness was understood throughout the republican movement at a time when the Free State was starting to make major advances in Irish foreign policy.

The year 1924 brought little respite for the republicans. The vastly superior resources of the Free State, combined with the administrative overhaul of External Affairs undertaken by Desmond FitzGerald and Joseph Walshe, began to bite. The Irish Free State won official recognition at the League of Nations. This was a major achievement, as it accorded the Irish government, in the words of Michael Kennedy, "a crucial listening post" on the international stage and broadened its diplomatic network.[27] External Affairs soon had its first minister plenipotentiary in the United States, belying the republican argument that the treaty precluded Ireland's development of a national and independent foreign policy. In response, the republicans struggled to collect funds even for a prisoner fund. Kerney again did his best: "A few months ago I was able to have collected and sent to Dublin about frs. 1300, but of this amount I contributed 500 frs."[28]

In de Valera's absence the envoy was coming under increasing pressure from the republican cabinet to justify the continued operation of his mission: "The policy of keeping a representative in this country seems to me to be a sound one. Paris is the most important center on the European continent. I have always understood that the enlisting of continental opinion on our side was held to be desirable and even necessary. If you withdraw from Paris, people here and elsewhere will conclude that the 'Free State' has definitely and finally replaced the Republic," he argued.[29] The uncertainty over future funding and his own employment weighed heavily on Kerney's mind, but he received little sympathy from Michael Colivet, the republican minister for finance, who repeatedly threatened to either close the mission or force the envoy to work for £30 a month, which amounted to roughly half his initial starting salary.[30] The only thing stopping Colivet from acting was de Valera's continued support of Kerney: "the value of his [Kerney's] services, which as you know are immense. The President had a very high opinion of him, and considered the salary he was getting much too small."[31]

On 14 March Kerney wrote an article that was well received by the French authorities titled "Alternative Markets—Or Else?" that favored free trade between France and the "Irish Republic."[32] On 16 March Andrée Viollis, a journalist and acquaintance of the envoy, wrote a favorable article in the large-circulation daily newspaper *Paris-Soir* on the republic. These publications and personal contacts were perhaps the envoy's strongest assets in overcoming the major financial and staffing limitations on his mission. On 19 March Vaughan Dempsey wrote to Walshe complaining again about the favorable press coverage Kerney was receiving. He feared such articles would confuse French public opinion about Ireland's legal government. The angry tone of his report might have been due to Kerney's early booking of the Palais d'Orsay restaurant for the annual Saint Patrick's Day celebration. Dempsey and his supporters had to wait in the hotel foyer until the republican guests finished their banquet. When Dempsey called into the offices of another publication, *Bonsoir*, the same day, he was astonished and indignant to see the editor phone Kerney in Dempsey's presence and assure the republican envoy "that the 'Bonsoir' was devoted to his principles and was entirely at his orders!"[33] Alongside this, Kerney's friendly relations with senior French civil servants convinced Dempsey, wrongly, that the Free State was losing the propaganda battle against the republic in France and on the continent and that Kerney's connections were far more numerous than they actually were. Writing to Joseph Walshe he said, "Might I suggest that you give me authority to employ a reliable Agency to have Kerney's movements watched during a fortnight. The report might be illuminating and give us useful information as to his activities, and the people with whom he is in touch."[34] Responding to Dempsey's reports, Walshe advised: "If at any time you have good grounds to believe that Kerney's activities are affecting the interests of the State, the Minister will be glad to have a further report so that he may take appropriate action."[35] Dempsey again recommended expulsion. FitzGerald, conscious of the broader picture, feared that a heavy-handed approach could upset relations with the French over such a minor irritant as the republican consulate. The minister was also aware at this time, through his close collaborative work with the Directorate of Intelligence, that the republic's overall position was fragile, despite Kerney's optimism: "The F.S. [Free State] seems to be moving rapidly to its doom," he wrote.[36] The republicans were finding it difficult to motivate the rank and file in de Valera's absence. Squabbles and a lack of discipline were breaking out. In one instance, Michael Colivet falsely charged Kerney with benefiting from the exchange rate, which drew a stinging response from Kerney: "The supposition that I have some such gain to account for is a gratuitous insult."[37] When de Valera was finally released in July, it injected the organization with renewed energy and optimism. Kerney wrote his best article yet in *Le Matin* on 24 July and received a standing ovation at the Club du Faubourg, where eight hundred guests listened to him give a political speech on Ireland. His counterpart from the Free State, Seán Murphy, declined the club's invitation to debate the treaty with Kerney.

All things considered, the envoy had done remarkably well during de Valera's imprisonment, especially given the disparity of resources allocated to him in comparison to the Free State. Kerney had shown that his skills extended far beyond commercial matters. He traveled to fairs, delivered political speeches, published articles, churned out copious propaganda materials, and built up his connections in Parisian society to publicize the republic and to challenge the validity of the Irish Free State at every turn. His superiors were always grateful for his devotion to and hard work for the cause, but this did not stop Colivet from repeatedly cutting the mission's expenses. As always, it was de Valera who defended Kerney the most and who saw the importance of his diplomatic work. His kind words were from one friend to another: "I am just now preparing to go to the North, and as I am likely to be arrested there, I take this opportunity to tell you how much your work is appreciated here. If only we could have such representatives in all the principal European countries, but that may come!"[38] Kerney replied to this handwritten letter. His wording shows the depth of loyalty he felt toward the "Chief":

> Your generously kind letter of 20th October is one which I shall always treasure, and it is for me a source of great satisfaction to know that my efforts, such as they are, are appreciated by those who have suffered so much and who continue to suffer in order that the Nation's honour may be saved. Your appreciation of my work strengthens in me that self-confidence which is so necessary at all times; on the other hand, I shall take good care that it does not develop any overweening or exaggerated notion of my own worth.
>
> Pray accept my assurances of profound esteem and my sincere hope that under your inspiring leadership the goal of liberty will soon be reached.[39]

Kerney was perhaps unique among his colleagues in that his health had remained relatively good during these years, probably because he had never faced imprisonment or been on the run, but he did devote every hour to the cause, and there is no doubt that this work came before family life. His superiors kept him informed about events in Ireland. The republicans had hoped that the Free State would crumble, but the state proved remarkably resilient, surviving the army mutiny in 1924 and the Boundary Commission crisis in 1925. As time continued, the republic became ever more illusory, and although Kerney never wavered in his enthusiasm, it was clear that de Valera had not yet found the imagined "high road," though his appeals to Kerney remained constant and helped foster a mutual respect and understanding between the men, as is reflected by this note from de Valera to Kerney: "Just a line to wish you a very happy Christmas. I am sorry that so far I have found it impossible to give to the Foreign Affairs

Department the personal attention I would wish. I fear also that it will not be possible to secure an improvement in this respect for a long time to come. However I wish to assure you again how very pleased everyone is with your work."[40]

THE REPUBLICAN MOVEMENT SPLITS AGAIN

Throughout most of 1925, Kerney was busy establishing political connections with other subjugated peoples of the British Empire. He met Egyptian and Indian nationalists to hear their grievances and to highlight the republican struggle against British oppression in an international context. Again he was encouraged in all these political meetings to use his own judgment rather than seek approval from his superiors first. De Valera made this point clearly again: "P [President] asks me to say that he leaves the conduct of these negotiations to your own judgement, knowing well how essential it is that you should have freedom."[41] Kerney, now an envoy (having been promoted to envoy once he went over to Dev's side), also met prominent Basque nationalist Elias Gallastegui. In one such meeting the importation of arms was discussed, which was rather peculiar given the envoy's previous lack of interest in any military consideration: "I suggested that a report as to possibilities of his country being able to supply light artillery, machine guns, rifles, etc the conditions of payment and shipping facilities would be of great interest to me personally."[42]

On the propaganda front, Kerney and a French associate, Baron Félix de Rosnay, worked throughout 1925 to secure private investment for a series of editions called *Inis Fáil: Bulletin de la Ligue pour l'indépendance de l'Irlande*. The editions were professionally made and well illustrated. Among the common contents were articles by Kerney extolling the legitimacy of the "Irish Republic" from 1916 onward, as well as pieces by his wife, Raymonde, and anti-treaty sympathizers. De Valera contributed an opening letter to the first edition extolling the righteousness of the struggle: "The Irish cause is just," he wrote.[43] *Inis Fáil* was designed to appeal to Catholic readers of *Le Figaro*, and its success marked the final stages of Kerney's mission in Paris. By the middle of 1925, however, Desmond FitzGerald and his colleagues in the Directorate of Intelligence had finally begun regular interceptions of Kerney's communications with the republican government. This intelligence coup provided the Free State with a window into the true state of the republic's most important continental mission. In one instance they intercepted reports from the republicans showing that their communication with Kerney was being severely undermined by Free State raids on covering addresses and arrests of couriers, as this note from the republican undersecretary of foreign affairs shows: "Bad news from Kerney, comms seems to have completely broken down from us to him. He has had no letter from me since one dated March 27th. The man is an invaluable worker and will do much for your department if not handicapped so terribly."[44]

The breakdown in regular communication between the Paris consulate and the republican government affected Kerney's mood. He felt quite isolated from his colleagues and events. His frustrations were often reflected in his communications, especially in his attitude toward the minister for finance, but despite admiring his "absolute frankness," his superiors urged him to be more accommodating toward his colleagues: "In these days, when many things are difficult for us all, there is a close and unbreakable comradeship in which you have a big place and upon which you can and must always rely even blindly. Distance, letters, the impossibility of talking things over—these things make the medium of exchange imperfect. One must make generous allowance."[45]

De Valera arrived on the scene again to reinvigorate Kerney's commitment to the cause. The Chief was impressed by a front-page photograph of Kerney in a French newspaper, *La France du Nord*, that Kerney had arranged. It captured the envoy meeting senior clerics, including Archbishop Daniel Mannix of Melbourne. Dermot Keogh has highlighted Mannix's known "anti-British sentiments."[46] This positive image was the kind of propaganda the republicans desperately needed to counter accusations that they were secretly in touch with communist Russia and to show that the republicans had clerical support in some quarters: "We want all the sympathy we can get, in every quarter, but, under present circumstances, the mere whisper of an understanding between the communists and ourselves can do us incalculable harm."[47] The photo was a major propaganda success, and de Valera was greatly impressed by Kerney's achievement. The Sinn Féin president wanted to reward the diplomat with a visit to Ireland to attend the Celtic Congress. The offer, coming from the republican leader, greatly enthused Kerney, who had not been back in Ireland for a considerable time. The envoy was delighted with the chance to meet de Valera again and to show his homeland to his wife, who had given just as much as her husband to the cause. But the minister of finance was against Kerney's traveling to the congress:

> Kerney presumably had property, and possibly cash, of Dáil Éireann in his possession when he refused to recognise the Free State Govt. May not a civil or even a criminal action lie against him now if he comes within the jurisdiction of the F/S [Free State] courts?
>
> Furthermore, the Treason Act is now practically in force, and he is liable to be proceeded against for seditious actions ABROAD against the FS Govt. Without a copy of the Act I cannot say definitely what the terms are but I have a recollection that they rope in action abroad as well as at home.
>
> Kerney is a great thorn in their side abroad, and they will jump at an opportunity of getting him. He is, for the same reason and others, a great asset of ours, and we cannot afford to have him arrested. Possibly the nature of the Conference may protect him. I doubt it very much.[48]

Responding to this decision, Kerney expressed his "disappointment" that he could not show his family his homeland and visit his father, Philip, whom he had not seen for several years: "It is a disappointment for me not to be able to meet you all in Dublin and to bring back with me fresh knowledge and a closer grasp of things, to say nothing of my natural wish to revisit the country and see my father and others, and bring Mrs K. and the children to know Ireland and its people still better."[49]

Clearly an element of fatigue was starting to impact every section of the republican movement. The Directorate of Intelligence was well aware that the Sinn Féin organization at home and abroad was in a parlous state. The agency copied another report Kerney wrote on 23 October in which he sought assurances from his superiors as to whether the consulate would remain open or whether he should begin looking for private employment. The Free State also intercepted communications between Colivet and Mary MacSwiney, the republican envoy in New York. In one critical letter, Colivet revealed the dire financial situation facing the organization. Sinn Féin's newspaper, *An Phoblacht*, was not selling enough copies and was becoming "a large drain on us,"[50] according to the republican minister for finance. The republic would have to close down the ministries of foreign affairs and economic affairs as well as overseas offices to facilitate "retrenchment."[51] The outlook was bleak: "We have no reserves now," wrote the same minister. "If we don't get £1,000 per month we might as well shut shop. . . . I just want you to know how we stand financially,—very bad at present."[52]

Kerney offered to return to Ireland and work there in some capacity, but this offer was rejected. The uncertainty about his future caused him great anxiety: "What assurance do you wish me to give to friends of our cause in France, who may be inclined to interpret the closing of this Office as being a sign of the collapse of the Republican movement, and not merely of momentary financial embarrassment?"[53] His anxiety was resolved again by de Valera, who asked him to stay on in Paris in an honorary and part-time capacity. Kerney agreed. He now worked tirelessly to secure seasonal work for some well-known republican activists on the run, like Seán MacBride, the future chief of staff of the IRA. With his family facing an uncertain Christmas, Kerney hoped the New Year would bring better times: "There is certainly a trying time ahead but I shall hope to weather the storm unaided."[54]

Politically, de Valera had gradually come to the realization that if he ever wanted to return to power he would have to recognize the fact that the Irish Free State was not going to disappear and could not be ignored. Such a major political volte face was in clear breach of republican policy, which he himself had advocated for years. As Diarmaid Ferriter observed, this new policy offered the only "opportunity to win the people over."[55] On 28 March 1926, at the Sinn Féin Ard Fheis, de Valera stated his intention to end abstention and enter the Dáil, if the oath was removed, and lead an effective parliamentary opposition to the government. His motion was narrowly defeated. With his policy rejected and the republican movement split yet again over a contentious political issue, de Valera and his followers formed a new political party called Fianna Fáil (Warriors of Destiny). De Valera and his lieutenants immediately canvassed for support from Sinn Féin national branches or cumainn throughout the country and began raising funds for Fianna Fáil. This weakened the Sinn Féin organization further. With de Valera's departure as Sinn Féin president, Art O'Connor was elected his successor.

De Valera and O'Connor tussled for Kerney's services, not knowing which side of the republican fence he stood closest to. This canvassing for Kerney's support reveals the level of trust both sides of the republican movement felt toward him. On 23 April de Valera first notified Kerney of the results of the Sinn Féin vote and his decision to form Fianna Fáil: "On March 28th, at a meeting of the Teachtaí by a vote of 19 to 18 my policy was not approved of. Though it is possible that at a full meeting there would be a majority in favour of the policy, I considered it better in the general interest of the movement to resign and let my opponents take the machinery, for the present at any rate."[56] He outlined his political vision and national policy for Ireland. He envisioned his economic program as making "Ireland an economic unit as self-contained and self-sufficient as possible."[57] Though Kerney was not himself an advocate of autarchy, this program for economic development would have found a welcome reception with him, as he strongly believed in the primacy of economics as an expression of national independence and progress. De Valera sent the envoy a signed copy of the Fianna Fáil manifesto with its five-point program, which also called for the restoration of the Irish language and national unification of the island. On 25 April O'Connor also wrote to Kerney advising him of the situation: "There is now a change in the administration. I unfortunately, have been placed in D's place."[58] Kerney was very seriously ill at this time with blood poisoning following a mosquito bite, yet he made the firm decision to stay out of the political commotion and remain on in his voluntary capacity at the consulate.

The envoy had never involved himself in party politics, even during the treaty debates, arguing that he served the republic and nothing else. Clearly he was a man still wholeheartedly committed to his principles, but he had not lost his shrewdness or instincts for survival. He kept the door open to Fianna Fáil by donating money to the party, and he wrote often to old colleagues like Seán T. O'Kelly to show his sympathies and to ask for a favor if need be. His wife, Raymonde, likewise wrote often to de Valera. Their personal correspondence revealed the anxiety de Valera was experiencing after he set up Fianna Fáil: "It is rather hard to be starting all over again here 'at the beginning' but good progress is being made."[59] Raymonde, for her part, was doing what any good wife in her position would—ensuring that her husband's services would not be forgotten and that he did not disappear off the political radar. This tactic would prove to save Kerney in a few years' time.

As these momentous political events were unfolding, Kerney and Raymonde welcomed the birth of a baby boy on 1 April. It was to be the couple's last child. In a mark of his personal admiration for and friendship with de Valera, Kerney decided to name his son Eamon, and he asked de Valera to be the boy's godfather. This decision reflected the bond of friendship that had been forged during these difficult years between the men. It also showed that de Valera's influence on Kerney the man was as powerful as John Mitchel's had been on Kerney the youth. De Valera kept the fires of Kerney's republicanism burning. The Fianna Fáil leader warmly accepted the honor, but, owing to his heavy workload, he asked Seán MacBride to stand in as a substitute baptismal sponsor at the ceremony. De Valera sent Kerney a small silver chalice that replicated the Ardagh Chalice as a token gift to baby Eamon. When he sent it, he wrote:

> I take advantage of the crossing of a friend to send Eamon Conall a small token. The coming of a new member into a household is such an occasion for joy that I am very grateful to Madame Cearnaigh [Kerney]

and yourself for giving me the privilege of sharing in it. I hope the boy will grow up to be as stout a champion of Ireland's cause as his father has been. I trust you are keeping well and I wish you all long years of happiness together.[60]

Throughout July and August, Art O'Connor had traveled around the United States in a desperate bid to continue funding the Sinn Féin organization. On his return he stopped over in Paris to give the envoy important documents relating to a bond litigation that he did not want to fall into "enemy hands," and also to inform Kerney that the organization could no longer fund the operation of the consulate, which finally closed for good in the middle of October: "I fear practically all activities at home which are not voluntary must be closed down," he wrote.[61] O'Connor admitted that he did not know if Kerney was supportive of Fianna Fáil or Sinn Féin, but he felt that he spoke for the whole republican movement when he wrote:

> I cannot too much stress the debt under which the Republic lies to you for the distinction you brought on it in the conduct of its affairs in Paris during the many years that you have been in charge. From all sides, I hear nothing but praise of your industry and ability and it is some little personal compensation to you to know that in this compulsory closing down of activities that you bear with you nothing but regret of those who are unable to utilise your services as they would wish and the sincerest wishes for success in your future ventures.[62]

This kind note was answered by Kerney, who declared his "most willing" commitment to stay the course and his conviction that the real enemy was, as always, England.[63] This letter marked the end of his official connection with Sinn Féin. He was now a private citizen, unemployed and walking alone on the road toward an increasingly distant republic.

CHAPTER 5

THE WILDERNESS
YEARS, 1926–1932

After the closing of the republican consulate in Paris by the president of Sinn Féin, Art O'Connor, Kerney found himself out in the cold with few prospects of securing private employment in France's depressed postwar economy. Small firms and traditional industries were reluctant to hire new employees given the economic uncertainty over the French franc throughout 1926 and in early 1927.[1] Things were little better in Ireland. Kerney also knew that the political views that had shaped his life over the previous years were not shared by his family back home, who had disagreed with his entire political outlook from the time of his recruitment to the consular service. No one was more critical than his "big brother" Henry.[2] Henry was a senior official in the British Civil Service who had been working in Berlin as part of the Reparations Commission, and he had always advised Leopold not to mix himself up in "absurd politics."[3] The brothers had frequently exchanged sharp opinions via letters during and after the War of Independence. In one such exchange, Henry had compared the Irish republican forces to a "wolf-hound" taking on a giant "elephant" (the British Army).[4] He had seen the republican struggle from the start as a fantasy: "asking for the moon—that is to say a republic."[5] Henry was a frequent contributor to the *Irish Times* defending the treaty and the Cumann na nGaedheal (Society of the Gaels) government after its ratification. He compared IRA soldiers to "assassination gangs" and described Éamon de Valera and his followers as "scoundrels" and "imposters."[6]

Leopold always responded to Henry's attacks on republicanism and the Irish struggle for independence in a forthright but friendly manner. He reiterated time and again his own innate belief in Irish economic and political independence. He did not want Irish people—men and women—to be "subjects" of the British crown, and he delighted in purchasing "nothing English."[7] During the height of the conflict in Ireland, he reminded Henry that the British Army was not so "almighty mighty as before 1914."[8] The different viewpoints held by both brothers toward the war and its subsequent aftermath were replicated in many Irish households at a time when the fallout from the treaty tore families apart.

Leopold's father, Philip, whom all the brothers referred to as the "Governor," was at this time particularly worried about Leopold and how he was going to support his young family after the consulate closed for lack of funds. Philip hoped his son would now leave the republican movement and take up a regular job outside of any political connections. He used the opportunity of a letter he wrote in December 1926 to implore Leopold to stop blindly following de Valera, referring to "the obstinacy of that man De Valera in causing the deaths of so many lives."[9] The tone of the letter is very much that of a patriarchal father admonishing his youngest son for being reckless in involving himself in the republican struggle. However, Philip reserves most of his criticism for his son's actions over the years toward de Valera personally. A belief that de Valera had hoodwinked or brainwashed Leopold into blindly following him appears to be Philip's main take on it all. He referred in the letter to de Valera as "that man" who caused "widespread evil" during the civil war.[10] The family left the door open for Leopold to return home if he so wished and to leave politics to one side. Kerney opted instead to stay on in Paris and find work there.

On 24 June 1927 Henry died suddenly of heart failure. His death shattered Philip, who never recovered from the shock of his son's untimely death. Philip died just a few months later, on 30 October. Inwardly their deaths hurt Leopold deeply, and he was wracked by grief. The deaths were compounded by anxiety over Mario, his eldest brother, who suffered with mental deficiencies and was unable to look after himself. Philip had always lived in rented accommodations with Mario. The cost of caring for his son meant that there was only a small inheritance to divide among the family members. With the other three brothers—Nicholas, Maurice, and Arnold—also living abroad, Leopold was worried about Mario's fate and financial security. When Maurice decided to look after Mario and move his family to London, Leopold continued to make his normal monthly payment toward Mario's care even though he could scarcely afford it. These were bleak financial times for Leopold and Raymonde. They were forced to leave the more prosperous area of Rue de la Terrasse and move to cheaper accommodations at 22 Rue Sarrette. The move was a symbol of Kerney's financial, emotional, and professional decline.

A FORGOTTEN MAN

In winter walks together with their children in the nearby Parc Monsouris, Leopold and Raymonde discussed how they were going to make ends meet. For Kerney this was a particularly hard time, as he agonized over the cruel hand fate had dealt him. He had once dreamed of extending Ireland's links with the continent across Europe after the success of the *Banba* project and had hoped to secure trade agreements with other countries he was familiar with during his travels in the 1910s and 20s—the Low Countries, Germany, Spain, and Italy. He wanted Ireland to use its agricultural and manufacturing base to connect with the continent and move its economy away from near-total dependence on the British market. This vibrant continental trade would finance the republic's social program and end class distinctions. He looked back at the well-heeled childhood that had separated him

so distinctly from ordinary Dubliners living in working-class tene-
ments and the Liberties (one of Dublin's most historic working-class
neighborhoods) and dreamed that another generation would never see
such inequality. But with his long-held plans ruined, his career apparently finished, and the whole republican movement again in chaos,
he could only lament the loss of what could have been. Raymonde
stood loyally by her husband through thick and thin, even though his
defense of his principles, rightly or wrongly, was the main reason they
now faced such a difficult financial situation. It was an indication of
their closeness and happy marriage that she would remain loyally at
her husband's side right until his death.

Following the assassination of Kevin O'Higgins, the vice president of the executive council and Free State minister for justice and
external affairs on 10 July 1927 while he was walking to Mass, the
Free State government acted swiftly against republican elements. A
Public Safety Act allowed for the reintroduction of military courts to
tackle the IRA, and an Electoral Amendment Act forced all successful parliamentary candidates to attend the Dáil.[11] This last act ended
Fianna Fáil's abstentionism and lack of cooperation with the state.
De Valera used a theatrical form of deception to claim he never took
an oath to the Free State, even though he had, and Fianna Fáil began
unloosing the tight ropes of republican dogma that had constricted
its popular appeal. When news of Fianna Fáil's attendance in the Dáil
reached Kerney, it shocked him. Writing to his close friend Hanna
Sheehy Skeffington[12]—who had resigned from the party over this
very issue—he lamented trusting politicians who repeatedly abandoned electoral promises:

> I never thought it possible that FF [Fianna Fáil] would go back on its
> constantly reiterated pledge. It seems an outright dishonest thing to do.
> But I am struck by the unanimity of the decision, and, in the dark I grope
> for the reason which led to it; after all, they are not all weak men or
> rogues, although possibly some of them might answer that description.
>
> I am wondering how opinion in Ireland will react to the new move
> and I fear that FF may perhaps lose ground. If that happens I see no

hope for many a long day to come because there is no likelihood of any other Republican body being organised to take its place.[13]

Fianna Fáil's move into constitutional parliamentary democracy did not, as Kerney feared, undermine its development but actually broadened its base of support, as Seán Cronin noted: "Sinn Féin faded into the shadows as de Valera drew a majority of Republicans behind him."[14] A confidential Garda report on the Sinn Féin party's Ard Fheis in December revealed that just 150 delegates had attended, and there was only £90 on deposit.[15] Kerney still detested the "ignominy of the oath," yet it appears that at this time he, too, was deviating from hard-line republican dogma: "I would have infinitely preferred it if FF could have first of all released themselves of their pledge to the electors before acting in direct opposition to that pledge. It is the breaking of that promise which saddens me, far more than if at another election FF candidates were to go forward with the avowed intention of swallowing the oath."[16]

With no prospect of immediate help from either republican faction, Kerney found himself in the wilderness and his services not required. It was a hard adjustment. Practical considerations were forcing him to secure private employment. Initially he thought about moving to Bordeaux, near Raymonde's family, and setting up a farm, even though he had no farming background or experience in intensive manual labor. The financial outlay required for such an undertaking would be great, and uprooting the family from Paris was another disincentive. Kerney then thought about setting up an Irish tourist service, but this again would require seed capital that he did not have or could not raise. In the end he managed to secure a job with estate agent Frank Arthur that he held for the next five years. His new job afforded him a regular income, and he was able to send his eldest children, Jean Michel and Micheline, back to Ireland to further their education. This separation from the children upset Raymonde, yet she and Leopold found solace in their baby boy, Eamon. In a letter to Hanna Sheehy Skeffington, Kerney wrote about how the little child brought so much happiness into their married life: "[The] happy natured, bright, clever little fellow is a big compensation for the absence of the other two."[17]

Both parents managed in the summer of 1929 to visit Jean and Micheline in Ireland. Jean was studying in the Jesuit-founded Clongowes Wood College, the exclusive private school of the Irish Catholic elite, while Micheline attended the Cross and Passion College in Kilcullen. Kerney realized that a private Catholic education was the best avenue for career progress for his children. During the trip back home the parents took the children on outings to Glendalough to climb into Saint Kevin's Bed, a cave in which the saint was believed to have lived. Photographs from the time show that at forty-seven Leopold was still quite fit and active. In one photograph he is shown climbing a rocky outcrop below the hermit's cave, while in another he is horseplaying in the lake. The photograph collection also reveals the esteem in which Kerney was held in republican circles. The family was joined on one picnic by Dorothy Macardle, Robert Brennan, Robert Briscoe, and Frank Gallagher—persons who would all be very close to Fianna Fáil and de Valera in particular. In another photo Kerney is seen playing cricket, showing that he had never entirely jettisoned some English traditions from his youth, such as serving as a cricket captain. Clearly the people he encountered in such activities saw him as one of their own, and these trips were useful for networking and keeping thoughts of him alive within influential republican circles as well as keeping an eye on his elder children's schooling.

Although Kerney was no longer a public servant, he continued to maintain contact with the Irish colony in Paris to keep the republican cause alive in France. He had not lost his imagination for daring exploits either, contemplating at one stage hiring a plane and dropping leaflets about Ireland across central Paris, writing: "Some day, for instance, I hope it will be possible to hire an aeroplane (but that means money too!) and drop leaflets in Paris and elsewhere; the aviator might be fined if he were caught, but he would certainly have no difficulty in getting press interviews."[18]

Kerney set up a "non-political" group called Le Cercle France-Irlande and continued to organize a Saint Patrick's Day celebration out of his own pocket.[19] The national celebration was well attended by some cosmopolitan figures, as well as by international guests (Basque and Catalan representatives), which showed how popular Kerney was in republican circles at home and abroad. From the Irish side, Lord Ashbourne, the aristocratic and extroverted Protestant president of the Gaelic League—a "picturesque figurehead" in traditional Gaelic costume,. as Kerney noted—chaired the event.[20] Erskine Childers also attended.[21] Hanna Sheehy Skeffington delivered the main speech of the occasion, titled "Ireland Today." On the French side, Joseph Crozier and the Marquis de Belleval attended. Both men were former intelligence agents who had written a sensational book detailing their exploits in the secret service against Germany in the Great War: *En mission chez l'ennemi, 1915–1918*. Kerney lamented the fact that he could not impart to the authors stories of daring from Ireland's war with England: "I wish I knew more about the workings of our 'Intelligence Service,'" he wrote. "A description of secret hiding places in houses where Dev and others were able to avoid capture."[22] The guests all wore the Easter lily and some a Fáinne (a pin worn to show fluency in, or a willingness to speak, the Irish language). An orchestra was hired to play traditional and contemporary Irish songs, including "We'll Crown de Valera King of Ireland." Some less-than-elegant poetry was also recited:

> Look round, the Frenchman governs France
> The Spaniard rules in Spain
> The gallant Pole but waits a chance
> To break the Russian chain
> The strife for freedom here begun
> We never will give over
> We'll own no land on earth but one
> We're Paddies evermore.[23]

REINSTATEMENT

Ironically, it was Kerney's continued organization of the Saint Patrick's Day celebrations that would become the focal point of his reintegration into the diplomatic service. In 1929 the French authorities finally recognized an Irish diplomatic mission in their country, and the Irish Free State opened its legation in Paris. The appointed minister reflected Walshe's identification of Irish foreign policy with Catholicism under his tutelage. Gerald O'Kelly, a Jesuit-taught student from Clongowes Wood College and a papal count, embodied the image of a Catholic diplomatic representative to another Catholic state. Before the treaty split them, O'Kelly and Kerney had been good friends, another indicator of how popular Kerney was in the consular service before the split. His friendship with O'Kelly had ended abruptly after Kerney joined de Valera's shadow administration. While Kerney worked as the republican envoy, O'Kelly worked for the Irish Free State and monitored the renegade's activities when Kerney visited Belgium for trade, publicity, and political affairs both during and after the civil war.

On 25 February 1931, O'Kelly wrote a revealing letter to Kerney, stressing the point that he was writing in a personal capacity and not as an employee of the Irish Free State. He wanted them to resume their personal friendship. O'Kelly was taking a big risk, and he was obviously writing to Kerney unbeknownst to Walshe, who still viewed the republican as a traitor and a "common thief."[24] However, as Gerard Keown has observed, O'Kelly shared a similar work style with Kerney, and also a "penchant for taking initiatives," often without sanction.[25] If either Joseph Walshe or the minister Patrick McGilligan had learned of this correspondence it could have jeopardized O'Kelly's career and reputation. Kerney was persona non grata as far as Walshe was concerned, and if the British had discovered O'Kelly's contact with anyone in extreme republican circles it could have caused an unnecessary diplomatic incident for the Irish government and its principled foreign policy. In his letter the count explained that he was busy finding new premises for the legation, and the Free State would therefore, as a consequence, not be able to organize a Saint Patrick's Day banquet. He knew Kerney was preparing his own annual event, and he used the pretext of the national holiday to urge reconciliation:

I hope, however, to be in a position in future years to organise an annual function to which all Irish men and women in Paris will come. This will give us an opportunity of meeting and knowing each other and, incidentally, of letting our French friends know that we are all essentially at one where the honour of Saint Patrick and the love of Ireland are concerned. I hope that you will accept this letter in the spirit in which it is written to all our fellow countrymen. It would give me great personal pleasure to see you again.[26]

Despite Kerney's innate stubbornness, he proved remarkably open to the invitation and replied to O'Kelly three days later. He stressed that he was willing to meet with O'Kelly in a purely "private capacity" and to put "conflicting views" on politics to one side: "We can be large minded enough to tolerate in each other these irreconcilable opinions," he wrote.[27] O'Kelly warmly received Kerney's response and willingness to discuss "old times," and he agreed to leave politics out of the conversation: "By definition, as a civil servant, I am debarred from participating in politics and have no intention of departing from that attitude."[28] The men met up for lunch a few days later. Given the vitriolic criticism that marked some exchanges inside the Dáil at this time between supporters and opponents of the treaty, the O'Kelly-Kerney rapprochement showed that the civil war divide could be bridged if men were willing to meet as equals and put politics to one side.

Around the same time that this remarkable reconciliation took place, an old friend of Kerney's, Robert Brennan—with whom Kerney had shared a warm friendship in Paris a few years before—contacted him. Brennan had also left the consular service over his disagreement with the treaty and had been replaced in his senior post by Joseph Walshe. Brennan was a staunch republican who had remained a loyal and close associate of de Valera's from the time of the treaty debates. At this time he was the general manager of the *Irish Press*, a national daily newspaper closely linked to the Fianna Fáil party. Kerney had been one of the first shareholders to invest in the newspaper, and Brennan notified him that a position was available in the company for a chief accountant with a salary of £400–£500 per annum. Although

Kerney was not a chartered accountant, he had plenty of accounting experience. The prospect of returning to Ireland and renewing his close friendship with de Valera was enticing. However, he withdrew his application when he heard that Matthew Healy, a business associate of de Valera's, was also applying for the post. It was a wise move. On 5 February de Valera wrote to Kerney about the vacancy. In the letter it is clear de Valera had a high opinion of Healy as a businessman, and he praised his work as "simply magnificent" at the time of the Dáil loan flotation.[29] If the board had to choose between Healy and Kerney the latter would most likely lose. Nonetheless, by withdrawing his name from the race and leaving it uncontested for Healy, Kerney had again won praise from the Chief. De Valera honestly admitted that if he alone had to choose, there was only one man for the job: "There is no man in whom I would have greater confidence to run the department successfully than yourself."[30]

Since its foundation, Fianna Fáil had grown stronger each year. As John Horgan detailed, it was not just "de Valera-style populism" that accounted for Fianna Fáil's rise, but also the party's republican credentials, its unique identity, its monolithic composition, and its social conservatism and acceptance of constitutional politics that swayed a sizeable proportion of the public.[31] In the background, Seán Lemass and Gerald Boland built up the party's efficient organization, and the establishment of the *Irish Press* proved a major success financially and played a significant role in raising the party's media profile. Hopes were high within the Irish colony in France that a Fianna Fáil victory would undo all the ground the republicans had lost since the treaty split: "Our hopes are once more high and with the help of God, His Blessed Mother, St Patrick and the souls of our beloved and martyred dead, surely we shall win at last!" wrote one supporter.[32]

The Kerneys were not as bombastic in their language as other members of the colony, but they certainly hoped that the "nightmare" of the past few years would soon end: "We are waiting for the elections as eagerly as you are in Ireland and we join in your hope of seeing this nightmare end within the next few months," wrote Leopold's wife, Raymonde.[33] Kerney had subscribed to the Fianna Fáil election fund in the expectation that if the party came to power he might gain favorable patronage. The 1932 general election saw an upsurge in support for de Valera and his party. As Seán Cronin noted: "Republicanism brought him [de Valera] to power."[34] Fianna Fáil won 72 seats and 44.5 pecent of the first-preference votes. Kerney sent the Chief a joyful telegram: "The West Awake."[35] With the support of the Labour Party, de Valera returned to power a decade after the treaty split and his fall from grace. For Kerney the occasion was memorable, but he was still not out of the wilderness.

The former diplomat quickly used every contact he had to secure a public job. This was not an easy task given the countless other supporters of Fianna Fáil who expected to be rewarded for their loyalty. Kerney's geographic remove did not help his case, either. Two close friends who kept him abreast of all events in Dublin were Frank Litton and Seán T. O'Kelly. Litton ran an engineering consultancy firm with Seán MacEntee, who was a senior figure in Fianna Fáil and who would be appointed minister for finance in de Valera's first government.[36] Their offices in Dawson Street became a hive of activity, with people calling in to see MacEntee, looking for favors and influence. Litton described the atmosphere of excitement and expectation in the air since the electoral success. The republicans rejoiced that William Cosgrave and Cumann na nGaedheal would now be playing "2nd fiddle" to de Valera.[37] Litton promised Kerney that he would put in a good word for him to MacEntee.

Seán T. O'Kelly was the former envoy to France during the War of Independence, and it was he who was the first to spot Kerney's talents as a consular official. In 1932 O'Kelly was de Valera's number two in Fianna Fáil and was, like him, working behind the scenes to get Kerney back into the service. O'Kelly was vice president of the executive council and the minister for public health and local government, and he took advantage of a letter he received from Count Gerald O'Kelly to sound out his old friend. The count proposed that he and Kerney appear together at their respective Saint Patrick's Day celebrations in Paris. Kerney was still a private citizen with no official status, and although he had mended fences with the count personally the year before, he saw that as a private matter between friends. A public and outwardly political display of conciliation was another matter entirely in Kerney's eyes. O'Kelly believed that the count was out to make "a big splash" for himself with the new republican administration, but nonetheless, he advised Kerney that it would reflect well on him and his chances of returning to the service if he accepted the invitation to attend the Free State celebration.[38]

This was a litmus test to a wider concern. There was great uncertainty within senior branches of the state—the police, the army, the public and civil service—about the transfer of political power from Cosgrave to de Valera. After all, the latter had once challenged the very existence of the Free State and had refused to recognize its legitimacy for years. Rumor and speculation were rife as to whether de Valera would cull senior officials who had sided with the treaty and replace them with his own supporters. Aengus Nolan explained the anxiety felt by departmental secretaries, especially the one who ran External Affairs: "Joseph Walshe had sworn his allegiance to the pro-treaty government. Others, including Walshe's predecessor, Robert Brennan, who had left the service in 1922 due to the government's anti-treaty affiliations, were now expected to return under the Fianna Fáil administration."[39] Walshe's fears of a cull proved unfounded, as de Valera chose to retain these experienced government officials. The secretary was delighted to discover de Valera's shared devotion to Catholicism, and, as Dermot Keogh noted, Walshe quickly began attending the same daily Mass as the Fianna Fáil leader to ingratiate himself with his new political master.[40]

Despite Walshe's accommodation with de Valera, many former republican diplomats felt they were entitled to a place back in the fold, and several Fianna Fáil activists viewed the civil service as pro-English in its outlook and staffed by senior officials completely opposed to republican policies. In the colorful description of Christopher Andrews, they were all "a crowd of Free State bastards."[41] De Valera was under pressure to secure posts for these republicans but wondered whether former colleagues who had fallen out over the treaty could work side by side in harmony. Dermot Keogh has acknowledged that the bitterness caused by the Irish Civil War was still very much present at this time and would, in fact, "muddy the waters of Irish politics for generations."[42] The vice president of the executive council, Seán T. O'Kelly, decided to use the private rapprochement between Kerney and Count O'Kelly to put this polemical issue to the test. He used the Saint Patrick's Day celebration to see whether former colleagues who had fallen out over the treaty could reach a public and mutual understanding, accept assimilation, and work together once again.

On the eve of this historic banquet, Kerney wrote an open and frank letter to Máire O'Brien—the former envoy to Spain during the War of Independence and a committed anti-treatyite—that expressed his dissatisfaction with the position he had been put in. The reconciliation would be a very public event with correspondents from the *Chicago Tribune* and the *New York Herald* in attendance. Kerney had initially refused point blank to "set foot" in the Free State legation, but after a phone call from de Valera and out of "deference" to the Chief, he did so.[43] Both he and Count O'Kelly attended both functions and read prepared statements to present a united front. Privately Kerney felt quite "disgusted" by the whole event because it appeared to him that de Valera wanted the anti-treatyites to make a bigger gesture than the pro-treatyites.[44] In Kerney's view, this was a public admission that the republican struggle was wrong: "So MacWhite was right. Joe Walshe was right and all those who deserted were right!"[45] Not for the first time did he seem lost in the jungle of politics: "I have finished worrying about 'politics,'" he stated, "as the views I held up to the present are so difficult to reconcile with those now held at home."[46]

The difficulty of the ceremony, "a painful sacrifice and an ordeal for me," was perhaps worsened by the sudden and devastating news that his employer no longer required his services and gave Kerney a month's notice.[47] The shock soon turned to anger, as he had increased the company's profits by over 70,000 francs in recent years. As a foreigner in France at the height of the Great Depression, the chances of his getting another well-paid position were slim. Kerney was left with little option but to gamble everything on being reinstated into the public service, and he hoped that his republican friends would help him out. He knew Fianna Fáil was officially committed to a policy of reinstating dismissed civil servants. Their Ard Fheis had passed a "motion to demand the reinstatement of National Teachers and other dismissed Civil Servants consequent upon their political activities."[48] The party also wanted to ensure that no black mark was placed on the record of any dismissed official: "That the status of all dismissed Dáil officials would not be less than those officers of similar grades who remained in the service."[49] When the party took power, it quickly established a Dáil "Committee of Inquiry into Resigned or Dismissed Civil Servants" to address this important issue of reinstatement to service of former civil servants and public officials who had resigned or who had been dismissed from state administrations for political reasons.[50]

For a man as committed to republican values as Kerney, reinstatement would also mean that he would have to take the unpalatable step of swearing an oath of loyalty to the Irish Free State, the very entity he not only despised but had deemed unlawful until recently. Even the name of the state clashed with his republican principles when he thought of the brutal Congo Free State and the racist Orange Free State. Then again, de Valera—whom Kerney looked up to as the leader of Irish republicanism—and de Valera's supporters had already crossed the constitutional Rubicon and faced up to realpolitik after wasting years defending lofty values and attacking the Free State's legality. It was de Valera's electoral commitment to dismantle the legal and political edifice of the Free State through constitutional means that had swayed Kerney to water down his own dogmatic republicanism. Rhetoric and reality were colliding, with the latter now winning out. Robert Brennan worked hard on Kerney's behalf: "Don't worry. Seeing Chief," he wrote.[51] Brennan reminded Kerney that de Valera and Seán T. O'Kelly always looked after their own: "Everybody very busy. Chief giving matter attention."[52] This did little to ease Kerney's anxiety. He agonized over his position and worried whether de Valera would come to his rescue: "My feelings are somewhat like those of a man condemned to death," he wrote, "waiting for a reprieve, expecting to get it, but by no means sure that it will arrive in time."[53]

Although conscious of the efforts his friends were making to help him in Dublin and of the workings of the committee of inquiry, Kerney felt his situation urgent enough to personally write to de Valera on

26 March. In this deeply personal letter, Kerney spelled out his years of loyal service to the republic and to de Valera specifically when he had been the republican minister for foreign affairs. He contended that it was the electoral result that had "materially altered" his opposition to the Free State, as well as de Valera's commitment to pursue republican principles through constitutional means.[54] He supported de Valera's commitment to "abolish the oath from the Constitution and the openly-expressed determination of the government to obey the Irish people," not militant organizations such as the IRA, as further justification for now recognizing the legitimacy of the Free State.[55] He asked de Valera for a "rapid and favourable decision" on the matter.[56] A telling trademark from the letter also reveals Kerney's neurotic concern with money, however trivial. He asked in advance for an allowance to defray the travel costs he would incur in going over to Dublin in May to argue his case face-to-face. Such a request could be viewed as rather brazen given the circumstances.

Despite the urgency that he attached to the letter, Kerney received no reply from de Valera. This seemed to him unfair. In a letter to his friend Frank Litton, who was working behind the scenes asking his business partner Seán MacEntee to find a place for Kerney, the former diplomat expressed his unease about the lack of a response to his official request and about rumors he kept hearing about the Chief: "I cannot help recollecting a criticism which I have heard pronounced concerning him on more than one occasion and according to which he is supposed to be more considerate of his enemies than of his friends."[57] Just as these doubts and concerns were occupying Kerney's mind, the committee of inquiry into dismissed civil servants reached its conclusion on his application and favored "reinstatement."[58]

Eunan O'Halpin, in his brief examination of Kerney's re-entry to public life, recorded that he had been "dismissed from the fledging diplomatic service during the civil war" and readmitted only in 1932 after a period of "rehabilitation."[59] In fact, Kerney had never been dismissed from the diplomatic service, nor had he ever been "rehabilitated"—a rather loaded term that implies a disfavor or disservice committed previously. Kerney, like de Valera and all other republicans, had modified his hard-line republicanism since the civil war, but he had not jettisoned the key tenets of republicanism. More-over, in his use of the word "rehabilitation" O'Halpin ignores the wording used by the Dáil committee that investigated Kerney's case and recommended reinstatement. Martin Maguire, in his analysis of Fianna Fáil's relationship with the civil service, correctly used the term "reinstated," in line with the Dáil committee's findings.[60] There had been no prior wrongdoing on Kerney's part; in fact, his skills and experience were now judged to be essential and necessary for the state's diplomatic service.

The committee had found that before the treaty was signed there had been the "nucleus of a complete administrative machine" with functioning government departments and that the 1920 Government of Ireland Act had split the British Civil Service in Ireland, meaning that before the treaty was signed on 6 December 1921 there had been three functioning civil services—a mainland British Civil Service, a Dublin Castle service, and a republican service.[61] The committee also recommended giving back pay to any dismissed republican servant going back to the first day of service. On 9 April Kerney received the full report directly from de Valera stating that his application had been approved.

Kerney wrote to de Valera on 13 April expressing "how grateful" he was and that "a great weight" had been lifted off his shoulders, and he thanked the Irish leader personally for all his efforts.[62] He looked forward to helping the new administration in its constitutional path toward republicanism: "I need not tell you how delight[ed] we are at the new spirit—or rather the old one—which is manifesting itself at home."[63] Kerney thus became the first of the four republican con-sular officials (the others being Seán Nunan, Art Ó Briain, and Robert Brennan) to be restored to their former positions without prejudice. In a letter to one of the other former republican officials, Robert Brennan, Kerney did not hide his unbounded joy: "I do not know whether you can hear the loud cheers, but you can imagine them."[64] The wilderness years were over.

CHAPTER 6

FROM FRANCE TO SPAIN, 1932–1939

At the age of fifty, Kerney returned to the Department of External Affairs with the rank of commercial attaché in the Paris legation, a grade and position similar to those he held at the time of the treaty split. In the ten intervening years, 1922–32, the diplomatic service had changed beyond all recognition under Joseph Walshe's direction. The secretary had transformed the department into a professional outfit and had spearheaded an independent foreign policy supported by overseas missions. In the overall assessment of Aengus Nolan, Walshe's biographer, the secretary had successfully "worked to convince the government that a Department of External Affairs was essential to the further development of the state."[1] Moreover, Nolan contends, Walshe was instrumental in the "formulation of Irish foreign policy," and this practice was not to change after de Valera took office.[2]

After securing the independence of External Affairs from the prying eyes of the Department of Finance and expanding Ireland's presence internationally within the Commonwealth, the League of Nations, and ambassadorial exchanges, Irish foreign policy under Walshe took, from the mid-1920s, a markedly Catholic turn in its identity and purpose that was to continue for decades. This was not surprising given Walshe's own personal devoutness and that of successive Irish governments. Diarmaid Ferriter argued that after centuries of British and Protestant control, the new Ireland wanted to celebrate the "ultimate triumph" of its Catholic values and culture to the world.[3] Obvious examples of the religious element that Walshe brought to Irish foreign policy were how he recruited staff and the type of staff chosen. Walshe wanted Irish diplomats to be the very embodiment of Catholicity, and he recruited from the elite Jesuit school Clongowes Wood College, where he himself had once studied. For instance, Tom Garvin noted that in the ambassador to Germany, Daniel Binchy, Walshe saw the embodiment of the "new Catholic Ireland," which was young, Catholic educated, well versed in languages, and pro-treaty.[4] Other recruits, such as Vaughan Dempsey and John Hearne, also fit the new mold, having at one time studied for the priesthood. Gerard Keown noted how the department employed "predominantly Catholic" personnel over Protestant officials.[5] Another manifestation of Walshe's alignment of religion and foreign policy had been the lengthy efforts expended in the 1920s to establish formal relations with the Vatican, Dublin's most prized overseas posting: "Walshe took a close personal interest in policy toward the Vatican and saw in the legation a means to consolidate the Free State's place in Rome as 'the most Catholic state in the world' and a defender of Catholic values."[6] In 1932, when de Valera came to office, Walshe played a key role in orchestrating this hyper-Catholicism internationally at the Eucharistic Congress held in Ireland when, as Dermot Keogh has written, "Irish Catholicism was made into a world showpiece."[7] This was the new diplomatic environment Kerney walked into in 1932 and to him, as an uncommitted Catholic convert, the department now seemed completely alien in its character to the one he had left in 1922.

Another distinguishing characteristic of Irish foreign policy was the caliber of recent entrants to the Department of External Affairs. Although Ireland still did not have a diplomatic school to teach and train candidates in the art of diplomacy and the responsibilities of working as civil officials abroad, a practice prevalent throughout its neighboring European states, the ad hoc appointments that had characterized the first generation of diplomats appointed to the service were discontinued. New entrants were required to earn their spurs both academically and professionally. These diplomats were highly skilled, and most were the intellectual superiors of the first generation of diplomats, Walshe included.[8] As Anne Chambers has noted, meritocracy was "the order of the day," with a Civil Service Commission conducting rigorous examinations and interviews.[9] Canvassing and favoritism were out. Not surprisingly, the circumstances surrounding Kerney's reappointment were seen as anything but normal in the eyes of the service, and he was viewed from the start as an outsider with influential political connections by some and with downright suspicion by others.

Kerney's anti-treaty stance did not help his re-entry either, and it naturally drew resentment from within the department, particularly from serving members of the first, "revolutionary," generation of consular officials, all of whom were pro-treatyites. Michael Mac-White's only view of Kerney was a narrow one, and he judged Kerney to be a traitor still. Count Gerald O'Kelly had mended fences with Kerney, but within the department he did not step out of line and remained distant toward his friend. Other officials from the first generation, like Seán Murphy, had worked tirelessly only a few years before to have the republican diplomat deported from France. At a more senior level, Joseph Walshe's attitude toward Kerney was rather interesting. In an official communiqué to the government, Walshe supported Kerney's reinstatement on the grounds of "public interest."[10] The report was glowing in its praise, citing Kerney's "intimate knowledge" of France, his "specialized" skill set, and the proven ability of this "keen and capable officer."[11] Yet this was typical of Walshe's doublespeak. He wrote his report only after the Dáil committee had published its findings and when he knew which way the wind was blowing. He had never supported Kerney's reappointment before that date. The secretary was mindful of the need not to fall out of favor with the new administration, especially with de Valera acting as both the president of the executive council and, more importantly in terms of Walshe's concern, overseeing his department as minister for external affairs. It is also noteworthy that after Kerney's application for reinstatement had been approved by the Dáil committee and the Irish government, Walshe made sure to stress the diplomat's skills for work overseas rather than back home in Ireland, which Kerney would have preferred. The secretary would show nothing but indifference toward Kerney's potential skill set, preferring to keep him on the continent for years, far away from the center of operations in Dublin. As far as Walshe and his colleagues were concerned, the republican was a political appointee placed in his position by de Valera.

For Kerney, the transition back into External Affairs was a difficult one because of both the treaty fallout with former friends and having to work side by side with pro-treaty men. Although no one discussed the treaty or the subsequent civil war openly in the confines of the Paris legation, the atmosphere in the small organization was toxic. Politics aside, Kerney also stood apart from many of his work colleagues because of his educational background, which had been Protestant. Tom Garvin has noted that one's schooling played a major role in how the Irish civil service treated entrants: "The learned middle class of the new Catholic Ireland was small and tended to be interlinked by family connections and school ties."[12] Many in the department, like Joseph Walshe, were former students of Jesuit-run colleges, which were on the pathway to career advancement and networking for the wealthier elites of independent Ireland. Kerney had never been educated by the Jesuits and thus was never a member of this exclusive old boys' club. At university level he had attended "Protestant" Trinity College Dublin and not "Catholic" University College Dublin. In a civil service that was dominated by men with a Catholic religious education and old-boy connections, Kerney was simply not one of the "lads" and never would be.

Kerney was also disappointed that he was being kept on in France after requesting assignment back home, and he felt that his reappointment to work on trade matters was something of a comedown from the more nuanced and politically centered work he had undertaken as a republican diplomat. He likewise found it difficult to adjust to Walshe's methodology, as it clashed with his normal working style. Kerney had always operated alone, often on his own initiative and without oversight, having been encouraged to do so for years by his superiors. Walshe opposed any such practices. Dermot Keogh attributes part of this management style to the secretary's own "secretive and mistrustful" personality.[13] The secretary operated a strict compartmentalized system whereby information was handed down sparingly and on a need-to-know basis and any initiative or financial expense was restricted without prior sanction. All matters had to pass before the secretary's eyes before being decided upon. Until the reinstatement of the other former republican officials in the next few years, this was a trying time for Kerney, who had only the grace of de Valera's support to keep Walshe and his supporters from hounding him out of his job. De Valera may have been aware of this atmosphere, as he stepped in on several occasions over the coming years to protect Kerney. He made one such move shortly after Kerney's reappointment by changing his official title in the Paris legation from commercial attaché to commercial secretary, which conferred greater prestige, higher status, and permanency to Kerney's position.[14] It was a subtle gesture of political protection that Kerney welcomed but that his opponents despised. Michael Kennedy has acknowledged that there was a "simmering resentment" generally toward anti-treaty men in External Affairs but that it was very much contained within the department.[15]

SOLDIERING ON

In 1932 France ranked third in order of priority as an overseas posting in Europe. The department attached greater consideration to its missions to the Vatican and Geneva, home of the League of Nations. Within a few months of his return to active service, Kerney built up business connections he had forged in the 1920s throughout France, Belgium, the Netherlands, and Spain to develop markets for Irish agricultural products on the continent. These overseas trade links became vital after de Valera's government withheld land annuity payments to the British government, which responded by placing a 20 percent duty on Irish exports, thus initiating the Economic War.[16] Although it is true, as Kevin O'Rourke has argued, that the Economic War "helped de Valera electorally," in the immediate term it presented immense economic challenges because of the need to replace overnight Ireland's main market for its agricultural products.[17] The Anglo-Irish disagreement forced de Valera to immediately seek alternative markets on the continent, and Kerney was one of those key individuals entrusted with this vital task of keeping the national economy afloat. The minutes of one of the department's meetings in 1932 state: "The Minister considers that every effort must be made to find markets other than the British markets."[18]

Despite the gravity of the situation, Kerney relished the challenge for several reasons. First, he had secured trade deals before in less-than-favorable conditions, the best example of which was the *Banba* flotation during the Irish Civil War. Second, the mission appealed to his perception of trade as a key component of Irish foreign policy, and establishing trade agreements was his strongest skill set. Necessity would force the economy to move away from its dependence on Britain and connect instead with the continent to enhance economic prosperity and independence. Third, nothing encouraged Kerney more in his work than to undermine Britain, as his political attitude was still vehemently republican. During the War of Independence he had relished distributing across France leaflets that urged the people to boycott British products. Now he was tasked with systematically altering entire trade networks away from the old enemy. Finally, Kerney was pleased, as were most republicans, that Fianna Fáil had upheld its election commitment to stop paying annuities to Britain. It was a clear signal that the new republican administration under de Valera's leadership was using constitutional means to dismantle the Anglo-Irish Treaty.

In June 1933 Kerney traveled to Spain to meet with companies in Barcelona, Bilbao, and Madrid. He followed up on this trip with regular meetings to hold formal discussions with the Spanish ministries of commerce and foreign affairs, and he extended these trips to Portugal to promote bilateral trade there. The results of these efforts were a historic trade agreement signed between Spain and the Irish Free State, as well as the acceleration of formal diplomatic ties between the countries. Walshe, on de Valera's instruction, wrote to Kerney commending his hard work, which had been done with no staff support or adequate financial resources. The letter shows no hint that Walshe felt any personal appreciation of Kerney for his accomplishment, nor does it demonstrate any sincerity on behalf of the department. Instead it takes a rather begrudging tone in describing the commercial secretary's achievement. Walshe wrote: "I am directed by the Minister to acknowledge the receipt to Mr Kerney of his minute of 14th June from Madrid enclosing Agreement made between the Irish Free State and Spain. The Minister has directed me to convey to Mr Kerney his appreciation of the very valuable work which he has successfully concluded in Spain."[19] Walshe's lack of enthusiasm for Kerney's achievement has been noted by other historians. Dermot Keogh has argued that Walshe saw his role as a rather narrow one that involved attending to top-level meetings, compiling confidential memorandums, and conversing with senior political figures.

According to Keogh, Walshe looked "askance at such 'plebeian' areas as trade and commerce, which had to be 'tolerated'."[20] Kerney, on the other hand, saw trade and commerce as indispensable to Irish foreign policy interests, and, undaunted by his superior's coldness, he traveled to Brussels to hold talks with the Belgian government to establish trade agreements to offset the loss of the British market, which had absorbed over 90 percent of Irish agricultural produce. These talks resulted in another historic trade deal. Ireland secured 17,000 tons of butter exports to Belgium.[21] Kerney again carried out these duties alone, and he managed to overcome the strict protectionist trade tariffs built up after the Great Depression on the continent to secure these vital overseas markets for Irish industry. This tiring work showed that he was still a dedicated official and a physically healthy man.

Despite Kerney's rapid success in his role, he was confronted with several attacks against him from the political sphere and from the department. On 11 July 1933, Desmond FitzGerald TD (Teachta Dála, which denotes a member of the Dáil)—former pro-treaty minister for external affairs—stood up in the Dáil chamber and made several personal and defamatory remarks against Kerney using parliamentary privilege, meaning he could not be sued for libel, a practice he had used before when he accused Kerney of treachery to the state in 1923. FitzGerald stated that the post of commercial secretary in Paris was an "unnecessary office" and that Kerney's appointment had come about because de Valera "may have felt he owed a personal debt to that man for past services."[22] FitzGerald raised issues of misappropriation of funds by Kerney for not surrendering the consular office and its furniture to the Irish Free State after he had joined the anti-treatyites, and he insinuated that Kerney had put "undue pressure" on de Valera to be reinstated.[23] The Fine Gael (Tribe of the Irish) TD further alleged that Kerney was a communist sympathizer—a serious allegation to make in 1930s Ireland—who had once acted as an "intermediary" in France between the republicans and an agent of the "Russian Bolshevik Government" code-named "Marino."[24] FitzGerald used republican documents he had seized when minister to name this man as Ciubranovitch. FitzGerald wanted Kerney to hand over his diplomatic reports from the time he joined the "illusory Government" to prove his point, and he stated that Kerney's reinstatement in Paris was "a direct affront to the French people," a "scandal," and "an appointment which this House [Dáil Éireann] and this whole country should protest against."[25]

FitzGerald's vitriolic charges and defamatory slurs stunned Kerney, but as an acting public servant the commercial secretary could not reply or interfere in the political melee. In a striking example of the esteem in which de Valera held Kerney as a friend and loyal colleague, the Fianna Fáil leader stood up in the Dáil chamber and offered a resounding defense of the republican official's appointment: "I find it very hard sometimes to get words to characterise the statements of Deputy FitzGerald."[26] De Valera then proceeded to give his strongest endorsement yet of Kerney's track record and loyalty to Ireland. It is worth quoting at length:

> The Deputy has made suggestions with regard to Mr. Kerney, and every one of these statements, as far as I am aware, is unjustified. Mr. Kerney represented the Republic, and when Deputy FitzGerald talks about going away with the loot and running away with the property of the people, I want to tell him that I still believe today, and that a large

section of the Irish people still believe today, and that history will yet prove, what is more, that the State established by the Irish people in 1919 continued to be the State and was the State which the Ministers, by their attitude in suppressing the courts and so on, tried to overturn by a *coup d'état*, and those who stood for the state—and Mr. Kerney is one—did not try to run away with anybody's property. They tried to defend the State set up by the Irish people and to hold the property of that State for the people, and neither Mr. Kerney nor I, nor anybody associated with that movement, are going to offer any apology for our actions to Deputy FitzGerald. Mr. Kerney represented us in Paris. He tried to maintain the position as long as possible. He gave accounts to the proper authorities—the people to whom he was reporting and, so far as I know, there is nothing that can be said about Mr. Kerney except that which is good.[27]

De Valera further lambasted FitzGerald for his accusation that Kerney's liaison with communist Russia had been an affront to France, calling his words "fairy tales," and he categorically dismissed any imputations of the ex-republican diplomat's unsuitability for the post by highlighting his proven ability and "special aptitudes" for the job.[28] The strength of de Valera's defense of his friend shows that loyalty mattered to the Chief but also that he needed men whom he could trust in key positions, particularly as he was trying to loosen the shackles of the Anglo-Irish Treaty behind the scenes and was uncertain about the support of some sections of the civil service. The record of the exchange between FitzGerald and de Valera would not have been lost on Joseph Walshe, who had worked under both men. As long as Kerney was performing his duties admirably, he would clearly be protected by de Valera. The secretary, however, used any instance to undermine and blacken Kerney's name.

Money was one issue that cropped up repeatedly between Walshe and Kerney. Kerney had always shown a forensic and at times neurotic concern for money, however trivial. His contract stipulated that he was to receive a salary of £400 pounds annually, which would rise incrementally by £15 pounds to £500. His salary was supported by allowances that included a local allowance (£275), a representation allowance (£150), and a rent allowance for married men (£175).[29] Kerney privately believed these sums were not enough to make ends meet. He wrote to the Revenue Commissioners to see if his pension entitlement could be extended to cover his services during the time he had been the republican diplomat in the 1920s, but his request was unsuccessful.[30] He began a long and tiring correspondence with Joseph Walshe to pressure him to petition the Department of Finance to increase his allowances. The commercial secretary argued that the rent allowance provided was not enough to cover rented accommodations in Paris and that contracts had to be paid in advance: "Rents for unfurnished premises in France are payable quarterly and in advance."[31] Kerney also took issue with the fact that allowances for married men were little more than for single men: "I, as a married man and moreover as a married man with a family, am entitled to a Local Allowance which should exceed the amount which I would be accorded if I happened to be a single man."[32]

However, an analysis of Kerney's expenses show that most of these expenditures were simply attributable to personal choices he made. It was his decision to send his children to private schools, for example. Jean had moved back to Paris, and from 1932 to 1935 he was attending the College Sainte Croix while Micheline was studying in Loreto Hall in Dublin. In 1936 Kerney likewise sent his youngest son to one of the most expensive private schools in Ireland, Clongowes Wood College. He still made a monthly contribution toward the care of his disabled brother, Mario, in England, and after his reinstatement the family had moved out of the one-bedroom flat on Rue Sarrette and relocated to a more expensive three-bedroom accommodation on Rue Jacques Dulud in Neuilly. It is interesting that when Kerney had worked for de Valera's republican administration, often on less pay but still struggling to make ends meet, he had not voiced similar financial complaints and, in fact, had paid for many expenses incurred during official business out of his own pocket without seeking reimbursement. It is perhaps indicative of his less-than-complete fondness for the Irish Free State that he now linked these expenses with what he perceived to be an inadequate salary.

One expense that irritated Kerney considerably was for official trips he made to various countries to promote trade, because he had to pay for everything in advance before he received any reimbursement, which could often take months, coming from the Department of Finance via External Affairs. Moreover, expenses he did pay were frequently challenged by Walshe, who queried the reasoning behind what in his eyes were any luxury expenses or quibbled about the exact exchange rate at the time of purchase. These deliberate obstructions and petty-mindedness exasperated Kerney, who often responded to Walshe's coldness by writing to him in a very frank manner. In one letter, dated 2 July 1932, Kerney responded to Walshe's estimate of how he could live more cheaply in Paris with this sharp remark: "No attempt is made to explain how you [Walshe] arrive at this figure!"[33] In another letter the language he used is quite abrasive, with Kerney demanding that Walshe bring to the "notice of the Minister [de Valera]" the issue of allowances and, should the secretary not do so, provide a justification for his refusal to notify the minister.[34]

The use of this tone to the secretary and the threat to exceed Walshe's authority reflected the underlying tension between the men brought about by years of mutual dislike and distrust. The issue of pay nearly forced a formal complaint by Kerney when he discovered by himself that increments owed to him had to be applied for and were not automatically sanctioned.[35] He blamed this entirely on Walshe. In a letter to a close republican friend he declared: "For my part I let it be known that I would refuse to go to Dublin [to resolve the dispute], even if called there officially, unless my full emoluments were paid, and I won."[36] It was clear to the commercial secretary that inside External Affairs he had few, if any, friends. Kerney finally went over Walshe's head and wrote directly to de Valera, in breach of the strict compartmentalized system Walshe operated, to let the Chief know how he was being treated by the secretary. In his letter to de Valera Kerney outlined all his financial concerns, particularly the continued slowness of reimbursement for official trade business to various countries, which he described as an "unduly heavy burden on me."[37] De Valera again sided with Kerney, and the Irish political leader saw to it that this matter was resolved favorably for the republican—something unlikely to please Walshe.

Beginning in the summer of 1934, Kerney met his Belgian counterparts again to secure more trade deals for Irish imports, thus offsetting the reluctance of French authorities to import foreign goods. He negotiated even more butter exports, and this time he also secured beef exports for that summer. However, during his negotiations with the Belgian government he was informed that some of the butter supplied previously had been moldy. Kerney passed on these concerns to the relevant authorities, the Department of Agriculture and the Dairy Disposals Board. He also opined that bureaucratic delays were hindering the development of a more permanent and profitable market in Belgium for Irish goods. Both of these viewpoints stung the minister for agriculture, Dr. James Ryan, who accused Kerney of "grave impropriety" for asserting that any Irish agricultural products could be deficient.[38] The secretary of the Department of Agriculture, Daniel Twomey, passed on Ryan's comments to his counterpart, Joseph Walshe. Armed with a ministerial riposte that accused Kerney of making sensational accusations, even though they were deemed facts by the Belgians who had purchased the goods, Walshe finally had something on him. He delighted in bringing the matter directly to de Valera's attention. On 16 November Walshe contacted Twomey to let him know that Kerney had been "admonished" by de Valera.[39] Eunan O'Halpin sees this incident as yet another example of Kerney's "hopeless judgement," but this viewpoint seems quite unfair when all the commercial secretary was doing was passing on the views of the Belgians, whom Kerney wanted to keep happy in order to maintain and enhance the essential trade agreements signed between the states.[40]

Kerney endured FitzGerald's public criticism and Walshe's resentment, but it was his close working proximity to the man in charge of the Paris legation, Minister Count Gerald O'Kelly, that caused a decisive break. Kerney could at times be his own worst enemy. Like de Valera, he constantly walked a political tightrope between recognizing the political status quo of the Irish Free State and its constitutional relationship with Britain in accord with the terms of the Anglo-Irish

Treaty and, at the same time, upholding sacrosanct republican principles. This dual responsibility was never better tested than when the annual invitation arrived from His Majesty's Government in June to attend celebrations in the British ambassadorial residence to honor King George V's birthday. While the pro-treaty members of the legation dutifully attended, for Kerney this was a bridge too far. In previous years he had declined these invitations with the excuse that he had a prior engagement or had a "diplomatic" flu. The commercial secretary could not have done this without O'Kelly's sanction. According to O'Kelly: "Mr Kerney had also received an invitation, but asked me if, in view of the special circumstances of his case, it would be possible, this year, for him to find a plausible excuse for not being present. As I recognized that there were special, if transient circumstances attaching to his case, I agreed to Mr. Kerney's not going—all the more readily as the presence of the Minister and first Secretary seemed to me to meet the needs of the case."[41] However, in 1935 O'Kelly suddenly changed his view on this matter and stood his ground, insisting that Kerney go and present a united front with his colleagues. When Kerney refused, it forced an open breach between the men: "There is no member of the Legation that is not aware of the position," he confided in a letter.[42] It was also an act of open disobedience to O'Kelly and to his position as head of the legation: "I expect he will find an early opportunity of reporting me for insubordination," Kerney wrote.[43]

O'Kelly had hitherto respected the independent role that Kerney enjoyed in handling all commercial matters relevant to his office. Following their acrimonious dispute, however, the minister decided to discontinue that practice and began opening correspondence and letters, even ones marked confidential, from businesses and firms that were addressed to Kerney. The commercial secretary saw this as an affront: "I must leave Paris at all costs and as soon as possible," he wrote.[44] For months the men refused to speak to each other even though they worked on the same premises. If they needed to raise an issue, they wrote to each other as "Dear Mr O'Kelly" and "Dear Mr Kerney." Eventually the whole farce proved too tiresome to the commercial secretary, who was constantly worried that O'Kelly would request that Walshe take action against his insubordination, though luckily O'Kelly had not done so up to that point. Fearing that Walshe would get word of the dispute, Kerney again turned to de Valera for help, but he did not notify the republican leader about the dispute via official channels, which should have been done through the president's public secretary, Maurice Moynihan. Instead Kerney used a back channel. He wrote to de Valera's lifelong private secretary, Kathleen O'Connell, whom he knew well. This was an obvious message that Kerney was sending—that he would not get a fair hearing if he went through the proper channels. Again he was in effect writing directly to the Chief as an old friend appealing for a personal favor and "fair consideration."[45] His position in Paris had become "intolerable," and he wanted out.[46]

At first there was a suggestion that Kerney could be placed in an auxiliary role or act as a consultant to the legation. Both of these offers were judged, even by a close friend of his, to be a "joke."[47] De Valera, in another clear sign of the friendship and rapport he had with Kerney, came down on the commercial secretary's side, and he acted swiftly on the matter. The Fianna Fáil leader took advantage of the personal feud to purge the Paris legation of its pro-treaty minister. Count O'Kelly was removed from his job and demoted to a new position as special counselor to the legation, a role he would now conduct from the office of his wine business, Vendôme Wines, on the Place Vendôme in central Paris. Kerney showed little sympathy for O'Kelly's fall from grace: "I suppose he will still try to cut a dash in society and misrepresent his country."[48] Art Ó Briain, a former anti-treaty diplomat and committed republican like Kerney, was put in charge of the legation by de Valera. It was a move with an obvious political subtext—de Valera wanted republican men whom he trusted in more senior positions in the diplomatic service, even if, as Niall Keogh argues, Ó Briain "lacked the formation and experience of a career diplomat."[49] De Valera clearly saw the need to break the pro-treaty monopoly of the service, and when he acted in such a unilateral way there was little that Joseph Walshe could do to stop him.

Ó Briain's appointment highlighted the political divisions that still bubbled below the surface of the diplomatic service. Kerney welcomed him with open arms while others adopted a more reserved attitude, seeing in the new minister many of the traits Kerney possessed—he was an anti-treatyite, a diplomat from the "revolutionary" generation, and was outspoken, politically well connected, unskilled in career diplomacy, and prone to independent action. The civil war rift was also evident in the constant clashes between Ó Briain and O'Kelly, with the former minister giving Ó Briain "nothing but trouble."[50] Paris was "Ireland's main listening post on the continent," and Kerney would have been happy to work alongside Ó Briain.[51] However, de Valera intervened again for Kerney in yet another benign way that was to have a major influence on his career. Twice before, in 1926 and in 1932, Kerney had written to request a transfer to Dublin, but on both occasions his request had been denied. A move to Dublin was out of the question given Walshe's animosity toward him. It would not have served the secretary's interests to have Kerney in close working proximity to de Valera, especially after the president had intervened so quickly against a pro-treaty diplomat. Rather de Valera took further advantage of the O'Kelly-Kerney fracas to promote his republican diplomat to lead his own mission in Spain and thus have two important European legations headed by republican officials and not pro-treaty men at a time of deepening political crises throughout Europe with the rise of fascism.

Catholicism was perhaps the strongest tie both then and historically between Ireland and Spain, although appointing a nonreligious Catholic convert rather than an ultra-Catholic was not the standard choice Walshe would ever have approved for such a delicate posting, and it went against a key element of the Irish foreign policy that Walshe had forged since the late 1920s of having an overseas diplomatic service staffed by Catholics serving in Catholic states. But Kerney's appointment was not made by Walshe. It was made by de Valera. There were also grumblings within External Affairs by others, who may have felt more qualified to be appointed to Spain rather than Kerney. However, an examination of Kerney's record shows that his appointment was an appropriate selection. Since his recruitment to the consular service in 1919 Kerney had acquired a relatively strong knowledge of Spain through commercial links with firms based there, trade deals he had negotiated with the Spanish government, connections with friends and family who lived in Spain,[52] and many trips taken in the course of official business.[53] He had a track record of initiating, negotiating, and securing trade deals. His time in Paris as a republican diplomat had given him valuable experience in reporting political matters. The mission would require a high degree of energy, independent action, and resourcefulness—traits Kerney had shown repeatedly in the past. He was still young and ambitious, and perhaps most importantly, he was someone de Valera knew to be loyal to him and whom the republican leader could trust to do the job. Ultimately the appointment rested with de Valera, and again he stepped in to help Kerney against his pro-treaty colleagues. He got the post and became Ireland's first official diplomat to Spain, with the title "Envoy Extraordinary and Minister Plenipotentiary."[54]

OBSTRUCTION BY WALSHE

Kerney's appointment to Spain, over Walshe's head, marked a dramatic moment in his career and in de Valera's confidence in his old colleague's ability. The diplomat immediately set to work throughout the summer of 1935, looking to acquire suitable premises for the overseas residency. There was much logistical work to be done as he traveled back and forth between France and Spain. Yet while his promotion filled him with confidence, within External Affairs Joseph Walshe harbored an ever-increasing grudge against Kerney. This resentment went back to before the treaty split, but the recent events in the Paris legation confirmed Walshe's opinion of the diplomat. Kerney's correspondence with de Valera's private secretary about the fracas, behind his back; the insubordination shown to Count O'Kelly; and Kerney's promotion to Spain all breached normal diplomatic protocol from the secretary's viewpoint. Walshe could do nothing against de Valera's backing of Kerney, but he could certainly make Kerney's mission more difficult, which he did through a process of deliberate administrative obstruction.

The first hindrance that Walshe imposed on Kerney highlights this pettiness. Kerney needed to transport his family, all their belongings and furnishings, as well as furnishings for the new residency to Spain. Walshe refused to dispatch an assistant to help the diplomat set up and equip the legation under the pretext of cost. When Kerney asked for specific books relating to diplomacy, Irish history, and culture to be lodged with the legation, his requests were turned down by Walshe, again on account of cost, even though most overseas legations need such materials for reference purposes.[55] Other basic requirements, such as temporary accommodations in a hotel, were turned down, and Kerney was not provided with any overdraft provisions and had to use his own money to pay for everything in advance. This led to endless correspondence to Walshe requesting reimbursements, which the secretary often responded to by requesting the exchange rate at the time of purchase or an explanation as to why the purchase was made, all of which delayed Kerney's repayments. When Kerney voiced concern that his allowances might not cover the cost of living given fluctuations in the exchange rate, his pleas fell on unsympathetic ears. In one instance Kerney wrote: "My object is to show you the position as I see it, so that you may understand why it is that there are serious and disturbing doubts in my mind."[56] Again it appeared to Kerney that Walshe was deliberately making his work intolerable and frustrating. He asked his friend Art Ó Briain for help in going above Walshe's head: "You would do me a favour if you were to mention something to Dev about my worries."[57]

At first there was no word about who was going to be assisting Kerney in his new post, something the diplomat had highlighted early on: "I am conscious of the fact that my task, at the outset, if I am unaided by a secretary, will be a heavy and difficult one."[58] Most diplomatic missions abroad are staffed by an ambassador or minister, a commercial attaché, a cultural attaché, a passport officer, consular representatives, secretaries, and typists, yet in Kerney's case Walshe made a considerable effort not to appoint anyone to assist Kerney, not even on a part-time or voluntary basis. This unwillingness to staff the new Spanish mission continued for years. For example, on 8 July

1940 a young lady named Olive Byrne wrote to Walshe after hearing from friends who had returned from the continent that there was a vacancy for a clerical officer in the Madrid legation. She cited Mother Aloysius and Mother Consiglio from the Loreto Convent as references that could vouch for her character.[59] Walshe replied on 13 July that there was no vacancy, even though her appointment would have been welcomed by the Irish minister in Madrid. On 6 August 1935 Walshe informed Kerney that he would have to perform the duties of a normal diplomatic station abroad without any of the normal supports, not even that of a secretary or typist.[60] The department also ruled out the appointment of any honorary consular agents to assist him, owing to Walshe's obsession with secrecy concerning state matters.[61] Kerney was therefore the only member of staff for the entire Irish mission to Spain. After he argued his case strenuously with Walshe, the secretary relented somewhat, and Kerney was allowed to have a typist. However, there were conditions attached: she had to be Irish, know Spanish fluently, and be resident in Spain, as the department was not prepared to dispatch an Irish girl to Madrid. Further, she was to be given only a temporary contract, as this would preclude her from any pension entitlements. Despite the difficulty of adhering to these excessive criteria, Kerney found a girl named Elizabeth "Maisie" Donnelly, who was working in Barcelona, teaching English.

Maisie Donnelly was a cousin of Lily Donnelly from Wexford, who had married Paddy Sheehan. Sheehan worked for Cables and Wireless in Barcelona, and Kerney had known Sheehan for many years from business and family trips to the Catalan city. The couple would, in time, have three children, the eldest of which, Seamus, Kerney became godfather to. As Kerney wrote to his brother: "I am the Godfather of one of them [the Donnelly children], Seamus by name, born in 1936, the first Irishman to be registered in the Register of Births at the Irish Legation in Madrid."[62] When Maisie accepted the appointment, she needed to get a train ride to relocate to Madrid. Dublin refused to pay her any travel allowance, as she had yet to sign contract papers. Furthermore, when Kerney sent her a telegram to confirm the time of her arrival in Madrid, Walshe refused to reimburse the diplomat for the cost of the telegram and for the fuel used in collecting her from the train station, as they were deemed unrelated to official duties.[63] So attentive was Walshe to these minor details that he frequently consulted train or bus timetables in Spain himself to argue with Kerney as to why he had decided to use the legation car to travel to a particular destination or event when a cheaper option, public transport, was available between this hour and that. In time Maisie would perform duties above and beyond her basic pay, working six days a week despite the knowledge that "her services are liable to be terminated on a week's notice."[64]

For weeks Kerney had bought furniture and other items to furnish the new legation, always conscious of Walshe's attention to any unnecessary expenditure. The secretary's interference with the most minute of matters clearly angered Kerney. The diplomat, as he frequently did, decided to literally cause a storm in a teacup. In early September 1935, some teapots and a cup in the legation were accidentally broken by a maid. Kerney decided to ask Dublin to send out replacement crockery. He gave an estimate of the price, knowing that this would provoke another clash between him and Walshe. The secretary argued that the department should not pay for the broken teapots and cup, and he challenged Kerney's estimate for replacing the crockery. That the secretary even concerned himself with such inconsequential matters reflects his enduring dislike of Kerney. But the diplomat refused to back down, so Walshe escalated the matter and brought it to the attention of the government. The minister for external affairs, Éamon de Valera, and the minister for finance, Seán MacEntee, concurred with Walshe over an issue as irrelevant as broken crockery. Only after the government backed Walshe did Kerney agree to recoup the money. Walshe wrote: "With reference to your minute of the 11th instant relative to the breakage and replacement of two tea pots and a cup, I am directed by the Minister [de Valera] to request that you will be good enough to report as to the possibility of having the cost incurred in this case recovered from the person responsible for the breakage."[65] In the end, the diplomat paid for the damage himself. The petty-mindedness of Walshe would continue for years, with the secretary often evoking the authority of the "Minister," to pressure Kerney at every turn to exercise rigid control of every item of expenditure: "The Minister has no doubt that in the interests of national economy you will see that all reasonable care is exercised in the use of fuel."[66]

DEV'S MAN IN SPAIN

On 3 September 1935 Kerney was officially accredited as Ireland's minister to the Second Republic. Yet Spain in the interwar period was a country on the threshold of anarchy, bloodshed, and civil war, and Kerney's confidential files to Dublin illuminate this gradual descent into violence, which marked Spanish life from 1935 onward and led him in one report to state: "Spain is heading for civil war unless the Government takes very prompt measures to render excesses impossible. The spirit of civil war is very manifest and is due to the fact that the extreme left believes in the policy of completely crushing the extreme right, and vice versa."[67] His eyewitness accounts shed new light on what conditions were like for ordinary people when strikes, violent street clashes, bans on political meetings, church burnings, and suspensions of many constitutional guarantees became a part of normal life.

The republican administration was made up of a pluralist political and social movement that enjoyed the support of the majority of Spanish society: peasants, laborers, small farmers, the intelligentsia, workers, trade unionists, and the lower middle class. Its supporters were politically identified as communists, socialists, liberal republicans, and Basque and Catalan regionalists. From the day the republic was constituted, these sections of Spanish society welcomed the government's commitment to redistribute wealth across all of society, especially in a country that was grossly unequal socially and economically and suffering badly from the Great Depression. Naturally the forces on the right, backed by industrialists, landowners, and bankers, opposed this political agenda. Monarchists still believed in the king. The army abhorred regionalism and saw it as a weakening of the state. Moreover, it grew uneasy when the government moved to trim down the bloated size of its officer corps. But of all its opponents, the government clashed the most with the Catholic Church—an institution that held enormous power and influence over Spanish public life at that time. The forces on the right were appalled by what they saw as the anti-clerical attitude of the government, and this perception was crystallized early on when, on 11 May, just one month after the government took office, churches were set alight across Madrid, Barcelona, and Málaga by anarchists and socialists chaffing at the bit for redistribution of land, title, wealth, and property. For historian Mary Vincent, this violent action by the left was "genuine persecution," which the right used as a just cause for preparing an armed uprising.[68]

Political violence was a hallmark of Spanish life from then on. Kerney noted: "All outdoor political meetings are banned, by a recent decision of the Government inspired by the fear that the gathering of huge masses of people might lead to acts of violence."[69] On 16 February 1936, after another general election, the left-wing coalition made up of moderate republicans, socialists, communists, and Catalan and Basque regional parties, known collectively as the Popular Front, came to power. But the election did little to stabilize the country. The political instability hampered Kerney's efforts to secure larger trade deals with Spain, and he could see for himself the gradual fragmentation of society. Just two days after the new administration took office, Kerney informed Dublin that the building complex that housed the Irish and Turkish legations now had four police officers stationed outside the premises twenty-four hours a day to guard the property. Neither he nor the Turkish minister had requested the additional security. Kerney inquired into the matter and discovered that the owner of the property, the Countess de la Sisla, a wealthy monarchist, had made the request for additional police protection.[70] To Kerney, events like this were a clear indication that the comfortable and conservative classes feared mob rule. In the months leading up to the outbreak of the civil war, attacks on property were replaced by attacks on citizens as ordinary people and public representatives were killed in the streets. Kerney attributed most of these killings to the fascists: "I was informed a week ago from 2 sources that it was a definite fact that 3 communists had been hanged in the Retiro Park and red handkerchiefs placed in their mouths."[71]

One important group that supplied the Irish minister with information was the Irish diaspora in Spain, who had enjoyed centuries of seniority and influence in Spanish society, occupying important positions in several governments and military commands. During a conversation with the Count of Cañongo, a descendant of the famous Irish nobleman O'Sullivan Beare, Kerney recorded that the count had already made travel plans: "He explained to me the arrangements he had made for escaping from his house with his daughters in the event of it being attacked."[72] Two weeks later Kerney met another prominent figure in the Irish diaspora, the Duchess of Tetuán, a descendant of the Ulster Gaelic chief Red Hugh O'Donnell, who told him about rumors of an immediate "coup d'état by certain elements in the army."[73] Another source of contact was the group of Loreto nuns who ran a convent in Madrid. The mother superior, Mother Aloysius, phoned him expressing her fear that the Irish nuns might be attacked by a communist mob at any time.[74]

In the weeks leading up to the outbreak of the Spanish Civil War, general strikes by workers fighting for more political change gave way to armed attacks against individuals. As Kerney revealed in one of his reports, it was not just the extreme left, such as anarchists and communists, who resorted to these acts of violence in order to achieve their political aims; the right was also culpable. In fact, he blamed right-wing fascists for most of the violence. What Kerney feared most was that the exaggerated charges that the Second Republic was communist and violently anti-clerical would legitimize the right's launching a coup and installing an authoritarian or, worse, a fascist dictatorship along the lines of Hitler's Nazi regime. He wrote:

> There are fascist elements whose creed is one of violence; their policy of reprisals leads to further excesses on the extreme left; this continued agitation creates an atmosphere of civil war; it tends to weaken the Government and may be aimed at forcing the Government to take action against some of its own supporters on the extreme left; if the Republican regime should be discredited, the fascists might expect a change favorable to their point of view. Spain is heading for civil war.[75]

Kerney's predictions proved accurate. On 15 April 1936, José Calvo Sotelo, a former minister for finance during the Primo de Rivera dictatorship and a notable hard-line right-wing politician, presented in parliament a comprehensive list of reported acts of political violence to the then prime minister, Manuel Azaña, since Azaña had taken office. Sotelo's report covered acts of political violence over only a two-month period from 16 February to 2 April 1936. During that short time, 74 people had been murdered and 345 wounded; 178 buildings set on fire, of which 106 had been churches; and 36 churches had also been ransacked.[76] Sotelo blamed all this violence on the left. Three months later, Sotelo himself was kidnapped from his home by officials of the state's security organs and was murdered. His death was viewed as the immediate and legitimate reason the right needed to launch a coup d'état.

Kerney's last official engagement took place on 20 May 1936, when the Irish minister and the rest of the diplomatic corps were in attendance at the National Palace to meet Manuel Azaña, who had assumed the role of president of the republic following yet another change in government. Kerney took advantage of the official occasion to talk with the minister of industry and commerce to finalize more trade agreements between Spain and Ireland and to extend a trade deal signed the previous year. The report on this was his last report from Spain before the outbreak of civil war. An evening or two later, while practicing his golf swing, Kerney noticed that he could not grip the club properly. He was suddenly struck down with polio, or infantile paralysis as it was often called at the time. He feared it was caused by contaminated water. The virus attacked his spinal cord and immobilized his arms and fingers, rendering him "powerless."[77] Raymonde applied heat compresses to his muscles, but these offered little relief. He underwent x-ray treatment and spinal injections before requesting extended sick leave and went to a thermal spa facility in La Toja, in the northwestern province of Galicia, just before the outbreak of the civil war.[78] On 4 August he left La Toja under armed escort and continued his sick leave in Ireland.[79] These difficulties were compounded by the death of his brother Nicholas from pneumonia in September and by his own contraction of sinusitis that left Kerney ill and fatigued and needing lengthy stays for recuperation and clinical treatment in France and Ireland that involved painful scraping of the sinuses. The bed-confined diplomat had always had great stamina throughout his life up to this point, but it is evident that from this time on he became increasingly afflicted with bouts of illness. In a rare show of sympathy on hearing his devastating news of his contraction of polio, Joseph Walshe wrote to Kerney: "Dear Mr. Kerney. The Minister was very sorry indeed to learn of your sudden illness. We all hope that you will make a rapid recovery to complete health."[80]

Around the same time as Kerney was struck down with polio, Maisie Donnelly's health also suffered. She was diagnosed with neuralgic sciatica on 24 May and needed medical treatment. Walshe, however, showed little concern for her and her requests for paid leave. Her temporary contract entitled her only to one day's leave per month served, and Walshe wanted all medical certificates forwarded to Dublin to verify her illness. The secretary refused to pay for an interim typist, so with Kerney and Maisie too ill to work, Raymonde Kerney took over the running of the legation on a voluntary basis until Maisie recovered. Thereafter the typist stayed behind at the Irish legation, ensuring that all Irish citizens seeking to be evacuated from Spain were assisted despite the dangers to herself from the fighting.[81]

In late January 1937, Kerney was healthy enough to resume work, and he rejoined his colleagues in the diplomatic corps stationed in the French border town of Saint Jean de Luz, where the international community had been reporting on the critical battle for Madrid throughout the winter.[82] The diplomat, like many of his counterparts, was forced to operate from the Golf Hotel. The Madrid premises had been sealed and secured before his departure. Yet, owing to the prevailing conditions in the country and his ill health at the time, Kerney had been unable to take equipment with him. In order to resume his work he needed official paper stamped with the harp and headed "Irlande." He asked permission to obtain paper from the Paris legation, but Walshe refused the request, arguing that this would cause a paper scarcity there and weaken the administrative efficiency of the French mission. Frustrated, Kerney bought plain paper and a typewriter. When he requested reimbursement for the typewriter, it was turned down on the grounds that it was purchased "without prior authority."[83] Kerney responded by handwriting all his reports—knowing that his handwriting was truly awful and barely legible. On 24 June, after three irritating months trying to read Kerney's handwriting, Walshe finally backed down and the diplomat was reimbursed his 3,700 francs for the typewriter. Kerney celebrated the occasion by using the money to buy a ring for Raymonde.[84]

These mini-battles with officialdom and the old boys' club behind the scenes were nothing compared to the real fighting and dying taking place inside Spain. Barry McLoughlin has recorded how the Spanish Civil War caused "a furore in Ireland, dominating politics for the next twelve months."[85] The majority of society, the press, the Catholic hierarchy, and the conservative and political elite supported the nationalists under General Francisco Franco, and a small but committed working-class minority supported the Republican government. Both sides sent volunteers to fight in Spain despite Ireland's noninterventionist stance.[86] Ireland's mission to Spain now became the spotlight of political and public attention. Inside the Dáil chamber the government was pushed early on to sever its formal accreditation to the Republican government and recognize General Franco's rebel Burgos government[87] by the Opposition Fine Gael leader William Cosgrave: "[I] ask the House to express the view that the Government should take the necessary steps leading to the recognition by us of the Government of General Franco in Spain. . . . The war in Spain is a war for the victory or defeat of Communism and all it stands for, with its denial of Christian principles, individual liberty, and democracy."[88] De Valera refused on the grounds that the situation was still uncertain, with no guarantees that Franco would win the war. Another question of recognition arose on 17 February 1937, with de Valera again refusing to recognize Franco's authority.[89] However, the next day de Valera cryptically revealed that his sympathies and those of his government were with Franco: "If the Deputy [James Dillon] will look at the map he will see that St. Jean de Luz is nearer to Burgos [the seat of Franco's government] than it is to Valencia [the seat of the Republican government]."[90]

This issue of accreditation remained a heated public and political issue in Ireland, as James Dillon TD pointed out: "The issue in Spain, the fundamental issue, is God or no God."[91] The Opposition parties clamored for the recall of Ireland's minister, and they were backed by the printing press, the pulpit, and the general masses. Michael Kennedy asserted that Kerney's advice to the government was very much in line with Catholic opinion generally: "Kerney remained accredited to the Madrid government, but he did not attempt to hide his preferences for Franco and the nationalists."[92] This claim is questionable, as Kerney supported nonintervention, and when he made sympathetic overtures to Franco's side, it was as a representative of the Irish government speaking on behalf of his government, in the same tone as de Valera's statement to the Dáil: "I had no doubt myself as to where the sympathies of my Government were," Kerney noted.[93] Stronger still, the diplomat informed Franco's supporters that the regime's alignment with fascism would clash with the "very strong democratic spirit in Ireland."[94] In a letter to his brother Maurice and in letters he wrote as a private citizen, Kerney recorded in late 1937: "Franco and his followers are blind optimists at the moment and hope the war will finish in a month or two; for my part I prefer to wait for the overdue offensive or series of offensives before making up my mind as to the probable result, or lack of result."[95] Even as late as August 1938, Kerney personally displayed his opposition to the recognition of Franco and his regime and advocated continued support for the Spanish Republic and nonintervention in the conflict: "if there is any question of recognizing a certain gentleman [Franco], this is <u>not</u> the moment to do so and I hope wiser counsels will prevail."[96]

The issue of more immediate concern to the minister was the welfare of Irish citizens inside Spain. Irish volunteers were dying in increasing numbers from 1937 onward as the war intensified, particularly at the battles of Jarama (February 1937) and Brunete (July 1937). Kerney had to concern himself with the repatriation of the bodies and with notifying their next of kin. Irish prisoners of war were likewise a top priority. Kerney liaised with the International Red Cross to ensure that these men were cared for in the best manner, but this proved difficult, especially as Franco's side frequently shot many captives after surrender.[97] The behavior of Franco's forces reminded the Irish diplomat of the brutal suppression of republicans by the forces of the Irish Free State during the Irish Civil War.

The largest of the Irish forces under General Eoin O'Duffy was proving itself completely unsuited to intense warfare in Spain. As Walshe wrote: "Reports are being received in Ireland that the soldiers of the 15th Tercio (Irish Brigade) of the Foreign Legion are to a large extent discontent with their lot. They complain of the bad food, poor clothing and of their treatment generally. They are said to be poor in physique, and with exceptions, bad soldiers."[98] O'Duffy's command was anything but satisfactory. He frequently showed up before his men drunk and disheveled. His own troops referred to him as "General O'Scruffy." In the end, Franco disbanded the Irish force and sent it back home in disgrace. Several soldiers stayed on, however, and joined the Spanish Foreign Legion. These men as well as their Irish opponents who had answered Frank Ryan's call to defend the Spanish Republic remained a constant concern for Kerney.

The care Kerney showed for his fellow citizens in Spain revived his health and spirits at a particularly bad time for him. He was still receiving "electrical treatment" for his joints, and he was forced to restrict his smoking after doctors detected heart problems.[99] These ailments had been aggravated by a long and bitter dispute between him and Dublin over exchange-rate payments that Kerney argued were depreciating his salary: "I have won my fight with Dublin over payment in Sterling; I cannot tell you how pleased I am to wiped [*sic*] the ground with those sourish officials in Finance. . . . I already knew from an inside source that Finance were pretty annoyed with me; I accused them of acting illegally, of being unjust, inconsiderate, unprincipled, etc. They had to stomach it all. Finally I wired Dev in such a way that he practically had to intervene. I threatened the Dept. that I would appeal for a transfer for me."[100] The beginning of the end for the Spanish Republic came on 25 July 1938, when its army launched a desperate counterattack across the River Ebro. The battle dragged on for four months and became an attrition contest, with sheer force of numbers and supplies eventually proving decisive for the nationalists, who enjoyed extensive military and economic assistance from Nazi

Germany and fascist Italy. The collapse of republican resistance in the eastern theater opened the entire region of Catalonia to a full-scale assault. The tide of the war had finally turned in Franco's favor, yet Kerney was still vehemently against recognizing Franco. Only after the nationalists entered a silent and starving Barcelona on 26 January 1939 did Kerney advise Dublin, on 30 January, to begin the process of recognizing Franco. On 10 February Dublin wired its approval, and the following day Kerney sent a note to Franco's minister for foreign affairs—General Francisco Jordana. The thought of returning to Madrid weighed on his mind: "I am not perturbed at the prospect of renewing the experience, however the limelight does not appeal to me and I shall soon be regretting and appreciating at its full value the couple of idle but happy and quiet years spent at St Jean de Luz."[101] The coming years would be far from idle and would, in fact, be the most intense and contentious of his life.

CHAPTER 7

FRANCO'S MOST FAMOUS FOREIGN PRISONER AND ESCAPEE— FRANK RYAN

During the Spanish Civil War several hundred Irishmen had joined the Republican Army to fight for the Spanish government against General Franco and his rebels.[1] Among the leadership of this Irish cohort was Frank Ryan, whose arrival in Spain was to mark one of the most contentious events in Kerney's career. Kerney's later perceived mishandling of the Ryan case, by indirectly contacting the Abwehr (German military intelligence) and opening himself up to German contact, marked him, in the view of Eunan O'Halpin, as a "monumental fool."[2] Michael Kennedy likewise saw Kerney's tenure in Spain during the war as indicative of his unsuitability as a diplomat: "[Kerney] proved to be something of a law unto himself," he wrote.[3] Both historians expressed these views in the context of other controversies surrounding Kerney, but neither provided a full in-depth analysis of these perceived controversies, not examining or referencing many critical files when they asserted these views and not providing the full context as to how it came to be that German intelligence and Kerney crossed paths beginning with the Ryan case. It is far too simplistic to place all the blame on Kerney once we assess the full facts available to us. In fact, other historians, like Barry McLoughlin, have understood the complexity of the Ryan case and have argued that, rather than bungling the affair, Kerney displayed "tireless" generosity and craft over a two-year period when faced with a "campaign of deceit, disinformation and denunciations against Frank Ryan."[4] It is only through a detailed analysis of Ryan's time in Spain that we can fully assess Kerney's performance.

THE FIGHTING IRISH

Ryan was a respected IRA fighter who subsequently fought on the anti-treaty side during the Irish Civil War.[5] He continued his association with the IRA until 1934, when he officially split from the organization because of a dispute over his and other members' socialist outlook, which clashed with orthodox republicanism over its obsession with ending partition as the prerequisite for establishing the "Irish Republic." A moderate socialist who still attended Mass, Ryan was not the communist his detractors would later describe him as, yet his was a voice in the wilderness in 1930s Ireland. That voice finally found an audience when news of the life-and-death struggles unfolding in Spain captured international attention. Ryan's views on Spain clashed with the majority of Irish public opinion at the time, but he was not afraid to voice his beliefs even to the Catholic hierarchy and its most senior ecclesiastic, the Primate of All Ireland, Cardinal MacRory:

> I am one of those Irish Republicans whom you consider "misguided" because we have sent to the Spanish, Catalan and Basque peoples a message of sympathy and support in their fight against Fascism. . . . It is

an historical fact that in the struggle for the Spanish Republic—as in the struggle for the Irish Republic—particularly in the periods 1865–67 and 1916–23 the Catholic clergy opposed the people. . . . I maintain that the real enemies of Christianity in Spain are the Fascist Generals who openly proclaim that they will set up a military dictatorship, suppress Trade Unions and prohibit the workers' right to strike. Is it Christianity to enslave and exploit the masses? . . . Our stand in 1922–23 is already vindicated: history will vindicate our stand on the Spanish question today.[6]

Ryan and other Irish supporters traveled to Spain in December 1936 to join fifteen thousand international volunteers from over thirty-two countries to help save the Spanish Republic from General Franco's fascist forces.[7] These Irishmen fought in national battalions as part of the 15th International Brigade. Ryan proved an excellent leader, particularly at the Battle of Jarama, where he rallied the retreating 15th to launch a counterattack that successfully repulsed the enemy onslaught. He helped to turn an impending defeat into a republican victory.[8] In March 1937 Ryan returned to Ireland for seveal months due to wounds received in combat, yet he spent these months recovering and campaigning for more Irish assistance and recruits for the Spanish Republic. He returned to Spain, but his war finally came to an end when he was captured by Italian troops in March 1938. A prisoner of General Franco, Ryan soon became a contentious political problem for de Valera's government.

On 14 June 1938, Ryan was tried by a military court in Burgos.[9] The charges against him ranged from engaging in "propaganda" activities to taking part in armed rebellion.[10] The five-member court found him unanimously guilty on both counts and sentenced him to death. Only Franco's signed commutation could save Ryan from a firing squad. The dictator kept Ryan's file open for months, as more charges were subsequently received against him. Only persistent diplomatic and political efforts finally moved Franco to commute the death sentence.[11]

The Irish government's de jure recognition of Franco's on 11 February 1939 finally accorded the Irish an official line of inquiry into Ryan's well-being. Kerney was eager to visit all Irish prisoners, not just Ryan. Some of O'Duffy's volunteers joined the Spanish Foreign Legion after their erstwhile commander had left Spain and were subsequently arrested for infractions or desertion.[12] Nevertheless, the Irish government attached the highest political importance to securing Ryan's release because of the prisoner's public profile and standing in republican circles. All avenues—diplomatic, political, religious, economic, and covert—would be explored and exhausted. The outcome in the end was Ryan's release, but not as the Irish had intended. Instead it was all done on Franco's terms. The entire case would dominate Kerney's time in Spain and would come to overshadow his career long after his own death.

THE FRANK RYAN CASE

On 1 May 1939, Franco's diplomatic representative to Ireland, Juan Garcia Ontiveros, arrived in Dublin to foster closer political ties between the states. The new minister was a staunch ally of Franco and a committed fascist. On 25 May Ontiveros had his first meeting with the Taoiseach (prime minister) and Minister for External Affairs Éamon de Valera in Government Buildings. In attendance was Joseph Walshe. The meeting was dominated by de Valera, who expressed unease that Ryan had not been released as part of a prisoner exchange. The Taoiseach said that he attached the utmost political importance to Ryan's release and that he viewed the prisoner's continued detention as an obstacle to friendly relations between the countries. He reminded Ontiveros that Irish public opinion generally "had always desired the triumph" of Franco and that men like Ryan represented only a minority viewpoint.[13] As the last surviving commander from the 1916 Easter Rising, de Valera could not be seen to be idle on this matter, and he stressed to Ontiveros his personal interest in the case. The Old IRA and "Frank Ryan Release Committees" in Ireland, England, and the United States were putting pressure on the Taoiseach to get his fellow Limerick native out of prison. At the meeting de Valera also stated with total clarity that in all matters concerning Ryan, Kerney was acting with the full authority and approval of the Irish government. De Valera's declaration is important for several reasons. First, it notified the Spanish that Kerney was lobbying not from a personal agenda but from official sanction to free Ryan. Second, it officially authorized Kerney to act as he saw fit in the best interest of the Irish government. When the Irish made their critical approach to the Germans later on, Kerney felt he had the approval to undertake such an initiative. Finally, the Taoiseach had made it abundantly clear that Ryan was the top priority in Irish-Spanish relations and that the government desired his freedom immediately.

If the Irish government thought that having a representative of Franco in Dublin to negotiate with would expedite matters, they were proven wrong. The minister, like Franco, viewed Spanish and Irish republicanism as essentially the same phenomenon—an anarchic, leftist, and extremist political movement to be crushed violently. Only de Valera's commitment to constitutional politics, his close association with Catholicism, and his being half Spanish kept the Fianna Fáil leader from being painted with the same "red" republican brush in the regime's eyes. Ontiveros's report back to Madrid described Ryan as a "mystical extremist," a rather exaggerated and unfair description that highlighted his own warped opinions more than anything else.[14]

Ontiveros knew about Ryan before this meeting with the Taoiseach. His residence had received letters from committee members and visits from prominent female republicans Hanna Sheehy Skeffington and Maud Gonne MacBride, as well as Ryan's sister Eilís. On 12 June Ontiveros called into External Affairs to complain about newspaper articles in leftist publications denouncing his government's treatment of Ryan.[15] He requested a postponement of a major rally organized by committee members in the city center. Walshe arranged to have the protest rally called off, but he did warn the minister that his life might be in danger after seeing slogans on walls reading "Release Frank Ryan or Else." Events like these convinced Dublin to postpone Ontiveros's official accreditation ceremony. They also reinforced the minister's view of Ryan and his supporters as extremists and dangerous people.

Ontiveros's views on Ryan were supported by the circle of associates he surrounded himself with. This support was best shown at a film screening at Saint Stephen's Green cinema, which he described as "the only one in this Capital whose business is not backed by Jewish interests."[16] The pro-Franco film, "Spain in Arms," was attended by staunch Catholics like the lord mayor of Dublin, Alfie Byrne; the fascist ministers of Italy (Vincenzo Berardis) and Germany (Eduard Hempel); and Ryan's nemesis in Spain, General Eoin O'Duffy. In his report the minister noted the large numbers of priests who were there that day to see the film, and he noted how they applauded and cheered General Franco when he appeared onscreen. To him these were the voices of true Irish Catholic people, while Ryan's supporters were, in his opinion, "leftists, communists and masons."[17] The minister also noted the repeated denunciations of Ryan in the press by ordinary people: "Everyone knows that Mr Ryan is a Communist. Instead of demanding his release we should be praying to God for being rid of such a person, for so long as his kind is out of our small country we will have peace. Long may General Franco keep him, because we don't want him."[18]

At this time the vast majority of visa applications from Irish citizens wanting to go to Spain were made by priests and nuns who wanted to help the Spanish church rebuild itself after the civil war.[19] Their public support for General Franco helped form Ontiveros's perceptions of Ryan and those who supported him. On several occasions Kerney had been informed by officials in the Spanish Ministry of Foreign Affairs that they had received countless letters condemning Ryan from Irish priests via Ontiveros. In one example, Ontiveros received a letter from James A. Cleary, who described Ryan as a "Communist."[20] The priest was angry that articles in the Irish press that condemned Ryan for his involvement in the International Brigade did not also detail his alleged involvement in atrocities: "Perhaps we have not heard the whole truth. If so, it is a pity," he wrote.[21] The words of religious men mattered in Ireland and Spain, especially the latter, given the murders of priests and nuns during the civil war, and these letters and discussions shaped perceptions of Ryan in Spanish eyes that were hard to counter.

Every demonstration that was organized by Ryan's supporters was also infiltrated by lay members of the Catholic Church who supported Franco. Ontiveros did not encourage these people to do this, yet he did not discourage them, either. On 2 July the minister was informed confidentially about a demonstration of some four hundred people—including the leader of the 1913 lock-out, James Larkin—who marched down O'Connell Street carrying banners demanding Ryan's liberation.[22] Ontiveros deemed these anonymous informants to represent sensible elements of the country. One unknown correspondent who attended such a rally wrote to him: "Your Excellency will see that the speakers, all Communists conceal the fact that he was condemned for murder, wholesale murder of prisoners."[23] When fifty Dáil deputies, seventy-two members of the House of Commons, the Old IRA Citizen Army Comrades' Association, and many others signed a petition in favor of Ryan's release, Ontiveros could contend that they were simply ignorant of the facts about Ryan.[24] He was determined to hold firm and offer no assistance in the Ryan case, as his supporters, whom he believed represented authentic public opinion, were expressing their opinions just as loudly. As another concerned member of the public wrote: "I hope the Spanish Government will show firmness and not release him."[25]

On 27 July Ontiveros finally presented his credentials as Franco's representative to Ireland. The significant delay was directly linked to the Ryan case and Dublin's fears for his safety. From the legation's residence on Shrewsbury Road right up to the gates of Dublin Castle, the streets were lined with soldiers and policemen to protect him against possible attack or assassination: There was "an extraordinary vigilance in operation and an uninterrupted barrier of police agents," Ontiveros informed his superiors.[26] He smiled when he saw some members of the public who "saluted in the Spanish [fascist] style with a raised arm."[27] The fact that the whole ceremony had to be kept secret from the press highlighted for him the extremist nature of Ryan's supporters. With no help or assistance coming from this quarter, any hope of releasing Ryan rested on Kerney.

"The nigger in the woodpile"

In 1939 Spain was ruled by a totalitarian dictator who commanded total power and ruled without any legislative, judicial, or constitutional restrictions. Public opinion counted for nothing, and anyone who found herself or himself on the wrong side of the regime, as millions of defeated republicans did, was in trouble. Kerney understood that only Franco could authorize Ryan's release, but also that access to the dictator was extremely difficult unless you were one of Kerney's German or Italian diplomatic counterparts. During the entire time that Ryan was imprisoned, Kerney only saw Franco once, on 10 April, the day he presented his credentials, and only for fifteen minutes. He therefore had to explore every possible avenue of inquiry, meet any official of the regime that he could, and rely on the Irish diaspora in the country to help influence Franco. The Irish mission's scant financial, human, and administrative resources were fully exposed during the case, as Kerney had to do everything on his own. This stressful situation led to further clashes between him and Walshe. The Ryan case also highlighted the Catholic romanticism of Irish foreign policy. Walshe had believed that because Spain and Ireland shared a common devotion to Catholicism, naturally a *modus vivendi* would be reached. In fact, the disappointing outcome revealed the impotence of Ireland's influence on the European stage even in countries with which it felt it had a historic and religious affiliation.

Ryan was held in an overcrowded military prison named Burgos Central Prison. His family used the Red Cross to send warm clothing to him via Kerney. The prisoner suffered from deafness and a weak heart. It was only when Kerney finally gained access to the prison that he saw for himself the deplorable conditions Ryan and his fellow inmates endured. Kerney had tried to meet General Jordana, the minister of foreign affairs, on several occasions without success. At a reception at the Portuguese embassy on 28 May he did speak with a leading official in Foreign Affairs who said they were "doing their best" but that Ryan was a "difficult" case given his reputation as a "stark communist," among other things.[28] Kerney asked if the military was the main obstacle to Ryan's release: "I put the question to

Casares—Is it the military authorities who constitute the real barrier? He replied that this was so. For the moment I do not see how we can bring any pressure to bear on these military authorities but at least it is well to know where the main opposition lies."[29]

Kerney's principal channel for gaining access to, and thence influencing, senior military figures in the regime was an Irish émigré named Walter Meade. Captain Meade had been General O'Duffy's interpreter and driver during the Spanish Civil War, and he willingly offered his assistance to Kerney. Meade had high-level contacts in the senior echelons of the army, which included the chief of staff and most of Franco's top commanders—Solchaga, Alonso Vega, and Yagüe. The general in charge of the sixth region, where Burgos Central Prison was located, was one López Pinto, and Kerney hoped Meade could use his contacts to persuade General Pinto to allow visiting rights for him to see Ryan. The minister was beginning to see that real power lay with the military in Spain and that Foreign Affairs had little, if any, pull with or influence over Franco. The British had discovered this for themselves when they inquired about access to their citizens.

On 16 June, a few days before a major demonstration of over two thousand people took place in London's Hyde Park, organized on Ryan's behalf,[30] Kerney visited Burgos Central Prison, having gained General Pinto's authorization through Meade.[31] He was greeted warmly by its director, Antonio Crejo.[32] From 6:30 a.m. to 9 p.m., prisoners assembled and stayed in an open courtyard. Most were housed in dormitories that accommodated anywhere from one to three hundred people. Crejo allowed Kerney to talk to Ryan for an hour, and the prisoner said that on the whole he was treated well, but that he suffered health problems. He asked Kerney not to permit his sister Eilís to visit him, and he inquired if people back home had forgotten about him. None of the prisoners were allowed to receive food from visitors, so Kerney gave him money, cigarettes, and clothing. During their chat Ryan said he remembered meeting Kerney previously through joint acquaintances—the Mulcahy family from Sligo. The minister could not recall this, and he did not know then how significant a role the Mulcahys were to play in Ryan's release.

The next day Kerney wrote to Frederick Boland, assistant secretary, demonstrating just how attached and determined he now was to free Ryan. The minister was angry that Ryan's enemies in Ireland could be so vindictive as to want him "to die" in such appalling conditions.[33] He believed Ryan was a good man, perhaps misguided, who did not deserve the vilification of being framed as a communist— an accusation that was reaching Spanish ears from his enemies back home. However, it was not just in Ireland that Ryan had enemies. Kerney discovered from a confidential conversation he had a month later with the *New York Times* correspondent in Spain, William Carney, who was known for his pro-Franco sympathies, that the British representative to Franco, Sir Robert Hodgson, had done his best to see that Ryan would never be set free. Hodgson blamed Ryan for the death of his relative, Vice Admiral Henry Boyle Somerville, who had been assassinated by the IRA on 24 March 1936 for allegedly recruiting men in Ireland to join the Royal Navy. Hodgson had passed on all this information to the Spanish authorities, Carney informed the Irish minister.[34] This uncorroborated revelation helped Kerney see just how extensive was the opposition, both real and alleged, to Ryan's release. Because of ongoing misinformation and rumor, he decided it would be best if only the Irish handled the Ryan case and he did not seek help from the British, who had offered assistance in the affair: "I shall most certainly decline to accept it, whilst clothing my refusal in as courteous a garb as possible," he wrote.[35]

Another contact Kerney used in the case was the Duchess of Tetuán, Blanca O'Donnell. Like Meade, she was of Irish descent and knew many prominent figures in the regime. The new minister for foreign affairs, Juan Beigbeder, who was reportedly pro-Irish, favored closer cultural and economic cooperation. Beigbeder had recently appointed the duchess to a senior position on his staff. Kerney asked the duchess to see Ryan, which she did, and she was so moved by Ryan's plight that she promised to see Franco and impress on him the necessity of early release. Kerney stressed to Beigbeder at several one-to-one meetings that Ireland had been one of the first nations to recognize the regime and that a Catholic nation that valued spirituality and religious morals, like Spain, would view clemency in the Ryan case as a major display of bilateral friendship. However, Beigbeder informed Kerney that every time he raised the matter with the *Caudillo* (Franco's title, meaning Warlord, equivalent to Hitler's title, Führer, and Mussolini's, Duce) he was confronted with a resolute obstinacy on Franco's part. Franco was not moved by Catholic sentiment in Ryan's case.

The only ministers who commanded real influence over Franco at the cabinet level were the armed forces ministers and the interior minister. Without the military and police forces he could not govern, and if he lost their support a coup d'état might just topple him from power. The *Caudillo* had a close inner circle of confidants who advised him in relation to many prisoners awaiting judgment. His legal advisor and close friend Lorenzo Martínez Fuset was bitterly opposed to Ryan's liberation, as his "mind was poisoned against him by Gunning and others," Kerney informed Dublin.[36] Thomas Gunning had been General O'Duffy's aide-de-camp and had spread rumors that Ryan had commanded firing squads. Together with Hodgson, who had condemned Kerney, men like Fuset were undermining Kerney's efforts to untangle the veil of lies that had been concocted against Ryan.

In addition to Fuset, Franco's other close advisor was his brother-in-law Ramón Serrano Súñer, who was both ambitious and conniving and wanted Beigbeder's post for himself. Súñer held the post of minister for the interior, commanded a senior position in the Falange—the only party permitted to exist openly—and had been the architect behind the political structure of the new state. Franco relied whole-heartedly on his brother-in-law and trusted his judgment implicitly. Súñer had been captured by the republican authorities during the civil war, and two of his brothers had been assassinated. He therefore had a visceral hatred of anyone who admitted to, or was simply accused of, being a communist. Kerney challenged the communist charge against Ryan by submitting a memorandum to Franco stating that two of Ryan's sisters were nuns and that he was known and regarded fondly by the archbishop of Dublin, Dr. Edward Byrne. Given the array of real enemies and fabricated stories about Ryan that circulated in Spain, Ireland, and Great Britain, it was proving increasingly difficult for Kerney to isolate and convince the one man that mattered, the one he called the "nigger in the woodpile"—General Franco.[37]

Kerney's monthly visits to Ryan resulted in the prisoner's receiving more parcels, clothes, and food, and also better treatment. Ryan was exempted from labor and allowed to see a doctor regularly. Furthermore, Franco had commuted the death sentence hanging over him to imprisonment, which could range up to thirty years. It seemed that things were slowly turning in the right direction. Kerney repeatedly asked Dublin to keep Ryan's supporters and the release committees at bay because their efforts only hindered matters. Instead he advised them to raise money to be used for Ryan's and his family's benefit. Ryan's family was in weekly contact with Joseph Walshe. Kerney also wrote to them. In one letter he informed Eilís: "I am sorry we are not yet able to give you the good news for which you have been waiting so long, but rest assured that we have Frank constantly in mind and that we shall not be satisfied until we succeed in obtaining his release."[38]

On 20 November Kerney had another meeting with Beigbeder, on the eve of a meeting between the minister and Franco, to again stress the Taoiseach's personal interest in this particular case and his anxiousness to "secure the release of Ryan."[39] Kerney wanted to assure Beigbeder that Ryan would be better cared for in Irish hands: "If there was any gaoling to be done where an Irishman was concerned, the gaoler ought really to be de Valera rather than Franco."[40] Beigbeder, however, felt that the rumors of Ryan's being an assassin were too serious to be ignored by Franco. After this meeting, Kerney suggested to Walshe that more pressure needed to be placed on the dictator. Following British and American moves, he proposed postponing any trade deals with Franco unless Ryan was handed over.[41] Walshe disagreed, seeing such a move as too high-handed.

On 16 December Kerney again met Beigbeder but was told that a general amnesty would not be granted soon because there were 75,000 prisoners already sentenced and carrying out their sentences, a further 100,000 awaiting trial, and another 65,000 awaiting interrogation. Only when all interrogations were done would Franco consider a general amnesty to include all foreign prisoners. Beigbeder said that when he opened the file on Ryan for Franco's attention at their last meeting, the dictator simply "shook his head."[42]

In one of Kerney's many reports back to Dublin he noted the name of a particular man, although he did not yet attach much importance to him. The person named was Dr. Antonio Vallejo-Nájera, and he in fact held the key to understanding Franco's paranoia regarding Ryan. Over a two-month period the doctor visited Ryan seven times and wrote a fifteen-page report on his findings. Vallejo-Nájera concluded that Ryan was a born revolutionary who possessed the "red" gene. This report was sent directly to Franco. Paul Preston, in his examination of Vallejo-Nájera's career, has noted the influence he exerted over Franco, urging him to scientifically identify the "bio-psychic roots of Marxism."[43] One of the reasons that the dictator's campaigns in the civil war had been so bloody and brutal was that he believed he was saving Spain and cleansing it of communism. In his eyes he was continuing a practice first begun by the Catholic monarchs when, at the close of the fifteenth century, they had expelled and expunged the Moors from Spain, a process known as *limpieza de sangre*, or cleansing of blood. In the same way that a genetically Christian people were healed from foreign contagion, so was Franco's own *cruzada*, or crusade, rebalancing society to its natural order. Anyone who opposed him must logically, he believed, have a genetic defect in their makeup. He found the expert scientific basis for this theory in Dr. Vallejo-Nájera's theories and work. Vallejo-Nájera became the regime's chief psychologist and headed an investigation unit made up of psychological laboratories during the war. Vallejo-Nájera's "research" proved Franco's beliefs. As genes represent the unit of heredity capable of mutation and replication, discovering a "red" gene could prevent a father who possessed it from passing his hereditary communistic tendencies to his son and thus save Spain another crusade. The simple cure for this disease was to kill the carrier of the gene. In Vallejo-Nájera's report he said that Ryan should have been killed immediately. In addition to all the other stories, rumors, letters, and denunciations against Ryan, the body of proof convinced Franco that he was indeed a dangerous man.

It would have been far easier for the Spanish dictator to have ordered Ryan's execution and be finished with the problem. However, this could have jeopardized the broader political game Franco was playing—establishing political ties with fellow Catholic states (Ireland, the Vatican, Portugal) to present a benign, respectable image of his regime; hence the speed of Ontiveros's dispatch to Dublin—less than a month after the civil war ended. Killing a captured Irish prisoner was not like other killings Franco had carried out in his life against Rif tribesmen, striking miners in Asturias, or political opponents. To be seen as a good Catholic in the international Catholic club, he forgave the sinner, showed clemency, yet made him atone for his crime with lengthy imprisonment. Perhaps he thought that simply locking the man up would put the issue to bed, but the persistence of the Irish government and Kerney showed that Ryan was a live issue, and they wanted him released or handed into their custody immediately. The only problem was that Ireland had no leverage over Franco. He was not moved to release Ryan by Catholic commonality. The weakness of Ireland's position to influence external matters was brutally exposed here.

Despite Irish efforts, Ryan was also a suspected assassin in Spanish eyes. His genetic impurity was confirmed by Vallejo-Nájera. He was a communist denounced by priests. He held a visceral hatred of fascism and was also an accomplished fighter and leader of men. These were the facts as Franco saw them. Handing him over to the Irish at once was one thing, but if they released Ryan in a few years there was always the possibility that Ryan might return to Spain and threaten Franco. Franco, like all dictators, suffered from paranoia. He lived in fortified complexes guarded by eight hundred elite Moorish bodyguards, and he traveled in armored convoys because he feared assassins. If Ryan was such a prized possession, Franco was going to make sure that a price was paid for his release. Franco held all the cards. He was going to decide in the next few months how to play them and on his terms.

End Game

Despite Ryan's improving material situation, things did not look good when it came to his release. The environs of the prison reported semistarvation. Hundreds of women waited outside the walls in the freezing cold for news of their husbands and sons, while all officers except Ryan were being systematically executed. In a prison designed to hold just a few hundred prisoners, there were 5,080 detainees by February 1940, many of them suffering from tuberculosis and wearing lice-ridden clothes, with hundreds more expected to arrive shortly.[44] Every month Kerney traveled the three hundred miles to see Ryan over appalling roads without claiming travel expenses. He was also procuring clothes, food (fatty foods to build Ryan up after his loss of body weight), vitamins, cod liver oil, and other supplies from France, as none were available in Spain. By now he was accompanied on these trips by Father Mulrean, who had been chaplain to General O'Duffy's Irish Brigade, to hear Ryan's confession. Kerney informed Walshe of the scene that confronted them in the main courtyard of the prison: "Fr. Mulrean and myself watched the prisoners in the inner yard, many less than 20 years of age, I should say, walking in groups, many miserably clad and apparently underfed."[45]

If things appeared chaotic inside the prison, they were equally chaotic elsewhere. The Franco regime was transferring the entire civil service apparatus from Burgos to Madrid, which hindered Kerney's access to various ministries for a time. The country was divided into military regions, with each general a virtual ruler of a territory and answerable only to Franco. Burgos was under General López Pinto's control, and Kerney secured several meetings with him to hear Ryan's case. The general expressed his own preference for a revision of sentences. He, like many senior generals, knew that the European war would have an impact on Spain, and he favored concentrating resources on military preparedness rather than having military men acting as security guards for prisoners. It seemed that the military men might hold the leverage needed to move Franco on the Ryan case.

Kerney's exhaustive endeavors were supported back home by Walshe, who stressed this point to the Spanish minister in Dublin. The secretary also emphasized that Kerney was acting with the full and complete authority and trust of the Irish government in his efforts: "In all his efforts on Mr Ryan's behalf Mr Kerney has acted and continues to act with the full approval and authority of the Irish government."[46]

This was the second time the department put on record that Kerney had carte blanche to act and do as he felt best in the Ryan case. The Spanish minister, however, washed his hands of the case, telling Walshe that "a further démarche by him would only tend to irritate his Government."[47] Suddenly, in March the regime announced that all foreign prisoners were going to be released. Kerney had argued to Walshe previously that economic pressure on Franco might work. The United States and Britain refused to sign new trade deals unless their citizens were released, and the tactic worked. Their citizens were released, while Ryan remained behind bars. Unable to get their last prisoner free, the Irish authorities looked weak in comparison. Walshe, however, refused to follow a similar approach, writing to Kerney: "I earnestly hope your splendid efforts on behalf of Ryan will soon succeed. The sooner he is released, the sooner we can have normal and more useful relations with the Spanish Government. I think your suggestion about bartering trade concessions for Frank Ryan's release or giving the slightest hint to the Spanish Government that you have such an idea in your mind would be thoroughly bad, and you should carefully avoid giving any such impression."[48] In his response to Walshe's rejection of this tactic, Kerney did not mince his words to the secretary: "I am afraid that we must agree to differ about that suggestion of mine which strikes you as being so thoroughly bad; I think I know the Spaniards better than you do; the Americans mentioned cotton and the Spaniards gave way; the English would not sign a trade treaty without a promise of immediate release of Englishmen; forceful arguments are necessary at times, at least in Spain."[49] This lost opportunity was hammered home to the Taoiseach, too, who was under considerable pressure to intercede personally in the case, as this example highlights:

> It is against all recognized rules of warfare to hold a prisoner of war for such a long period after the war in which he fought has ended, and to deprive him of the right of returning to his own country. The qualities of this staunch, courageous fighter for liberty, who proved his mettle in the struggle against fascism in Spain, must no longer be allowed to waste in prison. We call upon the British and Irish Governments, and

all public bodies and organizations, to make immediate efforts to secure his release.

As one who played such a prominent part in the Easter Rising of 1916 and the years immediately following, and as one who was an officer of that gallant body of men, the Irish Volunteers, you will understand, we feel sure, that it is to you more than any other public figure that we look to make the effort that will set Ryan free, in vindication of the ideals which he, as you yourself fought for.[50]

The release of the American and British prisoners again fueled the media coverage of Ryan, as ex-prisoners Tom Jones and Anthony Kerhlicker gave several interviews to the press and attended rallies on behalf of the release committees. Jones traveled to Dublin to see Joseph Walshe and some of Ryan's communist friends. In a letter to Seán Nunan he informed the Irish Communist Party about the scale of opposition to Ryan's release:

A British diplomat [Hodgson] tried to get Franco to shoot Ryan on two occasions (Personal vengeance). . . . Mr Kearney [*sic*] seems to be doing everything from an official viewpoint and also from personal friendship, to get Ryan released. I know that he has told Ryan that he will resign as soon as he gets Frank released. . . . Frank himself does not hold much hope for getting out soon, even thought [*sic*] Mr Kearney [*sic*] told him he expected his release within a few months. . . . Frank thinks that the jesuites [*sic*] in Ireland and Spain are working against him.[51]

Meanwhile, Kerney was meeting General de las Fuentes, secretary to War Minister General Varela. After more than a year, Kerney was now getting access to key men who held the real levers of power, and he came away with the positive impression that "Ryan's release seems certain within the next 2 or 3 weeks."[52] Varela held more sway over Franco as war minister than Beigbeder ever could. Kerney wired Walshe three days later, hinting that the end might be in sight: "Renewed hope exists as reported May 7th but pending possible developments discretion very desirable."[53] Ryan was moved to a comfortable five-man dorm, which again gave the impression that he was about to be freed. However, Franco was still the principal obstacle, as Kerney informed Dublin: "I have made the big discovery that Franco himself gave special instructions some considerable time ago that, in this particular case of Frank Ryan, nothing should ever be done in the way of reducing his sentence without his personal consent. . . . You can measure the difficulties we have had to overcome by knowledge of the fact that the obstacle to be overcome is Franco himself."[54]

The bizarre attitude of Franco baffled everyone, including the leader of the Labour Party, William Norton, who stood up inside the Dáil chamber to ask the Taoiseach the obvious question—Why was Ryan still in prison when "all other foreign nationals were released from imprisonment in Spain"?[55] Exactly a month later, Kerney notified Walshe that the "obstacle" (i.e., Franco) had finally been overcome and a pardon was imminent. He was wrong. Franco still held all the cards. He held Ryan's fate in his hands, and he was not going to let his last foreign prisoner, who had such obvious value, go without receiving something in return. The dictator chose in the end not to pardon Ryan but to hand him over not to the Irish, but to German military intelligence, the Abwehr, as a favor to Germany and to pay down his civil war debt to the Nazis. This was the worst possible outcome for Ryan, Kerney, and the Irish government. All their time, effort, struggle, and expenses counted for nothing. It felt to Kerney worse than a defeat, more of an injustice. Franco's ties to Hitler's spymasters had moved the Ryan case to a completely different level.

FRANCO AND THE ABWEHR

German intelligence operations in Spain originated during the First World War. Under the direction of Captain Kurt von Krohn, the Kaiser's Germany established a secret intelligence organization inside Spain—code-named "Etappe"—to fight a secret war against the Allies. At stake was control of the Mediterranean Sea and the critical supply routes carrying munitions, minerals, fuel, food provisions, and troops between the Straits of Gibraltar and the Suez Canal. The Germans wanted to acquire as much intelligence about Allied shipping in this area as possible in order to supply their submarine fleet with the information needed to locate and sink enemy cargo and warships. Among Krohn's staff was one Captain Wilhelm Canaris, who helped supervise a network of spies and maintained a successful surveillance of Allied naval flotillas. Canaris's network of informers relayed all Allied shipping routes to him. This information was then passed on to Berlin and from there forwarded to U-boat commanders in the area. In 1935 Canaris himself became chief of the Abwehr, and he wanted to revive, remodel, and intensify this overseas espionage network and to succeed where it had previously failed. The outbreak of the Spanish Civil War and the close association between General Franco and Hitler offered Canaris the opportunity to rebuild Etappe.

Rebuilding a network in Spain was not easy because of the rivalry that existed between the various intelligence agencies of the Nazi state. A cluster of three competing organizations quarrelled to undermine and hinder each other.[56] Reichsführer SS Heinrich Himmler's Geheime Staats Polizei, or Gestapo, acted as the Nazi state police but expanded its operations abroad as Germany annexed new territories and conquered European state after state; the Sicherheitsdienst, or SD, was the Nazi Party intelligence organization under Reinhard Heydrich that likewise operated outside Germany's prewar borders; and then there was the Abwehr, or military intelligence, charged with defending Germany and counteracting all enemy intelligence services. Canaris's Abwehr was under the remit of the Supreme Command of the German Armed Forces (Oberkommando der Wehrmacht, or OKW). The Abwehr served all branches of the Wehrmacht without being incorporated into any of them. This accorded the service protection from its rival SS services as long as the German Army could protect it. As German fortunes turned on the battlefield from 1942 onward, a suspicious Hitler eyed his own general staff with growing mistrust. The gradual purging of the OKW left the Abwehr without its safety net, and the SS moved in to tear the organization apart in 1944.

This was all in the future. For the moment, Canaris divided the Abwehr into several departments, or sections, known as Abteilung. The most important departments as the war progressed were Abteilung II (concerned with sabotage and infiltration) and Abteilung III (counter-espionage and security).[57] Canaris's fluency in Spanish, his time spent there during the First World War, and his naval background helped foster a good relationship between him and Franco, who owed the Germans, and the Wehrmacht in particular, 400 million Reichsmarks for the critical military and economic support supplied to his nationalist forces during the Spanish Civil War.[58] This leverage gave Canaris a major advantage over his domestic intelligence rivals. He personally traveled to Spain on several occasions to confer with Franco. The dictator approved closer intelligence cooperation between his services and the Abwehr, but in typical Franco style, on 25 November 1937 he also sanctioned closer cooperation between his police and Himmler's Gestapo.[59] The Abwehr mapped areas of the country, particularly around ports, secluded coastal enclaves, Gibraltar, and other strategic locations where radio transmitters, infra-red monitoring stations, agent cells, sabotage operations, submarine refueling depots, and so on could all be created and used for future operational deployment.[60] With the help of the German business community inside Spain, the Abwehr gradually built up an entire clandestine network inside the country and renamed it Kriegsorganisationen (KO) Spanien (War Organization Spain).

When war came again in September 1939, the Abwehr was well placed to launch aggressive intelligence operations against its enemies with the full backing and assistance of the Francoist regime. Lauran Paine has highlighted how, under station chief or leader (*Leiter*) Wilhelm Leissner, six hundred informers and more than seven hundred full-time spies and case officers stationed throughout Spain and its North African territories used the security of Spanish "neutrality" to spy on and attack the Allies on land and sea and in the air.[61] What transpired over the next few years was a full-scale intelligence war fought between the belligerents, with MI6[62] proving more than a match for the Abwehr, as some examples will show.

KO Spanien was divided administratively and geographically. Its center was not Abwehr headquarters in Berlin but rather the German embassy, to which every region throughout Spain reported. In Barcelona, for example, Friedrich Knappe—alias "Federico"—worked at a junior level and was responsible for recruiting foreign nationals. When war came, he recruited agents to infiltrate the United Kingdom, where they would be less likely to be surveyed or detained by the British authorities than would German citizens. These agent-recruits were tasked with sending back intelligence reports or committing sabotage operations. Most were successfully recruited, yet MI6 turned them into double agents, and they became part of the British double-cross system.[63] MI6 used the double-cross system, signal intelligence, and Ultra intercepts (deciphered intercepts of German Enigma machine code ciphers) to identify and target the Abwehr recruiters inside Spain, like Knappe. MI6 positively identified Knappe as a recruiter agent, and a request was made to the Spanish Ministry of Foreign Affairs, via the British embassy, to expel Knappe: "The British Security authorities are insistent that these hostile activities directed from Madrid against Great Britain should cease."[64]

At the highest level, the Abwehr liaised directly with the Spanish intelligence service (Dirección General de Seguridad). This cooperation was most active during Serrano Súñer's time as minister for the interior. Karl Eric Kuehlenthal, alias "Felipe," was secretary to the Abwehr *Leiter*, who was reported by MI6 to have "excellent connections" with Spanish intelligence and the chief of police, José Finat, who provided passports and visas for Abwehr agents.[65] Kuehlenthal was formally identified by MI6 as having "maintained personal contacts with representatives of the SIS [Spanish Intelligence Service]."[66] This direct cooperation between the German and Spanish intelligence agencies extended into the diplomatic service, where the Spanish press attaché in London, Alcázar de Velasco, headed a German spy ring run from inside the Spanish embassy. Throughout the war, critical intelligence information—including where Luftwaffe bombs were falling on London during the Blitz, the morale of the London people, and results of bombing raids over Newcastle, for example—were all dispatched to Madrid. These files were read by Franco and then handed over to the Germans with the dictator's approval, with the knowledge of British intelligence at the time.[67] Spain was the largest theater of Abwehr operations inside a neutral state. Understandably these operations were most prominent and active during the first half of the conflict, when it appeared to most outside and neutral observers that Germany was going to win the war.

WHO KNEW WHAT AND WHEN

The first link in the chain connecting KO Spanien to Kerney came via Jaime Michels de Champourcin, a lawyer attached to the Madrid legation. Champourcin had previously worked for Spanish intelligence during the civil war, and he had contacts with the Abwehr in Madrid.[68] In the most detailed report on Ryan that Kerney wrote to Walshe, dated 26 August, he described the events leading up to Ryan's "escape." Critically, he also informed the secretary that it was Champourcin, not himself, who had made the suggestion of approaching the Germans:

> Mr B [Champourcin] was in the Spanish secret service during the civil war and formed close contacts then with the German intelligence service; he is on friendly terms with certain Germans in Madrid; being aware of my concern for Ryan and having helped me in my efforts, he suggested some time ago that the Gestapo might serve to secure Ryan's liberation. About the middle of May (see my report 23rd May), I decided to fall in with this suggestion; I was beginning to doubt the likelihood of my direct petition to the War Office meeting with success; all our other appeals had met with a deaf ear; for some unaccountable reason, Franco himself was the stumbling block, and it appeared likely that Ryan's imprisonment would last as long as his own life or that of the regime itself.[69]

Champourcin's contacts in both German and Spanish intelligence were extensive, and he was able to secure two meetings with the chief of police, José Finat, who had direct access to Serrano Súñer and Franco. From this senior level the Spanish then liaised with the Abwehr, all the time keeping the name of the Irish minister out of the equation. On the two dates that Champourcin met with Finat, 5 July and 12 July, he was told that Ryan was not going to be pardoned, but

Franco "had given orders for Ryan's 'escape' to be officially organized as a solution; he would be put into France and the Director [Antonio Crejo] of the prison would be ordered to report that he had escaped."[70] Perhaps Franco and his henchmen felt they were doing the Irish a favor in disposing of a problem by handing Ryan over into German-occupied France.

Although Kerney had instructed Champourcin to keep his name out of the affair, approaching the Germans via a third party was risky. If the British got wind of this and traced it back to the Irish legation, it could cause political ramifications for the Irish government vis-à-vis neutrality. It is this point that has perturbed several historians, including Mark Hull, who has commented that "Kerney had worked with the Abwehr in freeing Frank Ryan."[71] This is not, strictly speaking, accurate, as Kerney had given Champourcin clear instructions to keep his name out of the approaches. Any perceived underhand contact with or possible assistance to a belligerent in wartime was always going to be viewed with suspicion, but this potential problem never in fact materialized, as British intelligence files reveal that the British were completely in the dark about Ryan and his whereabouts after his "escape" for a long time. Only an intercepted telegram dated 26 September 1940 from the International Brigade Association (IBA) in London gave them the first inkling that he was out of jail.[72] In March 1941, Colonel Valentine Vivian, deputy chief of MI6 and head of section v (counterespionage), contacted Captain Cecil Liddell, head of MI5's Irish section, to report that he had received no further news on Ryan's whereabouts.[73] Even by October 1941, neither MI5 nor MI6 had any clue as to where Ryan was, and their main source of intelligence was intercepts of communications to the IBA, the Communist Party of Great Britain (CPGB), or Irish sources, not their own agents in the field. Such reports as were coming from their own sources were wide of the mark for some time. For example, their report of October 1941 read: "Reported to be employed by a tourist agency in Lisbon."[74]

The other sticking point of an indirect approach to the Germans was that even if they were willing to take Ryan off Franco's hands, there was no guarantee that they would hand him over to the Irish or send him to republican friends in the still-neutral United States. It would have been naïve to think so. It simply did not serve Germany's interests to help get Ryan out for nothing in return, and it was not in Ireland's interest to owe Germany a favor if they did. Perhaps Kerney had not considered the full implications in this regard. As for Ryan, if the Germans decided to hold onto him and he refused to offer any assistance to Germany given his anti-fascism, there were some bad places he could end up in the Third Reich, places with conditions worse than those in Burgos prison. It is difficult to see if Kerney had given sufficient thought to this eventuality.

It is clear that Kerney felt that an indirect approach to German intelligence via Champourcin was necessary in order to do something for Ryan's welfare lest his health deteriorate further, and he felt that as minister he had the authority to initiate such an approach. Eunan O'Halpin disagreed and argued that the Irish diplomat breached normal diplomatic protocol in making contact with a belligerent's secret service, albeit indirectly through a third party and without official sanction to do so. For O'Halpin, this action confirmed that Kerney was a rogue diplomat whose performance contrasted sharply with that of his colleagues in Rome, Berlin, and the Vatican, all of whom, he argued, had displayed "common sense and professionalism" in the course of their duties.[75]

However, one can argue that O'Halpin missed key points in his judgment of Kerney. The diplomat had twice received clear confirmation that he acted with the full authority and with the complete backing of the Irish government to do everything he could to secure Ryan's release as the de facto representative of the Irish government in Spain. Walshe and the Taoiseach had repeatedly stated to the Spanish that Kerney was at all times acting with their total approval and that he had carte blanche to bring about Ryan's release. The conditions in Spain in which Kerney operated were tricky and constantly in flux. Kerney had no secure way of contacting Dublin. He could not simply pick up a phone and ring either Walshe or the Taoiseach to okay in advance an indirect move toward the Germans. All lines from Spain to Ireland were routed through Britain—in fact, Britain had been breaking Irish diplomatic cables since 1932 and continued to do so throughout the war, a point O'Halpin knew but failed to note in his judgment on Kerney.[76] The diplomat did not enjoy the benefit that other diplomatic colleagues, like the Portuguese ambassador, had, who could drive to Lisbon and see his political boss Salazar face-to-face in a matter of hours for a decision. Flights between Ireland and Spain were expensive and interrupted by the war. Kerney obviously acted with the best intentions for Ryan, but once he made this move he left the dealings and outcome entirely in other peoples' hands—people and organizations with their own vested interests.

Despite his left-wing leanings, Ryan was viewed as a prized asset by the Germans both in Spain and in Germany. KO Spanien saw the potential for Ryan to act as a sabotage agent to infiltrate and carry out operations against Britain in Northern Ireland. One important agent, Friedrich Wolfgang Blaum, of Abteilung II (sabotage and infiltration), was active inside Spain, carrying out extensive missions against British targets using captured British munitions and explosives. One operation involved the German freighter *Lipari*, anchored off Cartagena Bay. Blaum and his team converted the hull of the ship into a sabotage diving center to attach limpet mines on British ships. In another operation, they successfully used orange crates on the barge *Ravenspoint* to blow up the ship inside Gibraltar Port. Blaum was also busy attacking Allied underwater communications cables. When word was passed down the line from Champourcin that a former IRA fighter was being considered for release by Franco if German intelligence wanted him, Blaum took up the case immediately: "In May 1940 Blaum was instructed to contact Frank Ryan.... With the aid of Jaime Michels de Champourcin, Ryan's lawyer, Blaum was able to see Ryan at the prison."[77] Kerney reported to Walshe that a German, most likely Blaum, met Franco on 1 July and again on 3 July: "Franco was again seen and this time said definitely 'yes'; he was giving instructions to Finat, Chief of Police."[78] The fact that a German agent could see a head of state at any time while the diplomatic representative of a friendly neutral state could not highlighted the true nature of fascist Spain and the impotence of Ireland's influence as a Catholic nation on another Catholic state.

Inside Germany there were old acquaintances of Ryan who were also working behind the scenes to convince the Spanish to release him for Germany's benefit. These men were former Abwehr agents in Ireland, the most important of whom was Helmut Clissmann.[79] During Ryan's first meeting with Kerney, on 16 June 1939, Ryan said that he remembered meeting the diplomat previously in the Mulcahy household in Oakfield Sligo. Ryan was engaged to one of Elizabeth Budge Mulcahy's sisters at the time. Kerney knew Budge for several years and frequently visited the family home. He first met Budge in Paris when she was studying at the Sorbonne, and she frequently called at the Paris legation. She moved into the Kerney household in 1934 and taught the family Irish. As Kerney wrote: "Budge Mulcahy has become a great friend of ours and she has just come to live with us; she will, I hope, be as happy 'au pair' with us as anywhere else, and we are delighted to have her company. Raymonde, Micheline and myself are really the only students in her Irish 'class'. Budge is a tip-top teacher, and if we don't make progress the fault will not be hers."[80] She later married Helmut Clissmann on 29 December 1938. He worked in Ireland at TCD as part of a German student exchange program (Deutsche Akademische Austauschdienst). Kerney first met Helmut Clissmann at the Mulcahy home in 1937, but his friendship was with Budge. He had had no previous association with Helmut, and he did not know of Helmut's work in the Abwehr.

Irish army intelligence (G2), Garda crime and security branch (C3), and the Royal Ulster Constabulary (RUC) were all well aware of Helmut Clissmann's activities in Ireland before the war as an Abwehr agent. So, too, was British intelligence. MI5 "detected in 1937 and 1938" German efforts to use Ireland as a "base for operations," and several reports concerning three Germans (Franz Fromme, Helmut Clissmann, and Jupp Hoven) "alleging German contacts with the IRA were received in the early months of 1939."[81] During the 1930s the Germans were keen to establish links with militant Irish republicans, a practice begun in 1914, in case of a possible war against Britain, and so Clissmann and others were dispatched to liaise with the IRA in 1933.[82] Clissmann used the cover of his academic work to attend republican seminars, clubs, and commemorative events like the annual Wolfe Tone parade to Bodenstown Graveyard. Here he met leading republicans of a militant nature (Tom Barry) and of an ideological nature (Frank Ryan).[83] Most aliens, foreigners, or anyone with suspected extreme leftist or rightist views were under surveillance in the Irish Free State by G2 and C3 to gather data on their whereabouts and with whom they met.[84] Clissmann was put under watch by Chief Superintendant Patrick Carroll of C3.[85] G2 head Colonel Liam Archer notified the British War Office in September 1938 that Clissmann was under surveillance by them because they suspected that he was a German agent in league with militant Irish republicans in the IRA.[86] The Foreign Office also had "voluminous records" on him that were passed on to MI5.[87] Helmut had joined the Nazi Party in 1934, and a Special Branch report from September 1939 described Budge as "violently anti-British" and "ardently pro-Hitler."[88]

The Clissmanns moved to Germany before the war broke out. Budge resided mainly in Copenhagen, while her husband moved about as the war developed. He was assigned to Abteilung II of the Abwehr, run by Colonel, later Major, General Erwin von Lahousen, which concerned itself with sabotage, special operations, and infiltration. One of his main tasks was to recruit V-men—*Vertrauensmann*, or informant—who would build up an espionage network in Ireland to liaise with the IRA in the event of war with Britain. During the war Clissmann was also posted to an elite commando-style unit run by the Abwehr called the Brandenburgers.[89] The unit was composed of fanatically loyal Nazis of German extraction and *Volksdeutschen* (foreign nationals of German descent who spoke German) who fought alongside the German Army, infiltrating frontline enemy positions using enemy uniforms. Clissmann and his colleagues, like Jupp Hoven and Kurt Haller, were still "key men" in regard to Irish matters, and Ryan's lengthy imprisonment was not forgotten by them.[90] They pressed Berlin to get Ryan out. When France fell and Hitler turned his military-industrial machine against Britain in the summer of 1940, Abwehr chief Wilhelm Canaris finally saw the possible use Germany might make of Ryan. Canaris "intervened personally" and arranged with Franco to transfer Ryan to the Abwehr.[91]

On 12 July Kerney paid his last visit to Ryan to have a frank and friendly discussion about his impending "escape." They discussed politics, but differed considerably. Ryan opined that the war presented Ireland with possibilities, while Kerney upheld neutrality. As Kerney wrote: "He [Ryan] said that, if he got to Ireland, he would go to thank Mr de Valera for all that had been done on his behalf, but that, having done so, he would retain his right to oppose the policy of the Government; I told him that nobody would object to that attitude, but that it might be my duty to suggest that his movements in Ireland should be watched so that any opposition of a violent nature could be countered."[92] Before departing, Kerney joked that he was glad to be rid of Ryan: "I had many selfish reasons for being glad to get rid of him, as he had taken up a great deal of my time, given me a lot of worry and caused me no little expense, whilst the almost impassable road from Burgos to the prison had certainly shortened the life of my car."[93]

On 25 July Ryan was escorted out of the prison and placed in a car with Spanish and German intelligence officials bound for the Spanish-French border. Kerney paid Champourcin 1,500 pesetas for the expense of driving ahead of the convoy and making sure that Ryan did in fact leave Spanish territory unmolested and was not shot in the back by the Spanish while "escaping." Kerney wrote a summary of the whole case to Walshe. It is worth quoting at length:

> It also has to be noted that Franco rejected all Irish appeals in favour of Ryan, even when precedents had been created by the release of others; if he had granted a pardon, Ryan would have remained under Irish control and supervision; he authorised and ordered a very unusual procedure; as a concession to Germany and not as a concession to Ireland; he authorised the placing of this alleged dangerous communist at Germany's disposal—a gesture which could conceivably have unpleasant consequences for the Irish Government, and therefore anything but a friendly gesture towards Ireland.
>
> It is natural enough that relations between the German and Spanish intelligence services should be very close; there are apparently certain services which the head of the State is ready to render to Germans even if this means exposing himself to reproaches by other friends.

> If Frank Ryan is alive and at liberty today, we have no reason to
> thank the Spanish Government, and the result has been secured in spite
> of opposition from the highest quarter.[94]

It may have seemed natural for Ryan to feel some animosity toward
Kerney once he was in German custody, but he did not. The minister received a cryptic letter from Ryan that gave the impression that
"American friends" were behind the whole move to get him out, a
feint designed to make other intelligence services think that Ryan was
in the United States.[95] He thanked Kerney for his tireless efforts: "My
thanks again to you—and to all the other good friends—for all the
help you have given me. Someday—soon, let's hope—we'll meet to
celebrate, in the old Irish way!"[96] Several months later, a letter from
Budge in Copenhagen arrived for Kerney in which a passage read: "I
have seen someone who has many many reasons to be thankful to you
and who asked to be remembered by you."[97]

This was the first inkling Kerney had that Budge had a crucial role
in Ryan's "escape" and that Ryan was somewhere inside Hitler's Reich.
Kerney made no mention of Helmut because he did not know the role
the German had played in the case or that he was an Abwehr agent,
and all the evidence that the diplomat had at hand at this point indicated only Budge's role in helping to get Ryan out of prison in Spain.
The diplomat forwarded Budge's declaration to Walshe via a telegram:
"This can only refer to Ryan."[98] A few months later, in March 1941,
G2 director Colonel Liam Archer wrote to Walshe expressing his unease about Kerney's contact with Budge given her "previous associations with the IRA."[99] Kerney was unaware of Budge's alleged ties to
the IRA and of G2's alarm about his association with her. Walshe did
not inform Kerney about G2's concerns in March 1941, as the secretary was using Kerney's breaches of the diplomatic bag to undermine
his reputation within the department and with the Taoiseach. This
pattern of concealment was practiced by Walshe earlier in 1940, too.

Just a week after Budge's letter confirmed Ryan's presence in
Hitler's Reich, Walshe corresponded with Colonel Liam Archer in
December 1940 in relation to Kerney's notification to Dublin about
this revelation from Budge. Archer replied to Walshe that actually

it was Helmut Clissmann who was perhaps the real orchestrator of the "escape," not Budge, as her husband had a long association with Ryan and leading IRA figures: "I am in a position to say that Clissman [*sic*] met Frank Ryan in Dublin in 1936 and was seen occasionally in his company. Furthermore, Clissman's [*sic*] wife was known to have political leanings similar to those of Frank Ryan, consequently it is not at all unlikely that the Clissmans [*sic*] would help Ryan through their German friends."[100] The prewar intelligence files that Archer had on Helmut Clissmann showed that G2 was suspicious that he was an agent who had had links with the IRA during his time in Ireland and that that was why they had kept the German under surveillance. Based on this existing intelligence, Archer made the obvious point that Helmut Clissmann was the main instigator of Ryan's release and that he was a person of interest to them.

G2 and Joseph Walshe had enjoyed a close relationship with British intelligence for many years. Even before the outbreak of war in September 1939, the Irish authorities had met senior officials in MI5 to organize bilateral liaison and coordination in relation to any IRA-German activities that could be prejudicial to the security and safety of either Ireland or Britain or of both countries. On 31 August 1939, MI5, G2, and External Affairs agreed to a full "exchange of information" in this regard.[101] Once Helmut Clissmann's name surfaced in relation to Frank Ryan's release, both G2 and External Affairs should have fully briefed their British counterparts about this discovery. Not doing so not only went against the counterintelligence agreement put in place between the countries but also placed Kerney, unbeknownst to him, under the suspicious radar of British intelligence.

In the same month that Archer communicated with Walshe, Budge traveled to Madrid, ostensibly to deliver a letter from Ryan, but in truth it was arranged between herself and German military intelligence. Kerney met her at the Palace Hotel on 15 December to inquire about Ryan.[102] She had in her possession another letter from Ryan for Kerney. In it Ryan wrote: "If you have any qualms of conscience about possible bad results of your intervention on my behalf—then, Don't! . . . Let that be on record, as coming from me! . . . I sincerely hope that you will regard me as a worry no longer, and that you will have that so well deserved holiday. My best wishes to you, to your wife and family for Christmas."[103] For the first time, Helmut's name now came into the picture for Kerney. Ryan let Kerney know in his letter that Helmut had also helped in getting him out of prison: "Mr Mulcahy (Jr.) [Helmut Clissmann] and other old friends were the originators of the present trip."[104] Kerney now knew that Helmut had a role in Ryan's "escape," but he still did not know that Helmut was in the Abwehr, nor did he know that the German had been a source of interest to various intelligence agencies, including G2, even before World War II.

Throughout the Ryan case, Kerney furnished Dublin with detailed reports as events unfolded. Sometimes there were small delays in his reports due to wartime conditions or other factors that he had to bear in mind. For example, in one report he wrote: "My only justification for not giving you [Walshe] a full and detailed report immediately and for notifying the main facts in veiled language was the desire not to compromise or expose to possibly serious danger a friend."[105] He had promptly passed on his correspondence with Budge Clissmann also. Critically, though, he failed to pass on all his correspondence with Ryan after the latter's release, specifically letters handled by the Clissmanns. Some letters had been sent to Walshe, who then passed them on to Colonel Dan Bryan, the G2 director who succeeded Colonel Liam Archer.[106] However, others had not been passed on to Dublin, and this was a mistake on Kerney's part, as it fueled suspicion in the mind of Colonel Dan Bryan that Kerney was acting underhandedly. It also provided Walshe with further material with which to blacken the diplomat's name in the department in 1943. In reply to the request by Assistant Secretary Frederick Boland to have some of the letter correspondence with Ryan forwarded to Dublin, Kerney outlined why he had not furnished this material earlier: "My dear Boland, Many thanks for your kind letter of 30th December. I enclose copies of 2 letters, one dated 11th December, 1940, and initialled, the other dated 6th November, 1941, and signed. Hitherto I have treated them as private communications having no particular importance and to which it might be more prudent not to refer in official despatches."[107]

The responses of de Valera and Walshe to the whole Ryan case, Kerney's handling of the matter, and the revelation of German intelligence involvement was interesting. They did not give an opinion on Franco's role in the whole affair. The department did not even send a basic diplomatic note of protest to the Spanish legation, nor was any statement made on the floor of the Dáil to publicly express outrage at Franco's conduct. The Taoiseach's main concern appears to have been for the Ryan family. Both of Frank's parents were ill at the time, and when Kerney was notified that Ryan was well, de Valera instructed that this news be passed on to the family immediately. It appears that the Taoiseach felt that Kerney had done all he possibly could have for Ryan, given the scant resources available to the diplomat. If the Irish political leader had been dissatisfied with Kerney, the diplomat would have been recalled immediately to explain his handling of the case in person, or he could have been reassigned or even dismissed from the service. None of these actions were initiated by the Taoiseach, which shows that de Valera, the man whose judgment and opinion ultimately mattered the most at the departmental and government levels, still clearly trusted his man in Madrid.

Walshe was a different matter, and his response to Kerney's handling of the Ryan case is interesting. The secretary had in the past enjoyed flagging to his superiors any minor discrepancy or perceived error in Kerney's performance. The detailed content of the reports on the Ryan case that Kerney had sent to Walshe over a year and a half had perhaps been written in such a way as to cover himself should the secretary try to use anything against him. The secretary appeared to have had some misgivings about Kerney's actions and his handling of the case or felt he had not been entirely candid, because he contacted Colonel Dan Bryan, the head of G2, to examine the whole case and the documentation passed on from Kerney. The following October, when Kerney was home for an extended holiday and his daughter, Micheline, was getting married, the secretary told him, without prior notice, to prepare for a grilling by Bryan. This revelation stunned Kerney, who felt he was simply not trusted by Walshe.

The meeting began with Kerney putting on record that he had no documents with him,[108] but that he had sent the department "chapter and verse" on the Ryan case and that this interview was therefore being done entirely from memory.[109] Kerney outlined the entire case to Bryan, who compiled a memorandum. Kerney's account tallies with the reports he sent to Walshe, particularly the important one dated 26 August. He adds some more detail on certain points, such as the denunciations of Ryan by General Eoin O'Duffy and Thomas Gunning and states that he had "no means of getting a decision" from the department securely before authorizing Champourcin to approach the Germans, all of which also tallies with his reports and actions at the time the events occurred.[110] Certain passages of the memorandum are marked in black ink, most likely by Walshe, but the final sections are notes Bryan wrote on a chat the men had once the interview ended. He asked Kerney if he knew anything on the whereabouts of Seán Russell, the chief of staff of the IRA, who had left the United States for Europe. Kerney said he did not, but he did say that a lady named Annie Farrelly had had a conversation with him at the Gresham Hotel recently, asking if he had any news of Russell.

Bryan suspected that the minister was not being entirely truthful: "The Minister did not state whether he met Miss Farrelly by appointment or otherwise, but it was thought that the meeting was previously arranged."[111] It appears that Walshe and Bryan suspected that, given Kerney's past anti-treaty allegiance, he was in contact with dissident republicans. That this lady showed up at the Gresham should not have come as a surprise, as Kerney always advertised in the newspapers what hotel he was staying in when on holidays in Ireland, and he always found time to meet anyone, however brief the conversation that ensued. In that month alone, his diary records pages of names of ordinary people and public figures whom he met briefly or over a meal. Kerney's lack of frankness with Bryan was perhaps understandable—meeting Ireland's intelligence chief in the Department of Defense without prior notice to discuss official matters he had already reported on to Walshe reflected a clear lack of trust or even suspicion toward him from inside External Affairs. Bryan's pro-treaty stance would also not have endeared Kerney to him, and Kerney answered only the specific questions Bryan put to him, without elaborating further. Kerney was aware that Bryan had played an active role in the

Irish Civil War against republicans, and he mistrusted former anti-treatyites all his life.

The interesting point of the Kerney-Bryan interview was the Clissmann link to Ryan's "escape." Kerney had told Walshe via telegram that Budge had had a role in getting Ryan out of prison. At this meeting he revealed to Bryan that the "Clissmanns" had had a role in getting Ryan out, after Ryan himself had informed Kerney of this fact in his letter of 11 December 1940.[112] G2 already knew by this date that Helmut Clissmann had had an obvious role in Ryan's "escape," after Colonel Liam Archer had indicated this to Walshe in December 1940. In March 1941 G2 had also passed on to Walshe their concerns about Kerney's correspondence with Budge, given her past association with the IRA. Moreover, G2 had prewar files on Helmut Clissmann and his known associations with the IRA, as well as leading republican dissidents in Ireland, so they should have warned Kerney to break off any further contact from that side, as the diplomat was completely in the dark regarding this intelligence information on Helmut and Budge. Not only should Kerney have been informed of this fact, but so should de Valera, as Taoiseach and minister for external affairs, have been made completely aware of this link between Ryan and the Clissmanns. MI5 should also have been informed, given the exchange-of-information agreement signed in August 1939. A month later, Kerney wired Dublin with news of the death of Seán Russell and stated that his source for this information was Budge's husband, whom he had just met in Madrid.[113] Again no effort was made to warn him to break off all contact.

Perhaps this important information was not disclosed to Kerney because G2 wanted to trap him and see what he knew or what he might disclose inadvertently. Bryan's interrogation of Kerney did not go far enough to dissuade Walshe of his concerns that the diplomat was somehow connected to militant republicans and might be collaborating with them and a belligerent intelligence service to the detriment of the state. Obviously the doubts in Walshe's mind about Kerney remained, because in 1943 he would agree to covert investigations of the diplomat by G2 to blacken Kerney's name. Bryan would be the lead investigator again, believing until the very end that Kerney ought to be treated with a high degree of suspicion. As he wrote: "Certain remarks Mr Kerney had made indicated that he knew much more about German activities in Ireland than I or you [Walshe] had been previously aware of."[114] The failure by Walshe and Bryan, whether for personal, security, or possibly political reasons, to inform Kerney that Helmut Clissmann was a German agent in October and November of 1941—when both men had the chance to do so—would see the Irish diplomat walk into an intelligence scheme formulated by senior Nazis to alter Ireland's neutral policy during the Second World War.

Leopold Kerney as a young boy.

Kerney posing with his cricket teammates in Sandymount, 1896. He is seated first on the left, middle row.

Philip Kerney, "The Governor."

Kerney and his wife, Raymonde,
on their wedding day,
14 August 1914.

Baby Jean
with his proud parents,
Paris, 1918.

Kerney hosting the Saint Patrick's Day banquet in Paris. To his left is Lord Ashbourne. Note the portrait of Éamon de Valera hanging prominently in the dining hall.

On board the SS *Banba*, 22 September 1922.

The Kerney family enjoying a day out by the sea. Raymonde is holding baby Eamon, godson of Éamon de Valera.

Glendalough, 1929. From left to right: Frank Gallagher, Robert Briscoe, and Robert Brennan on a family day out with the Kerneys.

Kerney horseplaying with Frank Gallagher in Glendalough.

Still playing cricket! Kerney with writer Dorothy Macardle, Portmarnock, 1929.

With Robert Brennan climbing into Saint Kevin's Bed, Glendalough.

Kerney greeting Seán T. O'Kelly at Le Bourget airport, circa 1934.

Kerney with
Frank Aiken,
center,
minister for defense,
circa 1935.

Orense, Spain, 4 August 1936. The military escort of Guardia Civil troops that accompanied the legation car to the Franco-Spanish border after the outbreak of the Spanish Civil War.

Kerney with the Duchess of Tetuán, Blanca O'Donnell, center, alongside the legation typist, Maisie Donnelly, on the outskirts of Madrid. Note the destruction to the buildings in the background.

The Irish legation in Madrid. Kerney is in conversation with Irish Hispanist Walter Starkie, director of the British Institute.

Kerney presenting his credentials to General Franco, 10 April 1939. Note that the diplomat did not give an upright fascist salute.

Dreams of imperial glory—Franco's victory parade, 19 May 1939.

The Taoiseach and minister for external affairs, Éamon de Valera, alongside Kerney on the occasion of Micheline's wedding at University Church, Saint Stephen's Green, 30 September 1941.

Saint Patrick's Day celebrations at the Irish legation during the war. The legation's lawyer, Jaime Michels de Champourcin, is in the center in profile.

Kerney shaking hands with General Franco, circa 1946.

Kerney wearing the decoration of the grand cross of Isabel la Católica for the inauguration of Seán T. O'Kelly as president of Ireland, 25 June 1952.

Kerney holding a cigar alongside Seán MacBride, center, 11 August 1955.

With the "Chief" at the wedding of Eamon and Maud Kerney, 11 August 1955.

CHAPTER 8

INSIDE THE VIPER'S NEST

Kerney and German Military Intelligence during World War II

After Frank Ryan's release, Kerney resumed his normal diplomatic duties in Madrid and performed them until the following year, when he took two months' leave in Ireland. The Kerneys traveled from Lisbon to Foynes on 15 August 1941 and resided in the Gresham Hotel, Dublin. It was far from a relaxing time for Kerney, as his schedule was very busy with appointments every day to see colleagues, friends, or members of the public. Beginning on 18 August he had several meetings in External Affairs with Joseph Walshe, Frederick Boland, and former diplomat Art Ó Briain. He met Frank Ryan's sister, Eilís, on 15 October to discuss her brother's case[1] and had discussions nearly every day with leading government ministers (Seán Lemass, P. J. Little, and Jim Ryan) and departmental secretaries (John Leydon), as well as politicians (Robert Briscoe), republican figures (Seán MacBride), prominent officials (Frank Gallagher), and members of the public (José Camiña).[2] Kerney had official (15 October) and unofficial (21 October) appointments to see the Taoiseach at Government Buildings and at his home in Blackrock.[3]

For Leopold and Raymonde, the trip back to Ireland was also an occasion of great happiness, because their only daughter, Micheline, was married on 30 September at University Church, Saint Stephen's Green. The guest list was a "Who's Who" of high society. De Valera attended alongside nearly every government minister, from the Tánaiste Seán T. O'Kelly to Frank Aiken.[4] Some of Kerney's closest friends, such as the Sheehy-Skeffingtons and Frank Litton, were in attendance. His speech from the day survives, and from it, it is clear that he felt at home again. These trips back home fostered a sense of longing within him to be closer to family, friends, and home. Life in Spain did not compare to these happy occasions. As he said:

> It is a source of pleasure for my dear wife and myself that we should have the privilege of welcoming you here; we are happy that the wedding ceremony should have been honoured by the presence of so many distinguished friends—and more especially by the presence of one who enjoys widespread esteem and respect even far beyond the borders of this ancient Irish island of ours.
>
> . . . Many of you we first met in Paris twenty years ago or so and our friendship has ripened with the passing years; some there are whom I have known for thirty years and more; one or two were the friends of my boyhood or even of my childhood days.
>
> . . . I call to mind some lines that were scribbled out for me by an Irish friend of ours on the occasion of his marriage in Paris soon after the close of the last war, and which ran as follows—
>
> As years roll by in hurried flight,
> May friendship's ties more close unite,

The bonds that bind our souls together
In love of Ireland and each other.[5]

KERNEY PREPARES THE GROUNDWORK

It is clear from Kerney's diary records of this time and from family photographs taken of Micheline's wedding that within Fianna Fáil and moderate republican circles the diplomat was a close and trusted friend of everyone from government ministers down to root-and-branch associates. As far as de Valera was concerned, Kerney was clearly a loyal and trusted colleague, as these rare social events illustrated during the war years. Both he and Kerney had been through tumultuous events since the treaty split, and their association had endured many ups and downs to this point. German military intelligence, the Abwehr, knew of Kerney's close ties to de Valera both politically and as godfather to the diplomat's youngest son, yet they somehow came to the view that Kerney was a possible route of access to the Taoiseach to open negotiations to alter Ireland's neutral policy and reach an accommodation with the IRA.

Hitler's spymasters and henchmen, most prominent of all, the Reich Foreign Minister Joachim von Ribbentrop, supported an initiative of this kind, yet from the beginning they completely failed to see that such a plan was deeply flawed and was predicated on false assumptions. De Valera had marginalized, distanced himself from, and then clamped down on the IRA since coming to power in 1932, as one biographer, Diarmaid Ferriter, has shown: "Six IRA men were executed by army firing squad during the war; Charlie Kerins was hanged in December 1944, three others were allowed to die on hunger-strike, while more than 500 were interned without trial and another 600 were committed under the Offences Against the State Act."[6] He was no longer supportive of that organization. He had successfully used legislative and constitutional means to attain greater freedoms for Ireland and had negotiated the return of the treaty ports from Britain in 1938. This strategy had worked, and moderate republicans like Kerney, as well as the majority of the electorate, supported de Valera because his approach worked. Neutrality was a further expression of that independence. Any witness to Micheline's wedding that day would have seen that Kerney, like all his colleagues, was prepared to sacrifice anything for de Valera. It is quite astonishing how the Nazis got it so wrong right from the start.

It appears from the Germans' intelligence files that their reading of Irish republicans and republicanism in general was framed in a purely militant context and perspective. They believed that its adherents would be willing and ready to fight with Germany at the right moment against Britain to realize the dream of a united island, no matter what past actions demonstrated to the contrary. The different strands of Irish republicanism seem to have escaped or, rather, been overlooked by them. Their estimations of both de Valera and Kerney were profoundly incorrect. A natural assumption and overestimation was reached after meetings with Kerney, for example, that led them to think he was a militant republican who knew the inner thoughts of de Valera and could help shift Irish neutral policy to a more benevolent pro-German orientation.

One must bear in mind the historic context that also influenced the Abwehr's thinking in relation to Kerney. The Nazi war machine was fighting a titanic struggle against the Soviet Union, and victory appeared in sight that September. Many eyes were already arrogantly turning westward to the next theater and defeating the last remaining obstacle to German domination of Europe—Britain. The Germans were preparing the ground in advance and were considering Ireland as a possible ally. How Ireland was going to react to Hitler's triumph appears to have concerned top Nazi spymasters at this time. They pondered Irish neutrality and from their viewpoint judged that it had to be abandoned soon. Hitherto Berlin's main source of information on Irish matters had been Dr. Eduard Hempel, the German minister in Dublin. Hempel's argument that Irish neutrality already benefited Germany did not fit into the mental framework intelligence agents had conjured up about Ireland and the European war, so they looked to other views, either from within the Abwehr or from IRA exiles, such as Seán Russell or Frank Ryan, to verify their analysis.[7] None of these avenues proved entirely satisfactory, either, and so a more direct route to the official Irish outlook had to be found. They believed they found that source in Kerney.

HELMUT CLISSMANN MAKES CONTACT

The spiderweb of intrigue that led Kerney to meet Joachim von Ribbentrop's underling, Dr. Edmund Veesenmayer, began with Kerney's authorization of Champourcin's approach to KO Spanien during the Frank Ryan case, because it was the first time, albeit by association, that his name became known to the Abwehr. The second time Kerney's name was spoken of within the intelligence agency concerned an Irish citizen and an inheritance. In May 1940 Kerney was notified by Frederick Boland, the assistant secretary at External Affairs, that a Jim Doody had approached the department looking for information on a sister-in-law named Mary Pauline Mains, who was believed to be living in Spain.[8] Jim and the family were concerned for her well-being, as they had not heard from her for some time. Kerney was asked to look into the matter, and he discovered that she had been staying with a Señora Fournier, who had died and left her a legacy in her will. Kerney told Mains that her family was worried about her, and he forwarded her contact address to Joseph Walshe to pass on to her family.[9] Mains remained in Madrid because the will and her share of it was contested by the deceased woman's family. She approached Kerney for legal advice about the disputed will, and he passed on Champourcin's contact details to her.

Mains's entitlement to the inheritance soon came apart, and she blamed Champourcin for botching her claim. She turned up at the Irish legation to vent her anger at Kerney for recommending the Spanish lawyer, but the diplomat defended his actions and warned Dublin that she was potential trouble. In dire financial straits and unable to get home, Mains agreed to earn some money by becoming a courier for the Abwehr. Champourcin approached Abwehr agent Friedrich Blaum again: "Through Champourcin, Blaum met Mary Mains, an Irish citizen known to be an Anglophobe and Irish Republican Army sympathizer."[10] Kurt Haller later confirmed to Allied interrogators that it was Champourcin who recruited Mains, unbeknownst to Kerney: "The Spanish legal adviser to the Irish Legation in Madrid, Champourcin, put Blaum in touch with a client of his, an Irish woman living in Madrid, Mary Mains."[11] She was given the code name "Agent Margarethe" and left for Ireland on a liner bound for Galway in November 1940.[12] Her mission was to carry money and information to an Abwehr liaison agent with the IRA named James O'Donovan and a German spy who had parachuted into Ireland but had remained on the run named Hermann Görtz. Mains completed her mission and returned to Spain with letters from Görtz written in invisible ink.[13] She was quickly dropped by KO Spanien, however, because they feared, incorrectly, that she was known to the Irish authorities at the time.

For the second time, the legation's lawyer, Champourcin, had personally made contact with KO Spanien and had, by association, linked Kerney to the venture in the minds of leading German agents like Blaum, even though in truth Kerney knew nothing of Champourcin's or Mains's underhanded dealings with the Abwehr. The intelligence agency paid them both for their services. It appears that Dublin, too, knew nothing of Mains's clandestine activities until well into 1943, when Chief Superintendant Patrick Carroll of Garda crime and security branch C3 asked Joseph Walshe if he knew anything of her movements when she returned to Ireland from Spain in 1940.[14] It was not until October 1943 that Colonel Dan Bryan of G2 furnished Walshe with information that Mains was a definite rogue element who had carried money bound for the IRA and who had acted as an emissary for the Germans.[15] This knowledge fueled suspicion in both Walshe's and Bryan's minds that Kerney might somehow have been involved in the scheme. From their perspective, Kerney again seemed to be in collusion with dissident republicans who might constitute a threat to the security of the Irish state, but, in typical fashion, they did not recall Kerney to allay these fears.

On 21 June 1941, the day before the German invasion of the Soviet Union, Admiral Wilhelm Canaris, head of the Abwehr, approved Dr. Edmund Veesenmayer's request for the transfer of Helmut Clissmann to the Foreign Ministry for clandestine missions in Ireland.[16]

Veesenmayer believed Clissmann was critical to the grand scheme. He wrote: "He was five years in I [Ireland], is perfect in the language, possesses very good connections and consequently, 'hide-out' possibilities, has worked with me very closely for about two years and has full knowledge therefore of the political plan. . . . Apart from this he is also a confidant and collaborator of the counter intelligence service (Abwehr)."[17] Veesenmayer was a senior committed Nazi who was one of Hitler's "fixers." He had joined the movement in 1932 before the Nazis came to power. Veesenmayer became attracted to Hitler's SS, and he rose quickly through the ranks, thanks largely to his loyalty. By 1939 he held the rank of Standartenführer, or colonel, and Hitler entrusted him with the task of breaking up the state of Czechoslovakia.[18] Veesenmayer traveled to Bratislava and made contact with the ultraconservative and clericalist Slovak People's Party, urging the party leader, Josef Tiso, to secede from the Czechoslovak state. Tiso was persuaded and began immediate preparations for Slovak independence. After Hitler annexed the rest of Czechoslovakia in March 1939, Tiso declared Slovakia independent, yet under the "protection" of the Greater German Reich. During the war Veesenmayer was promoted and reassigned to many areas, including Irish affairs.

Veesenmayer planned several covert operations during the war involving German agents (Helmut Clissmann) and Irishmen (Frank Ryan and Seán Russell) to infiltrate Ireland in order to establish contact with the IRA, to transmit military information, and to prepare "underground resistance" in the event of an Allied invasion.[19] These operational plans proved rather fruitless because of a combination of bad luck (Russell's dying onboard the submarine in which he had been going to Ireland),[20] bad weather, and poor planning and coordination with the IRA. A new strategy or Plan B was devised, one that was easier to manage and far more clinical, whereby face-to-face contact would be initiated with Kerney. It needed to be done by someone the diplomat knew and trusted and with whom he would feel at ease. Helmut Clissmann had met Kerney before the war, Kerney was friends with Budge, and the diplomat knew that the Clissmanns had helped engineer Ryan's "escape." On 3 November 1941 the Reich

Foreign Ministry arranged Helmut Clissmann's passport, visas, and 2,000 Reichsmarks to travel to Madrid to see Kerney using the cover that he was carrying a letter from Frank Ryan.[21] In the letter Ryan informed Kerney that Clissmann was honorable: "Regard him as you do Budge. To his help I owe all that I enjoy here. He is more us than anybody else's!"[22] Ryan assured Kerney that he was not a Nazi collaborator: "I am not working for anybody here. I am not working for—nor even in communication with—any organization [IRA] at home. (I do not even know if such organization is aware of my whereabouts). I am, as I have already said, an individual claiming to represent myself, & only myself."[23]

Helmut carried this letter on his person and met Kerney twice at the legation on 8 and 11 November.[24] The main records of what was discussed by the men come from German accounts of the meeting and from Kerney's later recollections at the time of a libel action the diplomat took against UCD historian Professor Desmond Williams. A five-page report on Clissmann's summary of the conversations with Kerney reveals the politically sensitive topics raised as well as the diplomat's willingness to meet again to speak "very freely and frankly."[25] The first page of the German report noted Kerney's praise for de Valera's neutral policy and its wide support: "Ireland's inner political situation was described by K. [Kerney] as very satisfactory. De Valera represented the great majority of the people, whom he had convinced that only his policy of neutrality, which had so far been successful, could maintain for the country that measure of independence which it had up till now with great effort achieved."[26] Kerney also praised the country's economic survival under de Valera: "With a small merchant fleet of twelve ships a truly heartening beginning had been made."[27] Clissmann reported Kerney's praise for the 200,000 "well-trained" recruits of the "Irish Army Command," who were "prepared to offer serious resistance to any attacker."[28]

As the report goes on, Clissmann records Kerney as stating that "the danger of involving Ireland in this war mainly threatens from Great Britain and the United States."[29] Another critical passage on Irish attitudes vis-à-vis Germany and Northern Ireland reveals some astonishing declarations attributed to Kerney. It merits quoting at length:

For a German appreciation of the Irish situation the impression, which has been received from the Irish Government, that an English-American victory in this war would mean the permanent division of Ireland, while a German victory and a very great weakening of Great Britain which would result therefrom, could alone guarantee the freedom and unity of Ireland, is revealing. From this it follows that de Valera must see in Germany a potential ally. If England or America, or both, in spite of their reluctance, felt compelled to attack Ireland, German assistance after a request had been made by the Irish Government or her representatives would be heartily welcome. As England would utilize even the slightest pretext for an attack on Ireland, preparations for giving German assistance to Ireland would, in his opinion, unfortunately be impossible. K. [Kerney] explained that in the case of an English or American attack and the possible flight of the Irish Government from Dublin, when its isolation in the matter of information would have to be reckoned with, he would be prepared to accept extensive responsibility toward Germany.[30]

The report goes on to mention the discussions of Clissmann and Kerney on the IRA, the splits in the organization, and the concern of the Irish government about Seán Russell and whether the extremist and mastermind of the bombing campaign in England before the war was being safely harbored by Germany or was in fact dead. Finally Clissmann stated that Kerney "hoped one day to see Frank Ryan as a German go-between with de Valera."[31] On his first reading of Clissmann's report, Veesenmayer expressed his shock that the Irish diplomat spoke with such "unexpected frankness."[32] The Nazi drew some astonishing conclusions about Irish government opinion based on his agent's report: "From this, no more and no less can be deduced than that de Valera and his associates are already seriously considering, in the event of hostilities with England, the question of a call for help or a request for support from Germany."[33] Veesenmayer went on to believe that Kerney's far from discreet utterances must have been instructed by his superiors: "Kerney's desire to intensify the mutual contact, even leads one to conclude that Kerney had certain commissions or authority to approach the German Government in case of need."[34] Veesenmayer saw a golden opportunity here for Germany: "It should be considered whether the existing contact should not be strengthened."[35] He then stated his own willingness to intervene personally. He thought that Kerney's recent vacation in Ireland might have been politically arranged and that de Valera was now open to collaboration with Germany and the IRA against the "old enemy," England, especially with the war in the east nearly won: "I think that it might even be worth considering the possibility that I myself should have a conversation with Kerney. Kerney, who must be regarded as a cautious and reserved Irish Nationalist and a close friend of de Valera's, has clearly, as a result of his long leave in Ireland, which has recently ended, dropped this reserve to such an extent that it seems justified to assume that this altered attitude is due to de Valera's advice."[36] Veesenmayer hoped that through Kerney "a reconciliation between de Valera and the IRA" could be agreed to that would last for the duration of the war.[37] This first step would be followed by de Valera's abandoning neutrality, pursuing a pro-German policy, and assisting Germany against Britain in return for a united Ireland. Clearly Veesenmayer was impressed with Clissmann's work.

Some of Kerney's utterances are truly startling, so naturally one has to investigate the credibility of these assertions in Clissmann's report. It is common for intelligence agents across the world to exaggerate a source, a contact, an operation, or a scheme in order to gain career advancement or more money or to increase their prestige in an organization. After the war, when Clissmann was captured and interrogated by the Allies, the truth about his motives and the colorful statements he attributed to Kerney was revealed. Clissmann was the originator of the proposal to approach Kerney, and his colorful report secured for himself the role of Kerney's "handler" until early 1943. This activity kept him from being reassigned to a combat role with the Brandenburg Regiment for over a year and a half. The agent took advantage of Veesenmayer's interest in Ireland and Frank Ryan, as well as the success of the eastern campaign, to excite his superiors into thinking that Kerney would be a suitable mediator between Germany and Ireland when the inevitable showdown with Britain occurred. As Clissmann stated to Allied interrogators, "My enthusiasm influenced me to give the most favourable version possible."[38] This account was confirmed at the time of the libel action, when Clissmann agreed to appear in court on Kerney's behalf to testify under oath that indeed he had made his reports to Veesenmayer look more interesting than they were because of ulterior personal motives—with a young wife and family to take care of, he wanted to avoid frontline action and a transfer to the eastern front at all costs.

Clissmann also acknowledged to Allied interrogators that he took advantage of his previous acquaintance with Kerney to hide his clandestine mission: "He spoke to me as a friend of Frank Ryan."[39] It seems likely that Clissmann's cover, calling at the legation with a letter from Ryan, and his prewar acquaintance with Kerney, albeit through Budge, could have relaxed the diplomat's circumspection. What is not clear in the report is the degree of loosening of Kerney's tongue that he had achieved. The report mentions various topics discussed, from the general course of the war to de Valera's leadership, all of which were topics of normal discussion in wartime. The only notable information Clissmann provided, which Kerney passed on to Walshe as coming from Clissmann, was that Seán Russell was dead.[40] The revelation that Kerney looked favorably on a German victory and was willing to liaise with the Germans to further Ireland's territorial ambitions is striking. Whether Kerney expressed such a view or whether it was an exaggeration on Clissmann's part or a complete fabrication can be gleaned, in part, from British intelligence files.[41]

Michael Kerney, a nephew of the diplomat, had been born on 28 November 1904 in Plauen, Germany. He lived at various times in Germany, France, Spain, and Britain and spoke six languages. In July 1942 he informed his family that he had been called up into the British Army. He in fact had not; saying so was a "deception" on his part.[42] He underwent physical, mental, and military training for the British Special Operations Executive (SOE). The SOE was tasked with operating inside Nazi-occupied Europe to, in the words of Winston Churchill, "set Europe ablaze." Initially Michael was well thought of: "Straight from City life, but confesses to an innate urge for something more exciting; diffident at the start, by sheer ability has come to the fore-front; capable; personality and guts; esteemed rather than liked; latterly, progress accelerated; will probably outstripe [*sic*] most of them and prove a find."[43]

However, Michael soon proved "unsuited for subversive work of any kind."[44] The F [French] section then tried to employ him in clandestine communications in Spain, as he spoke fluent Spanish and Catalan and was knowledgeable of the geographic area, having lived there for years. British intelligence had a contact in the Anglo–South American Bank head office. H. Trevor Jones agreed to recruit an MI6 agent into one of the bank's branches in Spain to be a chief intelligence official for the Barcelona region after they could "teach him the rudiments of our work."[45] London put Michael's name forward for the post because he had worked for the bank previously; however, his selection was challenged by Jones primarily because he knew that Michael was related to Leopold Kerney. Jones revealed to London that he himself knew the diplomat personally and played golf with him frequently. He feared that Michael's posting might reach the ears of his uncle and perhaps spread further afield. More importantly, in terms of highlighting the diplomat's discretion, Jones also gave an outline of Kerney's view of the war, but only what he was inclined to believe or guessed were the Irish minister's views and thoughts toward the Allies and the Axis. In all their golf games together, the issue of politics and Ireland's alignment in the war had been "never talked about" because Kerney refused to divulge anything.[46] Perhaps his innate suspicion of anything or anyone English was a factor, but Jones's outline does reveal that Kerney knew how and when to be tactful, as he had spent a lifetime being discreet and diplomatic around people, especially anyone foreign and particularly at wartime. It is for this reason unlikely that he disclosed sensitive information to Clissmann as the agent led his superiors to believe.

We must also analyze the issue of Kerney and the IRA. The Germans believed that any operation linking their war aims with Ireland's territorial aspirations would require IRA assistance. Kerney had never been a member of any militant organization in all his years as a republican going back to 1919. He had never joined the IRB, the Irish Volunteers, or the IRA, and when he declared himself against the Irish Free State it was not the IRA that he deemed the lawful republican authority but de Valera's shadow government. The diplomat, unlike the Taoiseach, spoke little about Northern Ireland and showed little interest in it, which by 1940 was the last remaining area of contention in Anglo-Irish relations. Yet there is a revealing memorandum written by Kerney on 20 September 1940, when Britain was facing the threat of German invasion ("Operation Sealion") and its cities were being bombed, that shows his thoughts on partition, Irish politics since the treaty, and the attitudes of the Irish people toward the current war. It is worth analyzing as further evidence of Kerney's attitude toward dissident republicans as well as his antifascism.

The six-page typed report consisted of the diplomat's thoughts and considerations, as well as an evaluation of his own life during those tumultuous years. Kerney could make sense of all the events and the evolution of Ireland, it appears, only through de Valera's leadership. He began with the Anglo-Irish Treaty and then notes that de Valera and the IRA were "beaten in the civil war" but that, through constitutional means and "remarkable foresight," de Valera had "slowly but surely, deprived England of many advantages secured by the imposed 'Treaty.'"[47] He cited legislation, the abolition of the office of governor general, the 1937 constitution, and the 1938 Anglo-Irish Agreement as examples of how the Chief had wrestled away more independence for Ireland without resorting to armed violence. The only remaining issue of importance for republicans was the six disputed counties of Ulster, which for Kerney had to be resolved by dialogue: "There can be no doubt that the decision of the majority of the inhabitants [of Ireland], when they can be consulted as a whole, will be in favour of complete and absolute separation and independence. . . . Any settlement of any question decided by force has to be maintained by force, and, where inhabitants of Ireland are concerned, de Valera infinitely prefers the arguments of reason."[48]

He acknowledged that the issue of Northern Ireland was immeasurably complex and that, with the war going so badly for England, it might seem to some an opportune moment to grab these possessions back. He next turned his attention to the IRA. While de Valera had shown "wise statesmanship" in keeping Ireland out of the present war and "the utmost determination to maintain that neutrality," he recorded, the diplomat noted that there were militant republicans eager to take advantage of England's difficulties, and he expressed his abhorrence of any military campaign to unify the island by the IRA: "There are Irishmen, however,—and notably the IRA—who do not think so deeply, or perhaps so wisely, with a preference for force as the most desirable solution; they would hold that the 800,000 pro-English inhabitants of Ulster should give their loyalty to Ireland as their mother country or else be made to clear out of the country."[49] For Kerney, neutrality demonstrated that "Ireland chose the path of peace with England when she could not well do otherwise; she has no wish to abandon that path."[50]

Kerney then assessed Irish public opinion and noted how Germany's fascist dictatorship and British imperialism jarred with Irish attitudes. His thoughts merit extensive quotation:

> The state of opinion in Ireland is of course somewhat divided; roughly I would say that 20% are Anglophile, perhaps 10% Germanophile and 70% Irlandophile; the bulk of the people are glad that England should at long last "get a licking"; there is no great sympathy for Germany the people are mostly Catholic and do not approve of the German attitude toward Catholics and Catholic associations in Germany and elsewhere; they are truly democratic at heart because centuries of oppression and misery have placed them definitely on the side of the poor, the weak, the struggler, the sufferer; that is a profound feeling, and the Irish people have a lively memory of all their ancestors suffered from autocratic and tyrannical systems of government; democracy for them is the antithesis of rule by the wealthy, titled autocratic overlords from England; therefore their natural instinct is against totalitarian systems; de Valera has said more than once that no system of government is perfect, each one having its faults and imperfections, but that, all things considered, he thought the democratic one as good as any; events in the outer world have moved swiftly since but there is nothing to indicate that Irish opinion in this respect has undergone any change.[51]

Kerney then turned to the IRA and its history, its structure, its splits to its present form, and its members, whom he described as "dissidents."[52] He knew that their methods were violent at times: "They have put persons to death, usually as spies or informers, but sometimes for having made themselves otherwise obnoxious."[53] He noted that Ryan split from the IRA many years ago but that still men like Ryan were not popular at home: "Men of Ryan's stamp who have fought for Irish independence are respected by Irish nationalists and Republicans but there is nothing to indicate that they enjoy the confidence of the Irish people as leaders."[54] Kerney again weighed everything up and came down on de Valera's side, believing in his leadership, vision, and neutral policy as the best course for his nation and one that he and the majority of Irish public opinion supported. He did not see any value to Irish interests in linking up with Germany: "Opinion generally in Ireland holds that Germany is endeavouring to build up an empire in the same manner in which England built up hers, and that this is a struggle between two giants, neither particularly virtuous. . . . There is no desire whatever in Ireland that Germany should ever set foot in the island. . . . Most Irishmen feel, however, that Germany might just take England's place if she got the chance, and that it would be high treason to invite Germany or any other Power to come to Ireland."[55] Kerney understood that Nazi Germany could never be trusted to leave Ireland if invited there, given its track record of disrespecting neutral small states: "If Germany crushes England, Ireland may regain 'Ulster' and united Ireland might be independent, but this independence could be terminated at a moment's notice."[56]

Kerney concluded the memorandum by noting that the German political system was alien and repugnant to the Irish, with their respect for democracy and individual liberty: "There was no hostile feeling toward Germany in Ireland when this war started, and that may still be true, but brutal methods, whether totalitarian or democratic, are disliked there and tend to alienate sympathy."[57] Personal documentation such at this and Kerney's constant support for de Valera made it clear that he was opposed to any collaboration with the IRA or with any foreign power to unite the island despite Britain's difficulties at the time. It would therefore seem unlikely that the statements Clissmann attributed to Kerney were ever in fact made, particularly regarding

Ireland's willingness to alter its neutral foreign policy toward a pro-German policy. Other evidence can be found in letters sent between Kerney and Frank Ryan, which Clissmann couriered back and forth and were often the cover for his trips to Spain. These letters, unbeknownst to Kerney, were being read by Clissmann. In one letter dated 20 January 1942, Kerney made it crystal clear that he and the majority of Irish public opinion supported neutrality and were against any efforts to collude with the IRA or a foreign power to unify the island. It merits quotation at length:

> D's [De Valera's] attitude is that, as the Constitution removes all obstacles from the path of those who could, if they got the support of the people, easily remove him from office and change the country's policy, he cannot admit cooperation on any other than constitutional lines; to connive at violence by a minority would be to leave the way clear for violence by other minorities and would lead to anarchy and disaster; his neutrality policy is approved definitely by the vast majority. Those who suspect him of weakness or of secret agreements are, in my opinion, making a mistake; he will not give way to any pressure, however strong, from one side or from the other; he means what he says. . . . D must be on the alert for danger from all sides, and there is at least some foundation for his suspicions; it is necessary to avoid becoming a pawn in the game of others, who are not particularly concerned about Ireland for Ireland's sake.[58]

If Veesenmayer was reading the Kerney letters to Ryan as Clissmann was, it should have been obvious that a meeting with the Irish diplomat would be a complete waste of time. However, Hitler's underling continued to be impressed with Clissmann's reports to him, and it appears that Veesenmayer took everything at face value. The spymaster wanted to keep up the momentum, so he asked the agent to again travel to Madrid to discover if Kerney was open to a direct face-to-face meeting. For a second time, using the cover that he was carrying personal letters from Frank Ryan to him, Clissmann met Kerney at the legation on 17 and 20 January 1942. The German report on this round of conversations again warrants lengthy quotation:

Without giving names, Clissmann informed Mr Kerney that he knew a man in Berlin who had repeatedly carried out special commissions of an economic and political nature for the Reich Foreign Minister, without, however, being officially a political person. He had repeatedly discussed Irish questions with this man and he thought that there was a possibility here of acquiring a valuable contact in an indirect way. This man had shown great interest in the Irish problem and had asked him to enquire of Kerney whether it would not be advisable to bring about a personal discussion sometime. Kerney, who is known to be an extremely careful and reserved politician, indicated that he considered such an exchange of views would be extremely valuable and that, especially in view of the tense atmosphere in Ireland, he did not wish to miss making such a contact. On condition that the whole affair would be treated strictly confidentially he was therefore agreeable to such a meeting taking place on his own responsibility.[59]

Judging from this report and as subsequent events showed, Kerney agreed to meet Veesenmayer without first seeking authorization to do so from Dublin. Kerney initially suggested mid-February as a possible time for the face-to-face meeting. In making this decision to meet a senior Nazi without prior approval, the diplomat has been heavily criticized by many historians. Eunan O'Halpin believed that Kerney's meeting with Veesenmayer amounted to his "secretly negotiating with Germany."[60] Mark Hull saw it as confirmation of Kerney's ties with dissident republicans and belligerents, given his "existing history" with the Abwehr from the time of the Frank Ryan case.[61] Michael Kennedy believed that Kerney acted wrongly in agreeing to the encounter, stating: "Kerney unwisely agreed to the meeting."[62] The Germans themselves found it incredible that Kerney had agreed to a face-to-face meeting with Veesenmayer at the time. One Abwehr agent, Kurt Haller, later told his Allied captors that Kerney's openness to a face-to-face encounter without approval from his superiors "may have gone beyond the bounds of diplomatic security."[63] But whether Kerney acted incorrectly is entirely open to debate.

One of the fundamental responsibilities of any diplomatic head of mission is to engage in negotiations with the representatives of the host country in which they are resident or with any individual whose interest in seeing them is pertinent to the national interest of the country that the diplomat represents. Lauran Paine has discussed this issue in relation to various neutral European heads of mission during the war, including the Vatican, and noted that they regularly met intelligence agents from both sides.[64] It was, in fact, not only a common practice to agree to such meetings without official sanction but was also a vital part of any diplomat's work to gain information that could be beneficial or prejudicial to their country's national interests. As long as it was just conversations they engaged in, nothing was being committed to, and besides, as the diplomatic representatives of their nations, these diplomats themselves had the authority to organize such encounters. Kerney looked at the matter in the same way. He had ample time to contact Dublin, but he believed that as an official diplomat he had the authority to discuss issues with anyone, provided that it was only a discussion and covered only wartime information. We must also bear in mind the important fact that Kerney's official title was "Minister Plenipotentiary." This gave him fully authorized powers and an exclusive right—more commonly referred to as a prerogative in law—to act as he saw fit on behalf of his government.

At the time of the libel case, the British found nothing wrong with Kerney's agreeing to this meeting, and, in fact, their legal advisor judged his conduct to be "cautious and perfectly proper in every way."[65] British intelligence moved against neutral Spanish and Swedish officials during the war only when they had concrete proof of outright sabotage or clandestine activity that was prejudicial to British security, not mere discussions with an opposing belligerent. There was always the fear that such meetings with intelligence operatives could become known to the opposing belligerent side, but, in Kerney's case, British intelligence was singularly unaware of these Clissmann trips to Madrid. Only MI5's director of counterespionage, Guy Liddell, noted Clissmann's presence, but then not until 2 October 1942, several months after the critical Kerney-Veesenmayer meeting, and its true purpose was not known until years later.[66]

Clissmann carried with him another letter from Frank Ryan, dated 14 January 1942. Ryan confirmed Seán Russell's death, but not the place of his death (on board a submarine to Ireland) and outlined his support for de Valera's neutral policy: "In a time of national crisis like this, there must be a unified command. The country comes before party. So, in his neutrality policy—which is the only sane policy under the circumstances—Dev should get 100% support."[67] For the second time Clissmann made a report of his conversations with Kerney to Berlin that included passages bordering on the ridiculous, yet his boss, Veesenmayer, believed them and forwarded them up the line to Ribbentrop's Foreign Ministry for Hitler's ultimate consideration. Kerney was recorded as saying that he had tried to get explosives from Spain to be shipped to Ireland and that he was receiving detailed analysis of Ireland's military preparedness from, of all people, Joseph Walshe. Veesenmayer wrote: "Kerney still judges Ireland's capacity for military resistance favourably, although the lack of anti-tank guns and aeroplanes is very great. He based this on information which he had had from State Secretary Walshe, who in his turn had received it from Irish army circles."[68] At no stage did Veesenmayer question the veracity of such statements, perhaps hoping that the entire venture might further his own career. He believed Kerney's frankness was deliberate and was based on instruction from the Taoiseach. He now set in motion the arrangements for a face-to-face meeting.

Kurt Haller later detailed the purpose of this meeting from a German viewpoint. The Nazis wanted an "inside" perspective on Irish political opinion from a senior and reliable source close to policy-makers and to impress on this insider the strength of Germany as a useful ally: "Veesenmayer's main idea was to impress Kerney with the strength of Germany and the value of Germany as Eire's ally; he thought that Kerney would pass his views on to the Irish government, who, he considered, were getting only one-sided information."[69] A lot had changed since Clissmann's last trip in November however. Hitler had declared war on the United States in December after the Japanese attack on Pearl Harbor. The disasters that were unfolding on the eastern front as the Nazi war machine froze on the snowy steppes of Russia failed to convince leading German spymasters that, far from winning the war, Germany was beginning to lose it, although neutral observers could already see that the tide of the war was changing.

There were no further developments until 15 May 1942, when Clissmann returned to Madrid, this time with a Leica camera Kerney wanted, "for which I paid him 1247 pesetas."[70] He also carried another letter from Ryan: "The usual private half-yearly letter! Not that I have any startling, or interesting, news. But I feel it a duty—and find it a pleasure—to let you know all I know. Besides I have an interest in maintaining my Spanish connection—since I can't go home, I have hopes of becoming your successor when you retire, in another 15 years or so (of course, the Generalissimo will be encantado [delighted]!). Hadn't he already promised to maintain me in Burgos for the rest of my life?"[71] Ryan thanked Kerney for forwarding his sister's letter to him, which "cheered me up a lot."[72] This forwarding of letters through the diplomatic bag would later provide Walshe with hard evidence of protocol breaches by Kerney in the spring of 1943.

At this meeting Clissmann again raised the issue of an unnamed senior and influential German who wanted to discuss matters pertaining to Ireland with Kerney. The diplomat again said he was open to a conversation. As he noted years later, these meetings had no significance to him beyond that of friendly chats that also provided useful information about Ryan and his health to forward on to his family:

> These meetings obviously did not give rise to any official report of any kind by me. The proposed meeting with the friend of von Ribbentrop was of course a more serious matter, and I fully realized that at the time. I did not shirk the responsibility of taking a decision, knowing that I might possibly glean some information of value from this German, whilst he could not possibly learn anything from me other than what was public knowledge already. I possessed no secret inside information whatever and therefore was not in a position to reveal any secrets. I had not the faintest intention of "negotiating."[73]

Another long delay ensued. In August Clissmann for the last time traveled to Madrid, this time accompanied by Veesenmayer, who went with a false passport, name, and disguise. Another "personal" letter from Ryan gave cryptic clues to the man's seniority in the Nazi regime: "He has been most persistent and successful in preventing dealings with certain people in the little island. His attitude on all questions is that of his Chief [Joachim von Ribbentrop]; hence his insistence that the status quo in the little island is not to be interfered with is significant."[74] Here Ryan was being somewhat naïve and misleading. Veesenmayer had carried out military and intelligence operations that Ryan had been involved in that could have been potentially prejudicial to Irish interests.[75] Finally, at "6pm on Friday 21st August 1942," Clissmann again asked Kerney to fix an appointment to see this man in Clissmann's presence.[76] Kerney chose to meet both men in a café in Madrid's Retiro Park at 11 a.m. on 24 August. He still did not know the identity of the second individual, but he was about to meet one of Hitler's vipers who, barely two years later, helped Adolf Eichmann transport over 400,000 Hungarian Jews to the gas chambers at Auschwitz.

THE REPUBLICAN MEETS THE NAZI

This face-to-face meeting on 24 August 1942 between Kerney and one of Hitler's top SS officials ranks as one of the most famous encounters in Irish diplomatic history during World War II. The meeting has been the subject of historical debate among generations of historians, and it stands out as the most contentious episode in Kerney's entire diplomatic career. Mark Hull, in his analysis of this critical wartime meeting, argued that Kerney gave the Nazis "a green light" to become involved in Irish affairs, and he contended that the whole event was "incendiary" to Irish national interests.[77] Hull went on to write that "Kerney himself did not report the meetings [*sic*] with the Germans until well after the event—certainly after British Intelligence learned of them."[78] Although the first contention by Hull is open to debate, the second is not. Kerney wrote a detailed report on the day he met Veesenmayer, while the event was still fresh in his mind, to Joseph Walshe's attention. There are two versions that survive of what transpired at the meeting—Kerney's version and a German one. The important document from the German side is a

"Top Secret" synopsis of Veesenmayer's report, which he compiled on 28 September. The Irish diplomat, on the other hand, wrote his report himself; his secretary, Maisie Donnelly, did not type it. The two reports give contrasting accounts of what was said at the meeting, so to give the fullest outline of what was discussed and who said what, both versions need to be analyzed, beginning with the one from the German side.

The two-page German report marked "Top Secret" is dated 5 October 1942 and was typed up by Franz von Sonnleithner, an administration official on Ribbentrop's personal staff. It is a summary of Veesenmayer's 28 September account, written over a month after the meeting took place. The document was read by, among others, Walter Hewel—a diplomat and close confidante of Hitler's who was part of the dictator's entourage through most of the war. Hewel received the report at Hitler's Werwolf headquarters in Vinnitsa Ukraine, where the dictator was overseeing "Operation Blue"—the German offensive begun that summer on the south flank of the eastern front. This was an incredibly stressful time for Hitler at his Werwolf compound because he was coordinating the assault by the 6th Army on Stalingrad.[79] He was convinced that the Soviet Union was at the point of collapse and had used up all its manpower reserves. Despite these hectic commitments, we know that this top-secret report was sent to Hitler for his personal attention because "Note for the Führer" is typed as the heading.[80] The report also reveals that the Nazi regime was happy with Veesenmayer's work on Irish matters because by this time he had been promoted within the SS to the rank of Oberführer (senior colonel).

The report is divided into seven sections, each a summary of discussion points with Kerney's views on each outlined, from general attitudes regarding Ireland and the war (Point 1: that Ireland would resist an invasion by any aggressor) to fanciful points such as Point 3, which made the following assertion: "Kerney thinks that the differences existing between de Valera and the IRA would be automatically removed by an English-American invasion. De Valera himself came from the IRA; he had had a leading position in it and would never, in the event of war, be unfaithful to his fundamental principles."[81] The Taoiseach had introduced severe legislation already, such as the Offenses against the State Act, which allowed for the detention and arrest of IRA members and the organization's leadership, for the right to break hunger strikes, and for special courts to carry out hangings for capital offenses. De Valera was committed to neutrality and suppressing the IRA. The notion that he would suddenly turn volte-face and reach an accommodation with militants was absurd. Attributing this supposed statement to Kerney is equally far-fetched. The republican would not have continued to serve in de Valera's administration if the Chief was so supportive of the IRA because of the harsh measures the government was enacting against the organization at the time.

Point 4 states: "In spite of de Valera's determination to hold fast to his policy of neutrality he would not, however, in Kerney's view, pursue it to the utmost but would, as soon as there were justified prospects of success, take up the fight with the Allies with the object of liberating Northern Ireland."[82] In what context such a scenario would arise was not outlined in the German report, nor was it detailed who would be liberating whom. The Taoiseach had protested against the arrival of US troops in Northern Ireland in 1942 because he claimed sovereignty over the entire island, but in this scenario how was he going to convince US president Franklin D. Roosevelt that it was in America's interest to help the Irish government (and the IRA) clear all British presence from the statelet? The United States and Britain were wartime allies fighting across the globe against fascist aggressor states. The idea that the United States would abandon its ally to further Irish territorial aspirations is simply unreal and something Kerney was not likely to have said.

The final item of note concerns Point 5. Here a scenario was imagined during the Kerney-Veesenmayer conversation whereby Ireland would call on German support in the event of an Allied invasion: "Kerney thinks it essential that, in the event of the realization of German assistance, the German Government should simultaneously declare that Germany has no interests in Ireland and that German troops will only remain on Irish soil as long as this is required in the common fight against the Allies."[83] A short examination of Germany's conduct toward former neutral states in the war would have made such an assertion fanciful, as the Nazi regime had shown a complete disregard for international law, the rights of independent neutral states, and their territorial integrity. Germany had invaded neutral state after neutral state and occupied each territory by military force under a tyrannical Nazi administration. Hitler's totalitarian regime did not respect democracy, so why would anyone, even Kerney, think that the Nazis would leave Ireland once they had won the war? It is indicative of the German account of the conversation, unreal and incredible. How Veesenmayer even believed that by August 1942 Germany could launch an amphibious invasion of Ireland is in and of itself fantastic considering that the Allies were expanding their presence in Northern Ireland from 1942, whereas the Nazis were dissipating their strength in the west by committing the bulk of their resources to a war of attrition against the Soviet Union. They also lacked the surface vessel fleet needed to land troops on Ireland's coastline and hence could not protect them adequately from attack by the Royal Navy. Crete had also shown the deadly costs of an airborne invasion. It all seemed fantasy talk, but perhaps that is what Hitler wanted to read by October 1942—grand strategies to win the war quickly. Veesenmayer's report was providing solutions, not problems; it was telling Hitler what he wanted to hear.

It is interesting to note that in the criticisms leveled at Kerney for meeting Veesenmayer few historians have consulted or referenced either the German report or Kerney's report, despite making damning pronouncements against the Irish diplomat. Eunan O'Halpin described the meeting as "unauthorized discussions" and labeled the diplomat a "monumental fool," given his other perceived mishandlings, for agreeing to see Veesenmayer, yet at no stage did O'Halpin quote the Kerney report.[84] Michael Kennedy likewise was critical of Kerney's actions, writing: "Kerney was not a natural diplomat. He was prone to acting independently without ascertaining government policy, and his meeting with Vessenmayer showed he had forgotten that he was no longer simply a trade representative dealing with technical issues but the representative of the Irish government."[85] Kennedy also failed to take a single quote from any section of Kerney's 24 August 1942 report.

Kerney's version of what transpired at the meeting, written on the day he met Veesenmayer while the events he described were still fresh in his memory, is contained in a five-page document headed "Conversation with a German" and directed to "J.P. Walshe," marked "Confidential" and signed by him as "L. H. Kerney."[86] Kerney began by stating that only at the meeting did he discover the true name and identity of the second man he was meeting with, and he quickly detected something sinister about his business in Spain: "He was here under an assumed name, but his real name is Veesenmayer, and I was mindful of the fact that I was in the somewhat delicate position of talking to a gentleman who, if I had looked under the table, might have been capable of disclosing something in the nature of a cloven hoof."[87] He informed Walshe about the man's seniority in the Nazi regime, writing that "Veesenmayer is in the confidence of von Ribbentrop" and that he had come with a single-minded purpose: "I believe that he came to Madrid with the deliberate purpose of making known Germany's attitude in regard to Ireland."[88] Despite this, he felt it necessary to put aside his moral compass and, as a representative of his country, listen to the Nazi in the hope that "some information of value could be obtained by me"; moreover, the meeting had accorded the diplomat the opportunity to "leave him without any doubt as to Ireland's position of very decided neutrality."[89]

Veesenmayer dominated the early exchanges, spelling out Germany's supremacy in the war: the ongoing attack on the southern flank of the eastern front toward the Caspian and Black Seas would deprive Russia of its oil. Germany was already self-sufficient in fuel, and the war in the east would be over "possibly by the end of the year."[90] It was clear that this viewpoint was shared by Hitler because, as this discussion was taking place, tanks from the 6th Army were already entering the outskirts of Stalingrad to cut the city off from the great Volga River. The war in the east appeared to be on the point of victory. Veesenmayer said that the regime was already planning for the next phase: "Once the Russian campaign was over, they would turn their attention to England," which brought Ireland into consideration: "The policy of neutrality, like every policy, must play itself out in time, and he believed that a moment would come when it would have to be followed by a more positive attitude."[91] He further opined that Germany wanted Ireland to consider its future policy, as the Nazis would soon turn their attention again to the west to secure "the new order of the future."[92] That the Nazis thought they could deal with each of the Allies separately and not be attacked by combined Allied efforts across several fronts was indicative of the make-believe bubble that Hitler and senior Nazis like Ribbentrop and Veesenmayer lived in.

The German had stated that de Valera was much admired in his country and that Hitler fully understood the Irish claim to Ulster. Yet he reiterated that the Führer desired a more "positive attitude" from Ireland and wanted it to take an active part in the war in order to enjoy the fruits of triumph at the victory banquet.[93] Vessenmayer also opined that de Valera might "no longer be a man of action" and had spent too much time in parliamentary life.[94] He continued that Germany wanted to see Ireland "territorially united" and "completely independent of England."[95] His own knowledge of Irish affairs had given him an expert understanding of the Irish mentality and its fighting spirit, he argued.

After listening to these points, Kerney interjected and cited de Valera's repeated statements that any invader would be resisted. He told the German quite forcefully that, having known the Taoiseach for a quarter of a century, he had no doubt but that the man possessed the same fighting courage he had shown as a young commander and was now, more than ever, prepared to make any sacrifice in the national interest. This strongly worded defense of his "Chief" certainly impressed Veesenmayer, Kerney felt:

> I had no doubt at all that Mr de Valera had visualised every conceivable development of the situation, and had made up his mind, as far as could be done before the actual happening of events, as to what his attitude should be in determined eventualities; as I had had time and opportunity during the past 25 years to form a fairly reliable opinion of him, I was absolutely convinced that neither the years that had passed nor the life of a parliamentarian which he had led during recent years would lessen in any degree his power of decision, his readiness for action or his spirit of sacrifice in the face of new dangers which might arise; the

expression of this opinion, which is no more than what I believe to be true, visibly impressed and satisfied my listener, and, I think, removed any doubts he had.[96]

Kerney had declined to speak on behalf of any other policy than the present one of decided neutrality: "As regards the view that neutrality was of necessity a policy which some day would have to be succeeded by a more active decision, I could not venture to express any opinion."[97] He reminded Veesenmayer that although Ireland desired full territorial unity, military action against England would only foster "revenge" and "hatred" against Ireland's immediate neighbor and jeopardize vital economic ties.[98] If Germany invaded, the Irish government would ask Britain for assistance: "If Germany were to be the aggressor, England would, in her own interest, come to Ireland's assistance—and, I added, we would scarcely be in a position to refuse that help, even if we wanted to—and that the position would be somewhat similar if aggression were to come from the English or American side. There could be no question for us of abandoning neutrality in exchange for concessions of any kind."[99] The tone of Kerney's answers reflected a more mature man who had moved past his earlier anti-English attitude during the War of Independence and the post-treaty period. He had mellowed with age, and although he lamented partition, he did not take delight in England's being weak. It is at this point that he turned on Veesenmayer and, point by point, detailed how the one country that had done more harm to Ireland in the present war was in fact Germany.

Kerney began by stressing German violations of Irish neutrality: "If Germany was sincerely desirous of helping Ireland economically, it was a great pity, I said, that she had sunk some of the ships, such as the 'City of Bremen' and no doubt the 'City of Limerick' and others, of our budding merchant navy."[100] He reminded Veesenmayer of other breaches committed by Germany—"I reminded him of certain incidents, such as the dropping of parachutists" to undermine Irish neutrality as well as German efforts to liaise with the IRA—that had demonstrated anything but a friendly attitude: "An attempt to form contacts without the knowledge or consent of the Government."[101]

Veesenmayer had, throughout their meeting, lied about his part in such operations, claiming he never knew Seán Russell, and then said that, as far as Ribbentrop's Foreign Office was concerned, the Germans had never carried out clandestine activities but had always supported de Valera's neutral policy, which was a complete falsehood: "The Foreign Office (i.e. Ribbentrop, representing the Führer) was in complete control, and they had not entered into relations with any organisation of any kind—the IRA or any other—in Ireland; he [Veesenmayer] repeated that assurance solemnly when I ventured to express a doubt, and said that the last thing they wanted to do was to make things more difficult for Mr de Valera, whose policy they thoroughly approved of and admired, and he added that the only channel used by the Foreign Office was Hempel."[102] It appeared that Kerney saw through these lies and knew what type of man Veesenmayer really was, interjecting on several occasions to challenge him: "In reply to questions of mine, he said that Germany had no intention whatever of invading Ireland. . . . I suggested that it might suit Germany's purpose at some time to act without our knowledge."[103]

The last page of Kerney's report detailed Veesenmayer's assurances that Germany wanted nothing from Ireland and would never invade the island unilaterally. To this, Kerney, aware that the German was "reflecting the views of his friend and master, Ribbentrop," had asked for a memorandum outlining how Germany believed it was going to win the war because, as the diplomat reminded him, there was also the enormous military-industrial might of the United States to contend with in addition to the Soviet Union, Britain, and the Commonwealth of Nations: "I asked him to make and let me have a memorandum of the German position in the war and of the arguments which might go to prove that victory for Germany was as certain as he believed it to be. . . . I also made the suggestion that, even supposing the war in Europe were to be terminated by the collapse of England, there still remained the USA."[104]

Kerney had ended the discussion by inquiring about Frank Ryan and letting it be known that if the man should ever try to return to Ireland at any time, the Irish government ought to be notified: "I thought that it would be mere prudence on the part of the authorities to have him watched, and that it might even be desirable to have him interned as, otherwise, his return from Germany to Ireland might be misinterpreted in certain quarters and cause unnecessary complications."[105] He had again stressed this point, "I said, he [Ryan] should never be allowed to return to Ireland or be sent there without our knowledge and consent."[106]

This report made it very clear that at no stage during the discussion had Kerney divulged any confidential information to Veesenmayer, and in all his answers to the German he had reiterated his government's determination to pursue an independent neutral policy. Veesenmayer, on the other hand, had disclosed confidential information on German military operations then ongoing, as well as on captured munitions and oil supplies. Kerney's skillful handling of the meeting mirrored de Valera's clever handling of both belligerent sides. At a time when the balance of the war was still undecided, Kerney's robust defense of Irish neutrality over adventurism or vague promises of military assistance for the attainment of a united island serves as probably the best example of any Irish diplomat's defense of his country's national interests and neutral policy during World War II. He left the senior Nazi leadership in no doubt as to Ireland's commitment to stringent neutrality. This view is supported by Dermot Keogh, one of the few historians to cite the report: "Kerney gave the Nazi no words of support or comfort."[107]

ALL ROADS LEAD TO NOWHERE

What Dublin decided to do with this report is intriguing. Timelines, who knew what and when, and who was or was not in the know, come into play. We know that de Valera had heard of the report, because "Copies for T [Taoiseach]" is scribbled in pen on the top page of the original. We know that Walshe read it, as it was specifically sent and addressed to him that very day. There are also passages marked in the margins in pen, presumably by the secretary. What we do not know, first, is when the Taoiseach read Kerney's report. By now his eyesight was quite bad. The Spanish minister, for example, had noted as early as 6 January 1941 that de Valera's eyesight loss was "considerable."[108] When he passed a document across the table for him to read, the diplomat was amazed to see that the Taoiseach was unable to look at it properly. This loss of sight is confirmed by the clinical treatment de Valera was receiving from time to time and by the fact that secretaries of other government departments read reports to him throughout the war.[109]

It is plausible, given the Taoiseach's eyesight loss, that Walshe may not have shown this file to his superior when it was written in August 1942. The report was a resounding defense of neutrality by Kerney against a top Nazi, so there was justification—or a rationale, at the very least—for Walshe to withhold it to prevent Kerney from getting any credit for the meeting. On the other hand, it would have been a serious breach of duty for a senior civil servant to withhold from the Taoiseach such a critical file on German approaches to Ireland in the event of war with Britain. It is most likely, therefore, that Walshe read the document to de Valera, as many other secretaries did other documents on account of his eyesight trouble, and gave a sanitized synopsis of it that underplayed Kerney's strong defense of neutrality. The Taoiseach had in the past communicated via the secretary his gratitude to Kerney when the diplomat achieved a notable success, such as a trade deal, or when an important issue arose. This document was certainly of national and political concern, and for the Taoiseach to give Kerney no further instruction seems unusual.

Assuming that the Taoiseach was aware of the report on or around the time it was received, we encounter the next conundrum related to the report: Walshe's failure to pass it on to Colonel Dan Bryan of G2. In fact, Bryan was never shown this file by Walshe, and he became aware of it only thanks to Walshe's successor, Frederick Boland, in June 1946. Surely the record of this meeting between an Irish diplomat and a senior Nazi in Hitler's regime should have landed on the desk of Ireland's intelligence chief. Bryan was busy coordinating counterespionage measures against German infiltration and liaison with the IRA, as well as breaking German codes and cooperating closely with MI5's head of its Irish section, Captain Cecil Liddell.[110] He would have wanted to know what high-ranking German officials were thinking or planning in regard to Ireland. Kerney's report mentioned IRA figures (Seán Russell and Frank Ryan) in Germany that Bryan was interested in. In addition, the report noted sensitive military details, including information on captured munitions stock, oil supplies, and operational plans disclosed by Veesenmayer, all useful information for any intelligence agency.

Walshe and Bryan were frequently in contact throughout the war concerning any issue perceived to be a threat to Irish security from either a domestic or a foreign source. Walshe was passed files on Freemasons, foreign exiles, Jews, and dissident republicans who were monitored by G2 as suspicious elements and potential fifth columnists.[111] Walshe and Bryan corresponded and shared information on several German parachute drops into Ireland and also information on German-IRA collaboration. The two men already shared the view that Kerney was somehow suspect, so it is astonishing that Walshe did not show this pièce de résistance to Bryan. It was in the nature of Bryan's profession to find plots, conspiracies, and enemies. He would have quizzed Kerney about the meeting, how it had been arranged, who else had been involved, and why the Germans had specifically approached Kerney. If anyone could have gotten the necessary answers or had the doubts assuaged, it was Bryan.

By his very nature, Walshe was a peculiar man with notable "irascibilities," as Assistant Secretary Frederick Boland kindly put it.[112] Dermot Keogh noted, in his study of the secretary, that many of Walshe's failings in performance were entirely related to his obsessive "secretiveness" with information.[113] But perhaps the information in Kerney's report was even too hot or too sensitive to disclose to the Taoiseach fully or to Bryan at all, given the latter's working relationship with British intelligence, or perhaps Kerney's forceful defense of Irish neutrality in the report did not sit well with Walshe, who was using Bryan to tarnish Kerney's reputation behind his back.

The Germans expected a response to Kerney's report, but what seems to have happened is that no answer was given. The war was in the balance in August 1942 and was raging across the globe. Germany still controlled most of continental Europe, North Africa, and the western part of the Soviet Union. Only a few weeks before, an Allied landing at Dieppe had been repulsed with heavy losses. On the other hand, Britain and the Soviet Union were not yet defeated, and the entry of the United States was bound to have a major impact. No one could see who was going to win the war, so Walshe opted for staying on safe ground. If a reply to Kerney was given on behalf of his government saying that yes, Ireland was open to further discussions with the Germans, that could have led to future complications if the Allies found out and won the war. If a reply to Kerney was given that Ireland was not interested in any collaboration with Germany, that could have been dangerous, too, if Hitler won the war. Either option, viewed at the time, was risky, so no comment was given. With this approach, nothing was being committed to and nothing was being rejected.

From the facts available and the sequence of events that unfolded, it is likely that Walshe took this unilateral action because of one other important piece of archival evidence. Kerney did not disclose in his report that Clissmann was also present at the meeting with Veesenmayer and that it was Clissmann who had prepared the groundwork for the encounter. Walshe never asked Kerney how this meeting had been arranged in the first place, which was an obvious question to have been put to the diplomat. A top Nazi does not just show up and knock on the door of a legation. Someone had to have been a third party and arranged the meeting. Clissmann had been associated with Ryan in the past, he had had a role in Ryan's release, he had been familiar to Kerney and to Irish affairs, and he had been the source that confirmed Seán Russell's death, all of which Walshe knew. It is probable that Walshe suspected that Clissmann was the organizer of this meeting, given his role in the Ryan "escape" and his knowledge that Kerney had met Clissmann face-to-face in Madrid in November 1941, the outcome of which was that Kerney was able to confirm the death of Seán Russell via Helmut.[114] The secretary had not warned Kerney the previous year to avoid Clissmann given his known past Abwehr activities in Ireland. Walshe may not have done so because he was hiding something himself, a past association or even a past friendship with Clissmann that would explain why Bryan was not consulted on the Veesenmayer meeting and why there is no evidence of the

Taoiseach's reaction to or views of this German approach. In one of his postwar interrogations Clissmann had been given a list of names, from senior Irish politicians to civil servants, and asked whether he knew them through a brief encounter or personally. When Walshe's name was shown to him, the agent replied that yes, he did know him, and in fact he knew Walshe personally: As the record says, Walshe was "known well to Prisoner."[115] Walshe buried the file because he wanted to bury his own connections to Clissmann. If such a revelation had gotten into the public domain—that a senior civil servant was well known to or even acquainted with a former German agent in Ireland—it would have destroyed Walshe's career.

On the German side, the meeting had been disappointing. Clissmann himself already knew that the entire scheme was hopeless, yet he went along with it because it suited his own vested interests to do so. In his recollection of the meeting, he noted that Kerney had received Veesenmayer's statements "with a certain reserve."[116] Veesenmayer still hoped that something positive might materialize, but he himself knew that the scheme was, in reality, pure fantasy. Since 24 August the Germans had suffered a string of major setbacks: the North African landings ("Operation Torch" on 8 November 1942), defeat at El Alamein, and a crippling defeat at Stalingrad, all of which were beginning to turn the war against Germany. Ireland was no longer a consideration. On 23 January 1943 Veesenmayer wrote: "The question of the occupation of important harbours in Southern Ireland or in the whole of the Irish Free State, which in the Autumn of 1942 was much discussed, has for some time now been receding into the background."[117] He recommended that a handpicked detachment of SS noncommissioned officers (NCOs) that Reichsführer SS Heinrich Himmler had sanctioned for Veesenmayer's use now be redeployed to frontline combat: "The establishment of the special detachment of 120 picked SS men, mainly NCO's, which was sanctioned and carried out by the Reichsführer, in accordance with instructions of the Reich Foreign Minister and in cooperation with SS Standartenführer Schellenberg, will not now be proceeded with and [the men] will be freed for other and probably more urgent requirements."[118] Not surprisingly, Veesenmayer requested that he be excluded from any redeployment to a

combat zone and instead remain on as a central figure in Irish planning matters: "I would request authorization to continue this work
within considerably reduced limits so that in case of need a picked
group of ten to twelve men would at least be available, if called upon,
to go into immediate action. The task of this group, in the event of
their being ordered to go into action, would be to mobilise the forces
of resistance available in Ireland and to support them, and at the same
time to provide an efficiently functioning signal service."[119]

Kerney never gave Veesenmayer a deadline as to when he expected
to hear back from the Taoiseach. By January 1943 Veesenmayer was
skeptical that the Irish were taking the German proposals seriously
due to their long delay in replying to the approach: "My conversations
with the Irish Minister in Madrid, Kerney, as mentioned in my report
of September 28, 1942, have so far brought no results. From this we
must conclude that either Kerney, in spite of his promise, has initiated
no steps, or that de Valera because of his well-known over-cautious
attitude has, very probably, refused to take cognisance, even in the
slightest way, of our willingness to make precautionary preparation
for even modest assistance."[120] Kerney had, in fact, done his job and
passed the file on to Dublin for consideration. It was not until he
returned to Ireland in the spring of 1943 that he had his first face-to-
face meeting with de Valera. Veesenmayer hoped that this would be
the opportune time for a positive outcome for Germany.

The main record of what transpired at Kerney's meetings with
de Valera comes from diary extracts of the meetings he recorded and
from notes he took at the time of the libel case. On 27 March Kerney
and the Taoiseach discussed a variety of issues for over forty-five minutes in Iveagh House. The meeting was tense on account of Kerney's
misuse of the diplomatic bag but also because Kerney was threaten-
ing to resign from his position in Spain or else be reassigned unless
several grievances were addressed. These concerns mainly related to
his salary; the Department of Finance had made a sudden change by
lodging his wages in a Madrid bank account and not his normal one
in Lisbon. This had the effect of nearly halving Kerney's salary given
Spain's closed market, yet Walshe had done nothing to address this
issue up to this point. De Valera, who until then had shown nothing

but respect and care for Kerney, was rather harsh and stated his dislike of the fact that Kerney expected the Taoiseach to fight battles with officialdom on his behalf. For Kerney, however, these financial issues were life-and-death concerns. As he wrote to his brother: "We are both tired of this kind of life and long for a change. . . . I had a good deal of worry during the past year and so for some time I was anxious to clear out."[121]

At no stage was Veesenmayer's mission as Ribbentrop's emissary brought up by de Valera. Kerney found this surprising: "No reference whatsoever to Veesenmayer report of 24/8/42; not referred to by him [de Valera] nor by me," Kerney noted in his diary.[122] Further, the diplomat was not called by Walshe or Boland to give a debriefing on his mission in Spain, which he found extremely unusual, as he had expected that, at the very least, the Veesenmayer meeting would be the top priority for discussion, given the seniority of the Nazi he had met. As he wrote in his diary: "Also no invitation this time J.W. or FHB. Is it because suspect or in disgrace?"[123] Walshe's burying of the Veesenmayer report was later confirmed by Boland: "So far as I can recall, Kerney did not mention to me at any time during his stay in Dublin, the talks he is alleged to have had the previous year with emissaries of the German Government in Madrid. If he mentioned them to the then Secretary, the latter did not tell me."[124] The following month Kerney had another, longer, meeting with de Valera on 8 April from 4:00 to 5:20 p.m. during which the Taoiseach was very polite to him; they laughed and several issues of concern to Kerney were ironed out. Again there was no mention of the German approach. "Good-bye, good-luck" were the Chief's parting words.[125]

Kerney's notes from the time of the libel case provide more information on the Veesenmayer meeting, his reasons for seeing him, and how the report was received by Dublin:

> The interview must have lasted a couple of hours at least; I left them [Veesenmayer and Clissmann] there and returned home to my lunch; immediately afterwards I sat down (I had no siesta that day) and personally typed out a lengthy confidential report of our conversation whilst all the details were still fresh in my mind; neither my wife nor my assistant

[Maisie Donnelly] know anything of that report or of the interview which gave rise to it. It was sent home by the diplomatic bag, which of course was always exposed to violation in the post by the intelligence service of one country or another. I remember reflecting at the time that the interception of that document could produce no ill effect other than to show that the representative of a neutral country had dared to meet and converse with a high-placed German; I had indeed already rubbed shoulders with the heads of the British, American and Spanish intelligence services, in Madrid.

That report did not embody any offer or proposal or suggestion of any kind; it raised no questions; it showed what Mr Veesenmayer said and what I said; it did not call for any reply; it never received any acknowledgement or reply. When I returned to Ireland on a visit in February 1943, the matter was not referred to in any way by any official of the Department of External Affairs, nor by the Taoiseach, who was at that time also Minister for External Affairs. It had died a natural death. I was not the subject of any rebuke, sharp or otherwise.[126]

In July 1943 Kerney and Raymonde were in Bordeaux visiting her aging mother when Clissmann arrived in Biarritz to get feedback on Dublin's reaction: "We put up at the Carlton Hotel, where I met Mr Clissmann—whether by accident or design I do not clearly recollect, but it is possible that I may have given my prior assent to such a meeting."[127] The next day, 21 July, Kerney again met Veesenmayer for an hour in a park by the seafront at 8:30 a.m. He had little to say to the German except the facts:

I stated that I had sent home a full report of our previous conversation (24th August, 1942), but that it had not evoked any reply or any comment of any kind, and that, during my visit to Dublin in February, 1943, no reference whatsoever had been made to my report in any official discussions. Mr Veesenmayer appeared to be disappointed; he had apparently expected a reaction of some kind; I could do no more than acquaint him with the fact that there had been none. There was nothing more to discuss. I did not even remind him that he had not fulfilled his promise to furnish me with a report showing that Germany's position in the war was invincible. That was the last I saw of Mr Veesenmayer.[128]

The triangular meetings between Kerney, Clissmann, and Veesenmayer that had promised so much from a German viewpoint came to nothing in the end. The Germans lost interest in Ireland starting in 1943, not only as a result of this failed mission but also because the balance of the war was turning against Germany. Clissmann was reassigned to frontline service in North Africa, fighting in Tunis. He was captured by the Allies after the war and interrogated about his intelligence activities. The defeat of his grand project did not undermine Veesenmayer's career in the Nazi elite. He was promoted to SS Brigadeführer (brigadier) and reassigned by Hitler to Hungary to act as his plenipotentiary. The Nazis knew that Hungarian admiral Miklós Horthy's regime had sent out peace feelers to the Soviet Union, whose armies were massing on Hungary's borders, so the German dictator annexed Hungary. Veesenmayer, a virtual Gauleiter (regional Nazi Party leader), cajoled and threatened the Hungarians to round up the country's Jews. Veesenmayer worked with Adolf Eichmann to transport over 400,000 Hungarian Jews to the gas chambers at Auschwitz. After the war he was tried at Nuremberg and sentenced to twenty years' imprisonment for crimes against humanity. He was freed early in 1951. For Kerney the meeting with Veesenmayer was to overshadow his latter years after a prominent historian named Thomas Desmond Williams made this meeting public knowledge.

CHAPTER 9

CONFIDENTIAL REPORTS FROM FASCIST SPAIN, 1939–1945

Tom Garvin, in his analysis of the Irish economy during the war years, concluded that the senior echelons of the civil service, in particular the Department of Finance, did not want Ireland to reach out to the world economically. Instead, Garvin opined, the secretary of the Department of Finance, James McElligott, alongside other mandarins like Joseph Walshe, hoped Ireland would remain agricultural, non-industrialized, and effectively a nineteenth-century economy rather than a twentieth-century one: "[They] expected to see, and perhaps actually looked forward to, an Ireland which would be more or less as it had been previously: rural, pastoral, static, small-town and Jeffersonian in virtue and religiosity."[1] The problem with this insularity was that, unless Ireland reached out to Europe, not only its economy but also its diplomacy would suffer.

Economic nationalists had long advocated "protectionism for nascent Irish industries."[2] This had been a core principle of Sinn Féin and then Fianna Fáil. Kerney, like most, understood the need for some form of limited protectionism to build up indigenous manufacturing, and on one of the few occasions when he reflected on self-sufficiency he praised the government's efforts during the war: "We are struck with the change for the better since we were last home; much tilled land and many wheat fields all the way from Foynes to Dublin."[3] However, his overriding economic philosophy was to engage in free trade and to use diplomatic relations as the means to foster closer bilateral trade, particularly with continental Europe. Even before the war, it was clear that trade statistics did not lie. Irish manufactured products were simply not desired by continental countries. Instead these countries wanted Irish agricultural products. However, Finance was unwilling to move Ireland's agricultural economy away from Britain in the long term, and so Ireland kept producing industrial goods not wanted by other European states, with the inevitable outcome that the country was faced with a balance-of-payments deficit with almost every partner with which it traded. For example, Spain exported to Ireland £188,764 worth of goods in 1935 and £283,957 worth the following year.[4] The goods Spain exported (wine and fruit) were in demand by Irish consumers. By comparison, Ireland could export to Spain only £70,836 of goods in 1935 and £27,213 in 1936, with the balance met in hard cash. Kerney saw the opportunity caused by the Spanish Civil War and its destructive impact on Spain's crippled economy, which had made that country an ideal market for Irish agricultural goods and products to flood the market and rebalance trade in Ireland's favor with the commodities the Spanish wanted. Lively trade there would also naturally forge stronger political ties between Ireland and the new regime in Spain. Yet it is evident that Kerney's efforts were disregarded by Walshe, who clung to his conservative, anti-materialist outlook. An examination of certain files reflects this apathy.

On 10 April 1939, Irish political relations with fascist Spain were normalized following Kerney's official presentation of credentials to General Franco. Within a week, Kerney worked to open Spain up to Irish agricultural products, ensuring that Irish producers would get higher prices for their commodities than the British paid for them. On 17 April he sought Dublin's approval to travel to Bilbao to see the minister for industry and commerce, Juan Antonio Suances, to open negotiations on trade, but by 9 June he had received "no reply" from headquarters.[5] Undeterred, he decided to go "without authorization" and received formal permission only on 17 June, two months after he had made the request and after the trip had been concluded.[6] The outcome of the Suances meeting was that Spain was anxious to conclude a trade deal with Ireland as soon as possible. Kerney wired Dublin on 30 August for instructions and again on 2 September but received no reply despite the eagerness of the Spanish for a trade deal: "I wired again stating that the Minister for Foreign Affairs was anxious to foster trade with Ireland and that the Minister for Commerce was willing to start negotiations."[7] On 23 September he requested "permission to enter on preliminary negotiations," but again he received no reply until 23 October, and then only with instructions to begin asking "informally" about the parameters of a trade agreement.[8] On that same day he responded with trade analysis for the department as well as draft proposals. Not until 4 March 1940 did he receive any further instructions to begin formal negotiations on a trade agreement, and by 31 March there were no "further developments."[9] This negative response from Dublin stood in marked contrast to Ireland's Spanish counterparts, who believed that a negotiated trade deal could be reached easily, writing: "The Spanish authorities are now ready to begin negotiations on arriving at a speedy settlement for a Trade Agreement."[10] For Kerney it was another missed opportunity: "I now understand that the fomenting of direct trade is no longer a matter of prime importance."[11]

Clearly, for Walshe the priority in Irish foreign policy regarding Spain was not trade or economics but religion. He wanted Kerney to use all his time to build up Ireland's historic Catholic ties with Spain, which stretched back to the Irish colleges there, and he saw in a bloc of Catholic states a useful place for Ireland in the international community. When he did direct Kerney on Irish-Spanish relations it was usually around this issue of extending the hand of Catholic friendship to General Franco and letting the dictator know that all of Ireland, officially speaking anyway, had been behind him in the recent Spanish Civil War. The secretary pressed Kerney, for example, to personally hand a telegram from the Scouts of Ireland to Franco to show this Catholic sentiment. It read that the organization would like to bestow its "congratulations on his glorious victory in Spain."[12]

Behind this palaver Kerney discerned the realities of Francoist Spain and knew that from Franco's perspective religion was mere window dressing to disguise his authoritarian rule and fascist sympathies. Far from being a bastion of law-abiding Catholic virtue, the dictator was constructing a totalitarian state that impoverished his people and humiliated the defeated republican side. In a letter to his brother Maurice, Kerney revealed how he abstained from ever making an "outstretched arm" fascist salute at official occasions despite the extension of the gesture by other members of the diplomatic corps and said that he wished he could show his friendliness with the bygone Second Republic and its socialist identity "by saluting with a clenched fist."[13] Kerney's disdain for the Francoist regime would reflect itself in his wartime reports, which shattered official Irish perceptions of Franco's Spain. In one year alone, 1939–40, he furnished Dublin with over 134 political reports, many of which concerned crimes against humanity.[14] Walshe's ignoring of these compelling confidential reports stands as an indictment of his tenure as secretary of external affairs.

In July 1939 Kerney first informed Dublin that Franco's regime was killing people indiscriminately. He noted hearing of "unofficial arrests in Madrid and of corpses being found daily in the vicinity of a Madrid cemetery."[15] Kerney believed that Franco's continued killing of his political opponents would have drastic consequences for millions of people: "There are no signs of increased production. With hundreds of thousands killed, hundreds of thousands in exile and hundreds of thousands in concentration camps, Spain is deprived of a very large proportion of skilled and unskilled workers."[16] When World War II broke out, Franco declared the "strictest neutrality" in the conflict, which was what the nation needed—time for reconstruction and rebuilding—and said he backed the Vatican's call for peace.[17] However, Kerney was unimpressed by Franco's appeals for peace and by his styling himself as a man of faith while organs of his regime were still arresting and murdering opponents. On 21 October Kerney passed on to Walshe a list of newspaper cuttings from *Ya* and *Arriba* that detailed the arrest of forty-two people that day. Some detainees listed included a German Jew whose extradition back to Germany had been requested by the Gestapo, which cooperated extensively with its Spanish counterpart under a secret agreement signed on 25 November 1937.[18] The rest had been arrested for "red activity," "assassination," being members of the "communist branch," and having signed "death sentences."[19] All these people were subject to the retrospective Law of Political Responsibilities, which had come into being on 9 February 1939. Enríque Súñer, professor of medicine at Madrid University, was the president of the "National Tribunal for Political Responsibilities."[20] In the opinion of Mary Vincent, such repression was symptomatic of the dictatorship: "The Francoist regime was born in violence and depended on violence. Killing was essential to its initial display of power."[21]

Kerney could rely on other sources of information to ascertain and verify the scale of the arrests and persecutions being undertaken by the security organs of the Spanish state. In a conversation with the Belgian ambassador, the envoy was informed that four hundred people, including priests, had been arrested at a church for demonstrating alleged separatist sympathies.[22] He informed Walshe not only that people were being "arrested and imprisoned daily" but that mass executions were being carried out.[23] One of his reliable sources was an unnamed doctor who voiced privately to Kerney his shock and disgust at the scale of the crimes being committed. The doctor was ordered to be present at one execution in Alcázar de San Juan to certify the death, and he described his complete revulsion toward a priest who argued to him that there was a rational and sound basis for the killings—purification of the race.[24] The doctor's information was entirely reliable, Kerney said, and he declared: "I have just got very direct proof of the shooting of a batch of 50 prisoners, ten at a time."[25] He himself regularly heard shots fired in nightly executions throughout the capital: "I have often heard in the middle of the night (generally between 3 and 4 a.m.) shots fired in the vicinity."[26]

Kerney had a high-level contact "close to one of the Cabinet Ministers" who furnished him with detailed and secret information that the public was not hearing.[27] First, the regime had begun the "export of oranges from Valencia" and bananas from the Canary Islands at a time when famine, malnutrition, and disease were widespread throughout the country.[28] Everywhere, he was informed, people were suffering. In Bilbao, a coastal city with access to fish as a source of food, the people were suffering from severe "hunger."[29] In Asturias, too, the people were living at subsistence level because all of the male population, which traditionally had worked in the mines, was "interned" for being politically suspect.[30]

Spain appeared on the edge of a precipice in the summer of 1940, and Kerney feared that Franco might throw in his lot with the Axis powers. He advised Dublin to plan emergency measures for Irish citizens should Spain join the war as direct air and sea links were cut between the countries and "starvation" threatened Spain.[31] The Spanish minister in Dublin, Juan Garcia Ontiveros, spread rumors that Kerney had advised all Irish citizens to leave Spain immediately. Kerney demanded an apology: "Please do not believe any false rumours spread by Spanish Legation. I have taken no such action. Request Spanish Minister to justify his attitude by giving details or else to apologize."[32] Instead Walshe backed the Spanish minister and accused Kerney of causing "mischief" and "friction."[33] The diplomat openly challenged Walshe, writing him: "You left me in the dark. . . . All Irish citizens are entitled to the protection of this Legation under any circumstances."[34] The tone of this correspondence highlighted the deep-rooted animosity between the secretary and the diplomat that regularly surfaced during the war.

Undaunted by Walshe's personal enmity toward him, Kerney continued to furnish reports about mass killings. In another report in March 1940, Kerney recalled that from 10:30 until 11:30 p.m. he "listened to almost continuous shooting which began not far from the Legation."[35] The diplomat also sent Walshe visual confirmation of Franco's crimes against his own people. Visual imagery can be an emotive medium for transmitting the reality of a situation better than words or a written account can, and inside the confidential file for this period is a photograph that Kerney had acquired from Ocaña prison. In the photograph are shown over forty men, young and old, "mostly Basque" priests who were still dressed in their cassocks.[36] This evidence of Franco's arrest of priests highlighted the emptiness behind the façade of Catholic virtue in which he shrouded his regime.

It must be remembered that back in Ireland the public was being told on the leading broadsheets, like the *Irish Independent*, that Franco's regime was popular and rested on the "sound base of the will of the united Spanish people."[37] Their editors freely admitted that they had done "all that in us lay to secure the enthusiastic support of the Irish people for the Spanish Nationalist cause" during the Spanish Civil War.[38] They continued this deception with articles that made Franco's rule sound like a paradise for workers, who enjoyed "free treatment in spas and health resorts, family allowances, workers' insurance, loans, medical assistance, old-age insurance."[39] Not surprisingly, the majority of the Irish public, pressured by the Catholic hierarchy and the political establishment, read these newspaper accounts and welcomed Ireland's ties with a fellow Catholic state.

Kerney's wartime reports were not known to the Irish people, and the truth was not revealed or disclosed in any way by Walshe. At no stage did the secretary call in the Spanish minister in Dublin to account for, verify, or refute Kerney's reports. At no stage was the department's legal advisor, Dr. Michael Rynne, called in to draft a protest note to the Spanish. At no stage was any utterance about the department's knowledge of mass crimes raised in the Dáil by the Taoiseach. This again raises the role of Walshe in his handling of these sensitive documents. It is entirely probable that the Taoiseach and minister for external affairs, Éamon de Valera, was not being shown these pieces of damning evidence on account of his poor eyesight. These unread documents belied the perception that it was the Second Republic and its supporters who had been the criminals in the Spanish Civil War. The guns had fallen silent, yet Franco, despite his victory, was still executing people without any judicial restraint or accountability. Recent research has corroborated Kerney's wartime accounts. Paul Preston argued that the true number of Franco's executions "may be in the region of 130,000."[40]

Kerney did broach the topic with Franco's all-powerful brother-in-law and Minister for Foreign Affairs, Ramon Serrano Súñer, by using the pretext of religion to discuss Ireland's experience after its civil war. He outlined Ireland's path to reconciliation as initiated by de Valera, whose subsequent efforts to "reunite our divided forces" had healed many deep wounds in the body politic, as Kerney contended.[41] De Valera had adopted a "non-victimisation" policy toward his political opponents that had been "far-sighted" at the time, Kerney argued.[42] This measure had stabilized the nation, and now all grievances were aired and resolved within a national parliament and not by the use of violence. The inference was clear: Spain should use the example of Ireland, combined with its Catholic faith, to bind and heal the nation's wounds. Súñer listened but was not persuaded because his mind was driven by a political ideology that overrode all other considerations. Kerney, from his own past experiences, naturally felt sympathy toward the plight of the defeated side in Spain's civil war, but his words fell on deaf ears. Just two days later, the German ambassador sent a "Top Secret" message to Berlin: "In reply to the request made by the Embassy in accordance with instructions, the Foreign Minister has now stated that the Spanish Government has agreed to the disposition of German tankers in remote bays along the Spanish coasts for refuelling German destroyers. The Foreign Minister strongly urged that the utmost discretion be observed in carrying out these operations."[43]

Kerney's exposures continued regardless of Dublin's indifference. In four separate reports, three titled "Death Sentences" and one titled "Executions," he exposed, through informants and confidential contacts that reached into the Spanish cabinet and army, the gruesome and sinister scale of Franco's retribution, the extent to which it turned neighbor against neighbor, and the military's role in the macabre process. At the time that he wrote these reports, it had been over four years since the Spanish Civil War had officially ended.

The first report, compiled on 8 June 1943, concerned a group of people on trial for alleged communist activities. Kerney's informant was a devout Basque Catholic and ardent anti-communist who was "pulling every string to save the life of his nephew, one of the condemned men."[44] The condemned man was on trial for his life on a charge of "having endeavoured to re-organize the communist party," Kerney informed Walshe.[45] There was no shortage of witnesses to corroborate the charges against him. Many who had supported Franco in the Spanish Civil War, and who had lost relatives as a result, held a bitter "vindictiveness" toward those who had lost, the diplomat noted.[46] Their attitude was "unforgiving," and they continuously denounced those in the Basque regions: "[Especially] in places like Santander, Bilbao and towns of smaller size, life is made difficult if not impossible for any who were associated with the 'red' side."[47] Kerney was aware of one such woman, who had lost her husband and son during the conflict and who was unsparing in her efforts "to see that sentences of death" should be meted out by the military, whose courts carried out such sentences "with so much ease."[48]

Kerney believed that all this killing would only exacerbate the schisms within Spanish society, remembering as he did his own experience of the tragedy of the Irish Civil War. Even the appeals of ecclesiastics failed to halt the persecution. On 17 June Kerney reported that there were "150 persons awaiting execution in one Madrid prison [Porlier] alone."[49] He reported that even the papal nuncio, the Vatican's representative to Spain, had tried to intercede with the minister for war, General Cabanillas, and with Franco himself, on behalf of a "Basque nationalist."[50] His efforts were unsuccessful, as the regime was determined to unmask all its enemies and solidify its position through the use of arbitrary terror, which was unrestricted by law. There was no compunction of conscience against arresting women, and the diplomat was aware of several girls of "high moral character" who had been arrested for allegedly "ridiculing the head of the State" and for passing on "military information to France."[51] They faced a mandatory sentence of thirty years' imprisonment if found guilty by the court.

On 23 September Kerney passed on information he had received from an officer attached to a military court.[52] The young officer imparted what it was like to be present at an execution. His job was to sign the death sentence of the court and to be present at the execution site to ensure that the sentence was carried out. Normally the condemned were shot in batches of "usually about 40."[53] The men were "roped together, wrist to wrist," and marched toward the firing squads, which normally consisted of ten or twelve soldiers.[54] The officer stated that "a man awaiting his turn to be shot often has a dead or dying neighbour pulling him down on one side."[55] Kerney's reliable contacts reached into the upper echelons of the regime to "a member of the Government."[56] He informed Dublin that at a meeting of ministers it was proposed that they commute 470 death sentences and carry out "44 other death sentences."[57] The cabinet knew of and sanctioned these executions. One must also bear in mind that, in addition to continuing the killings, the regime was forcing thousands of republican prisoners to work as slaves to build an enormous monument to the nationalist dead in Cuelgamoros Valley outside Madrid. This project had begun in 1940 and took over eighteen years to complete. Franco personally chose the site, which, from an engineering perspective, was most unsuitable. The land was composed of granite, yet the regime supplied the prisoners only with basic tools and primitive machinery. The project cost a fortune at a time when the nation could hardly feed itself. Like Hitler and Mussolini, Franco wanted a monument of gargantuan proportions that would project his greatness and power in architectural form. Carved inside the granite hill was an ornate basilica, and atop the hill stood a five-hundred-foot cross. When it was completed, the site became known as the Valley of the Fallen, or Valle de los Caídos.

The killing of opponents on the grounds that they were suspected to be communists and former supporters of the Second Republic continued throughout the war years, and in fact continued until after the war in Europe had ended. On 29 January 1945, nearly six years after the Spanish Civil War was officially declared over, Kerney detailed how the regime had constructed a new prison on the outskirts of Madrid where mass executions were carried out in the courtyard: "On Sunday 21st January there were 77 executions."[58] On 13 June, in another report, titled "Executions," the diplomat informed Walshe of the following: "As I lay awake; in the early hours of Tuesday, 12 June I heard a volley of shots in the vicinity, followed by several 'coup de grace', and I presume that a batch of condemned prisoners was disposed

of on that occasion."[59] These reports, based on the diplomat's contacts within the Spanish Army and the cabinet, as well as confidential
informants, offer a window into the appalling crimes committed by
the Francoist regime in the post–civil war period, crimes that Paul
Preston has labeled a "Spanish holocaust."[60]

That a democratic state like Ireland, which prided itself on a constitution that enshrined and recognized the rights and civil liberties of
its people, continued to maintain diplomatic relations with a deplorable regime in the face of overwhelming evidence of state-led and
state-orchestrated murder is in itself an indictment of Irish foreign
policy in this period and of those in charge of its stewardship. Moreover, that a nation whose international outlook was so intertwined
with principled Catholic rectitude chose to remain silent about crimes
committed by a Catholic ally highlighted the moral bankruptcy of this
position. De Valera had always championed an independent Irish foreign policy as an expression of sovereignty, and being aligned with
a repressive regime was not in Ireland's interests, especially in view
of the inevitable triumph of the Western liberal democracies against
German and Italian fascism. The Irish public had been appalled by
the anarchy and lawlessness of the Spanish Republic, yet Franco's
crimes dwarfed these in comparison, and Ireland's representative on
the ground was providing indisputable proof that unchristian acts of
violence were being sanctioned by a Catholic head of state and fascist
regime. By remaining silent, the Irish state was in effect siding with
the oppressor against a horrifying injustice.

It is astonishing that Walshe remained silent on these reports
and took no action beyond filing them away. Perhaps their explosive
content seemed too much to show to his superior, and de Valera's
poor eyesight accorded Walshe the flexibility to act in this manner.
However, if the Taoiseach was being notified about these reports, his
silence reflects poorly on his political leadership as does his failure to
stand up, as the democratically elected representative of a Catholic nation that respected human rights, and denounce these killings. It seems
that the Irish government's deliberate blindness to these crimes against
humanity was in keeping with its overall silence on other atrocities in
Europe of which it was well informed. Thomas Bartlett highlighted

the case of the Nazi crimes against Jews, to which he found a similar moral indifference: "He [de Valera] chose to ignore this moral dimension to the war and he continued to do so even as the first footage of Buchenwald and Belsen concentration camps was being shown in cinemas everywhere in Europe (though not in Ireland)."[61]

Despite the fact that a significant proportion of his wartime confidential reports exposed crimes against humanity by a fascist state, Kerney has been singled out for criticism by some historians for one act—offering condolences on the death of Adolf Hitler, the Nazi dictator responsible for the Holocaust among so many other crimes against humanity. Michael Kennedy highlighted this incident and noted that the diplomat "again proved to be something of a law unto himself," having acted without sanction.[62] Kerney always paid close attention to de Valera's speeches and actions, and when the Taoiseach himself called at the German legation in Dublin and offered his condolences on the death of Adolf Hitler, the diplomat did so as well in accordance with diplomatic protocol, as Ireland retained diplomatic relations with Germany, in spite of the many unneutral acts Germany had committed against Ireland during the war. As de Valera himself said at the time: "I acted correctly and I feel certain wisely."[63] Kerney acted likewise and in accordance with de Valera's actions, actions the Taoiseach deemed correct: "It is of considerable importance that the formal acts of courtesy paid on such occasions as the death of the head of a State should not have attached to them any further special significance, such as connoting approval or disapproval of the policies of the State in question or of its head. It is important that it should never be inferred that these formal acts imply the passing of any judgement good or bad."[64]

A NEUTRAL ALLIANCE—PLAN D

Ironically, it was through the mystical chords of religion that one of the few acts of bilateral cooperation between Ireland and Spain took place during World War II. Beyond the rhetoric of Catholic affinity, Ireland had no means to reach out to Spain to cooperate on an international level even in this sphere, and Walshe provided little or no encouragement for such a venture. Any act of cooperation between these two supposedly Catholic, neutral nations during the war was always initiated by Spain. On 10 September 1942, Kerney secured a personal meeting with the minister for foreign affairs, General Francisco Jordana, who was eager to align Spain more closely with neutrality and other Catholic states.[65] He greeted Kerney warmly with an *abrazo*, which the diplomat informed Dublin was "an arm around the shoulder, in the way customary between Spaniards who are good friends."[66] He perceived the symbolic gesture to be an indication of Spanish perceptions of Ireland as one of its closest allies in the international arena. The men discussed neutrality, with Jordana assuring Kerney confidentially that he would fight to pursue a more stringent neutral policy. Kerney reiterated his government's adhesion to "unswerving" neutrality.[67] The meeting was perceived by the Spanish as very important, as Jordana, without disclosing his proposal at this meeting, was looking to Ireland to form a neutral bloc of Catholic states to broker a peace agreement between the Allies and the Axis.

Jordana followed up on this meeting by traveling to Lisbon on 18 December to hold high-level talks with the Portuguese minister for foreign affairs and prime minister, Dr. Oliveira Salazar. Portuguese foreign policy had maintained a benign neutrality that favored the Allies, but Salazar had always desired, in tandem with this, a closer working relationship with Spain that would slowly accustom Franco to stricter neutrality. On 20 December the first soundings of a possible Bloque Ibérico, or Iberian Bloc, began to be discussed. Spain had signed two treaties with Portugal during the war,[68] and Jordana believed that a mutual alliance would safeguard the Iberian Peninsula from invasion, cause Spain to gravitate toward the Allies, hinder the furtive provisioning of U-boats and other clandestine activities by senior Falangists in the regime, and serve as "an instrument of peace and safeguard of the highest moral values."[69] He wanted the Bloque Ibérico to propel Spain into the international arena by playing the role of honest broker between the warring sides. Franco liked the idea of being perceived as an international statesman and mediator. It could enhance his standing with the Vatican, the Spanish church, and Catholic nations like Ireland by propagating an image of him as a pacifist. It could possibly also assist the Axis during this difficult period for the New Order by splitting the Western Allies from their friendship with the Soviet Union. On 6 January, at the annual New Year's dinner for the diplomatic corps, Franco spoke at length with the British ambassador, Sir Samuel Hoare, and outlined his theories on the future course of the war. His theory was that a stalemate akin to the one that had occurred during World War I would ensue and that the West could not defeat Hitler but rather should join forces with him to stop the advancing Soviet armies from enslaving Europe. Franco thought that the time was ripe for an "honourable peace."[70]

On 7 January Jordana called on the Irish legation to have lunch with the Kerney family and build on his personal rapport with the diplomat.[71] Over coffee the topic of discussion revolved around Jordana's recent visit to Portugal. Kerney was intrigued to learn about Jordana's proposal for a bloc of neutral like-minded states that would work to implement peaceful reconciliation in the world based on the principles expounded by Pope Pius XII on 24 December 1939. Jordana informed him that this idea had been outlined in a memorandum he had presented to the Portuguese ambassador on 6 November titled "Plan D." Following this conversation Kerney met José María Doussinague, the director general of the Political Section in the Ministry of Foreign Affairs, on 11 January to receive a copy of the memorandum. In his postwar memoirs Doussinague recalled that at that meeting the Irish minister had said that he completely identified with the proposed intentions of Plan D and that, as he knew the "intimate thoughts" of the Taoiseach, he was confident that Ireland's adhesion to such a neutral bloc of nations was all but assured, something Kerney strenuously refuted after the war.[72] It was politically expedient for the Spanish to encourage Irish participation in Plan D, as Ireland's standing in the international arena as a Catholic and staunchly neutral nation had long been established. Furthermore, because direct air and sea links between the nations had been closed for some time owing to the war, it was hoped that Plan D offered a platform for both nations to reinvigorate and enhance bilateral relations.

On 9 February, shortly before the Kerney family was recalled back to Dublin for a long-overdue holiday, Doussinague compiled a report on his interpretation of the third meeting he had with Kerney, which took place over lunch at the Irish legation that day.[73] As a consequence of this meeting, he informed Jordana that the moment had come to give "greater consideration" to the implementation of Plan D.[74] The Spanish sought "closer contact with the countries that are remaining outside of the conflict," especially with those that shared a similar "spiritual and religious" formation—Spain, Portugal, Ireland, and the Vatican.[75] These countries could unite, under Spanish leadership, to form a bloc based on Christian "civilisation" and justice that would cooperate to end the "violent waves of passion and hate" that afflicted mankind.[76] The Spanish hoped that Ireland and Spain would adopt a "similar international position" that would champion the cause of peace, morality, and ethics above materialism and belligerency.[77] Plan D was therefore a program to be implemented prior to the inevitable "Peace Conference" between the warring factions, at which Ireland and Spain would act as moral advisors to both sides.[78] In another file Doussinague recorded his own hopes that Plan D would also "make Spain a great power" and showcase the nation as the "number one Catholic country" in the world.[79] He put great store in Kerney to be able to win over the Taoiseach to the idea.

To Kerney the whole plan was ludicrous. His reports detailing the murderous crimes of the Spanish regime made it clear that Spain was the most unsuitable candidate to lead any mission of Christian peace and harmony. Nevertheless, he duly passed on the Spanish proposal to his government. In External Affairs, Joseph Walshe looked with skepticism on Plan D: "While we are interested in it, we do not consider that our best interests would be served by involving ourselves in any commitments in the matter at the present juncture."[80] It seemed to Dublin to be a rather impractical plan, as the Allies had already rejected any notion of a peaceful détente with the Axis at the Casablanca Conference, during which they had stressed their insistence on unconditional surrender. Equally, Hitler's desire for *lebensraum* in the East had not abated despite suffering a crippling defeat at Stalingrad.

It seemed equally incomprehensible that either side would be will-ing to listen to peaceful overtures from Franco, given the insignificance of Spain and the distrust with which the Spanish dictator was regarded by both warring camps. The Irish did not like the idea of Spanish hege-mony over such a neutral bloc and believed it would be manipulated for purely political ends, though again no mention was made in Exter-nal Affairs of the crimes committed by the regime, which made it from the start an unsuitable candidate to lead such a bloc. For Dublin, the Vatican was a much preferable leader for any neutral grouping. If the Spanish were unwilling to acquiesce in this regard, the Irish believed the only achievable outcome for Plan D was the formation of a neu-tral bloc based not on political affinities but rather on humanitarian concerns to help the thousands of impoverished and displaced people whose lives had been dislocated by the war. Dublin passed on this suggestion to the Catholic hierarchy, which responded favorably to the proposed formation of a humanitarian rather than a politically ori-entated organization.

At the same time that Jordana and Doussinague were sounding out Irish opinion on Plan D, Joseph Walshe had received correspon-dence from the Irish Red Cross Society (IRCS) outlining that orga-nization's viewpoint that Ireland could play a role in the "Christian work of relief" throughout Europe.[81] Its chairman, Conor Alexander Maguire, was president of the High Court and a fervent supporter of the Spanish regime. From other channels the department also re-ceived requests concerning the formation of a Christian and humani-tarian organization. On 21 January the Irish high commissioner to Britain, John Dulanty, had met with Bishop David Mathew and the former British high commissioner for refugees under the protection of the League of Nations, Sir Neill Malcolm, and reported the out-come of that meeting to Walshe. The Irish Women Citizens and Local Government organization also contacted the department in the hope that Ireland would use its international standing as a devout Catholic nation to begin to help war refugees in Europe and, if need be, to work with other neutral nations to achieve this goal.

One of the few admirable services that Franco rendered during World War II was to refuse to close the Spanish frontier with France.

Economic and political considerations lay behind this decision, but nonetheless it enabled countless numbers of Allied airmen who had been shot down over German-occupied territory to escape over the Pyrenees and pass through Spain en route to Gibraltar. In addition, the Nazi persecution of the Jews, which accelerated in the later years of the conflict, forced thousands of Jews to use this escape route to prevent deportation to German concentration camps. We must not forget that the Francoist regime was openly anti-Semitic.[82] When the German Army overran the Greek port city of Salonika, Franco did nothing to protect the Sephardic Jews living there. The city was the center of Sephardic religious and cultural life, and many of its inhabitants, who were descendants of the Jews that had been expelled from Spain in the fifteenth century, spoke a Judeo-Spanish language and still identified themselves with their Spanish heritage. The German persecution of the Sephardic Jews began with their obligatory wearing of the Star of David and eventually led to their forced deportation to concentration camps in the spring of 1943. Despite this failing, Franco must be acknowledged for indirectly saving thousands of Jews from the gas chambers by keeping the Spanish border with France open.

Once these Jews entered Spain, they were confronted with the same problem that afflicted the Spanish people—lack of food. The nation could not shoulder the burden of more mouths to feed, and the Jews had few belongings left once the German authorities had seized their homes and goods. It was these Jewish refugees that the IRCS, the Catholic hierarchy in Ireland and Britain, and other humanitarian organizations particularly wanted Joseph Walshe to aid. On 12 February 1943 Dulanty contacted the Spanish embassy in London but was informed that "there are no refugee children in Spain."[83] The Irish counsellor in London, John Belton, knew this to be untrue, as he was aware of "certain Spanish Doctors who kept drugs supplied for refugees and either gave them to their own private patients or sold them in the Black Market."[84] The high commissioner for refugees informed Walshe that by the commission's estimates approximately ten thousand Jewish refugees, including women and children, were in Spain in December 1942. Many were located in makeshift camps, with no money and hardly any food during the winter. On 19 February 1943

Belton approached the Spanish to verify or deny these figures but was informed that "to cross the Pyrenees by difficult mountain passes, [was] a journey that no child could make."[85] That thousands of republican children had done just that to escape Franco's armies after Barcelona was captured was a fact not advanced by Belton to his counterpart on this occasion.

As a result of these conversations and meetings, the Spanish began to realize that Irish interest in Plan D was a purely humanitarian one based on religious charity. Their ambassador in London, the Duke of Alba, wrote to Jordana on 25 February to make him aware of this reality.[86] He confided that it had been "absolutely impossible to discourage the Irish Government from its intention, without offending them."[87] He outlined a conversation that had transpired between himself and John Dulanty during which the Irish high commissioner had said that both Spain and Portugal, owing to their "political tradition and geographic position," were ideally suited to forge an international center for Christian aid that would help the "bereaved civilian populations of the continent" in the reconstruction of Europe under the guiding influence of the Catholic Church.[88] Alba informed Jordana that all this was a direct result of the commanding influence that the "hierarchy" exercised over all facets of Irish life and that the Church wanted to rechristianize Europe after the war under the guise of humanitarian work.[89] Based on Alba's report, Jordana realized that Ireland had no political desire to become part of Plan D unless it related to the formation of a neutral bloc of nations that worked for humanitarian relief. He therefore permitted the IRCS to organize such aid to help war refugees in Spain because "the initiative taken by the Irish Government is so generous in its intention and so expressive in its high ideal of Christian and Catholic collaboration" that refusal to acquiesce would be unthinkable.[90]

It was the Catholic hierarchy in Britain that first sent goods and officials to Spain to prevent a calamitous humanitarian disaster. The Dominions Office informed Dublin that it would allow an Irish ship to transport a thousand tons of goods for humanitarian relief, despite British scruples about having navicerts for all naval cargo, and confidentially informed Belton that they would not attempt to claim any credit for the relief effort.[91] On 25 February Walshe called on the Spanish minister, Juan Garcia Ontiveros, to set "a proper official footing" for Ireland's desire to "feed and clothe some of the thousands of refugees who were destitute in Spain."[92] Here was Walshe's dream of Catholic nations working together in international unity for the good of humanity. Ontiveros promised to "give every help in his power" to the enterprise.[93] It seemed that the approximate figure of ten thousand refugees given previously had been misstated. Kerney informed Dublin that the Spanish authorities did not classify children separately but rather counted only adults. In addition, Hitler's takeover of Vichy, France, after Operation Torch had precipitated a sudden influx of four thousand war refugees, who were interned in conditions of "great hardship and suffering."[94] The Spanish were, in Kerney's estimation, "not organized to cope with this sudden inrush."[95] At this critical time, even Protestant ecclesiastical leaders were prepared to put aside Franco's hostile attitude toward their faith in the hope that thousands of lives could be saved. Reverend G. Allen of the Presbytery of Letterkenny contacted the Department of External Affairs, urging them to aid these Jews who had escaped persecution by the Nazis.[96] De Valera preferred relief to asylum, and at a cabinet meeting held on 26 March he delegated Frank Aiken, minister for the coordination of defensive measures, with the responsibility of organizing the supply of two cargo ships for travel to Spain.

In order to do this, the Irish government needed the cooperation of the public. Aiken used the *Irish Press* to publicize the urgent need to supply foodstuffs and clothing to thousands of war refugees in Spain.[97] It could have been an arduous undertaking to persuade a people to donate tons of supplies given the debilitating impact that the war had had so far on domestic consumption and peoples' living standards, but the Irish public responded positively to the request. The fervor with which the public generously gave to the relief effort was entirely linked to missionary zeal and the Catholic connection. After all, the Irish public had always been informed that Franco was a pious and religiously devout Catholic head of state. Two hundred tons of sugar, potatoes, peas, powdered milk, and blankets were donated to the assigned depot and then shipped for the relief of these refugees under the auspices of the IRCS. It was a triumph for that organization, too. The mission was its first overseas enterprise since its foundation in 1939.

The IRCS dispatched two delegates: Colonel T. McKinney, director of Army Medical Services in the Irish Army and senior member of the central council of the society, and Captain Joseph G. Healy, a University College Cork lecturer in Spanish and former delegate to the Irish Manuscripts Commission in Spain. Both men flew from Foynes to Lisbon to await the arrival of the vessels for overland transport to the Spanish border. No news was forthcoming for some time except a report issued by the IRCS chairman, Conor A. Maguire, which stated that the "mission was successful, and that the Spanish Government and Spanish Red Cross had expressed their gratitude for the relief supplies of food that had been sent [to] them."[98] But Maguire was either ill informed or inclined to fantasy due to his pro-Franco sympathies, and the secretary of the IRCS, Martin MacNamara, felt obliged to contact Joseph Walshe to seek his assistance on 27 October. Alarmed by the news that the mission was not going quite as Maguire had stated, Walshe wrote to Ontiveros on 18 November 1943: "Dear Minister, no communication has been received from the Spanish Red Cross by the Irish Red Cross Society or by the Irish Representative in Madrid concerning the disposal of the relief supplies sent to the Spanish Red Cross Society in the Spring of this year. It would be encouraging to know that this first effort at collaboration between the Irish and Spanish Red Cross Societies had been a success, and I shall be grateful; if you can let us have information as soon as possible."[99] Ontiveros had known since 7 August that there was a major problem with the overseas mission, but he had chosen to deliberately withhold this information in the hope that news of the scandal would not surface in Dublin. On 14 August Jordana wrote to Ontiveros that if Irish ears heard of the calamity it would diminish the "prestige and noble tradition of Spain" in the eyes of the "generous donors" who had so willingly contributed to the effort.[100] Even after receiving Walshe's letter, Ontiveros said nothing in his report to Madrid to convey Dublin's concerns for the well-being of the refugees.

It was left to Kerney to inform Dublin about what had transpired. Since 15 June the relief aid had been held up at the Spanish border because the customs authorities wanted to charge an import duty on the goods.[101] The problem was that the import duty amounted to the cost of the goods. On 16 June Kerney had met a senior official in the Spanish Red Cross, Count Granja, to discuss the problem and see if the authorities would be willing to transfer the ownership of the goods to his name.[102] As a diplomat, Kerney would not have to pay an import duty, and the cargo could continue on its way to the camps of northern Spain. Bureaucratic delays between the customs authorities and the ministries of foreign affairs and finance delayed the consignment for so long that by August "the potatoes had already rotted," Kerney informed Dublin.[103] The Spanish Red Cross was unable to pay the duty, and the Falange's social wing, Auxilio Social, seized the consignment. This was another major blunder. The British Passport Control Officer in Madrid, a Mr. Crofton, confidentially informed his Irish counterparts that it was rumored that "Germany had secured possession of all of the supplies."[104]

The Falange had seized control of the goods so that individual members could sell them on the black market and make a handsome return. The secretary general of the Spanish Red Cross, Dr. Valero, privately scolded his government and senior officials for their behavior, which had made him "very much upset" owing to the humanitarian need in the country and the sincerity of the Irish in making their donations.[105] But neither he nor his colleagues could express their indignation publicly, as it "would land them in prison."[106] Valero wanted to bestow some award on Colonel McKinney, Captain Healy, or some senior "ecclesiastic," but Kerney objected.[107] Officially the Falange claimed that the consignment of peas had been given to the "needy populace" of Madrid and that the powdered milk was distributed to institutions for child assistance.[108] Walshe, a devout Catholic who had hoped that this gesture by Ireland would foster a new progressive direction in Irish-Spanish relations based on Christian charity and humanitarian concerns, did not mince his words in a note to Kerney. The whole scheme was "a complete failure," he wrote.[109] The

Spanish regime was riddled with "incompetency" at every level, and those who needed the aid would suffer the most as a consequence: "It appears that only a few pairs of blankets actually reached the refugees."[110] The neutral bloc was in tatters. Yet Walshe had gone along with the whole mission in the naïve belief that he was dealing with a morally upright regime. Despite report after report from Kerney during the war that had flagged the repressive, unchristian, corrupt, and dictatorial nature of Franco's regime, it took a disaster like this to finally awaken the secretary's eyes to reality.

With Ireland firmly opposed to forming a politically oriented neutral bloc under Spanish hegemony, the regime decided to continue to make peaceful overtures on its own. On 9 May 1943, at Almería, Franco spoke before cheering crowds declaring that a stalemate had been reached in the war as neither "of the belligerents has the strength to destroy its opponent."[111] On 16 April General Jordana spoke before diplomatic officials articulating his country's readiness to instigate peace overtures and to convene a peace conference between the warring sides. Spain's "dispassionate" plea for a "just and fraternal peace" would not only save millions of lives but forestall the insidious communist encroachment on European civilization, he argued.[112] Not surprisingly, Plan D came to nothing. It was an ill-conceived idea by a regime that had yet to realize the international opprobrium directed at it.

A DIPLOMATIC CONFERENCE AT IVEAGH HOUSE

When World War II ended, it brought to a close an intense period in Irish diplomatic activity. The country's diplomats were all but exhausted, and the war years had exposed major shortcomings in the operation of missions abroad, particularly concerning interdepartmental relations. Although embassies and legations were deemed essential for the Irish government, providing eyes and ears close to international events and to help form foreign policy, all foreign missions were chronically underfunded and understaffed, and their employees were poorly paid. Men like Kerney were willing to endure these privations and work industriously throughout their careers because they were patriotic and proud of their nation's achievements as an independent state, yet by the end of World War II they had had enough. An examination of the quarrels between Kerney and Joseph Walshe show that many arguments were caused by or directly related to the paucity of services made available to diplomats. Equally frustrating was the failure of Dublin to act on so many critical wartime reports, particularly, in Kerney's case, in relation to the department's silence on his reports of mass executions. For Kerney, like his colleagues on the continent, a sense of disillusionment crept into the diplomatic service as well because these men had been stationed away from home for far too long, and none were shown much sympathy by Walshe.

After the war the department recalled all its overseas diplomats for an important conference at Iveagh House on 11 September 1945. According to Walshe's biographer, Aengus Nolan, the purpose of the meeting was straightforward: "The aim was to initiate an assessment of its own foreign policies and procedures as it was recognised that it was important to analyse and reassess the organisation of External Affairs in light of the new international environment."[113] What Walshe did not expect in calling this important meeting was that it would provide a platform to Kerney and his colleagues to air their opinions, grievances, and shortcoming. De Valera was questioned about the outcome of the meeting in the Dáil by Opposition TD John A. Costello of Fine Gael. The Taoiseach responded that the meeting had been arranged for an "exchange of views and suggestions" and to coordinate a future strategy to promote "Irish interests abroad."[114] De Valera did not impart just how strong the exchange of views had been. Men like Kerney were no longer idealists. They were realists, and they were determined to highlight the grave deficiencies in Dublin's handling of their reports.

The diplomats compiled a joint résumé that castigated the department for failing to provide adequate staffing and financing to promote Ireland abroad. The situation was, they all judged, "so bad that an altogether disproportionate amount of routine and clerical work is thrown upon the Head of the mission."[115] De Valera was present at this meeting and was informed that despite his wishes to disseminate information on Irish culture and grievances over partition, the missions had no cultural attachés, were not provided with any books or translations of books in the languages of the resident countries, and were not supplied with any propaganda materials. Some diplomats argued that Ireland was further away from European integration now than in the past, recalling— "our [better] position in the 7th and 8th centuries when we were nearer to Europe, in spirit, than now."[116] These shortcomings reflected badly on the secretary and called into question his performance as the most senior administrator in External Affairs. For too long he had ignored repeated complaints by overseas mission heads about inadequate staffing and support, but, by extension, such criticisms naturally applied to the Taoiseach as well. A picture emerged of a department whose ministerial head might not have been allocating sufficient time to the running of the organization and who had allowed the secretary undue independence of action without regular and proper oversight.

In his relationship with Kerney, Walshe had never displayed any compassion for his plight, but Kerney had not been unique in this regard, as Dermot Keogh has noted. The secretary had had fractious relationships with many overseas mission heads.[117] When Walshe was presented with the résumé, he dismissed its criticisms as unfounded and misplaced. In the margins of the document he scribbled his own observations. He believed that Kerney and his colleagues undervalued good, hard, honest work. A more industrious attitude and dedicated performance would overcome many of the deficiencies noted, he argued, but by saying this the secretary was, incredibly, deflecting grumblings away from himself and back onto the authors of the résumé. He questioned whether, as a collective body, they were appreciative of the important role that they had undertaken for their government. The turn of phrase Walshe used indicated the types of diplomats he wanted overseas mission heads to be and how he envisioned Irish foreign policy—the diplomats should always behave as if they were "Apostles for this country."[118] This phrase shows the obsession with religion that had been a feature of Walshe's life from his time as a Jesuit seminarian. Whereas Serrano Súñer had dreamed of a Spanish diplomatic corps enthused with fascist zeal and ideology,

Walshe, in contrast, wanted a bizarre priestlike representative abroad. If this was his psychology, that of an extreme orthodox Catholic, it is not surprising that Kerney, as a convert to Catholicism and a less-than-strict adherent to the faith, was, in Walshe's eyes, less than acceptable as an overseas mission head to a Catholic state like Spain.

The secretary did endorse some proposals the diplomats had made, such as their suggestions that the department get Irish music and poetry aired abroad, but he disagreed with the idea that this should be done by the department using shortwave transmitters that would beam the broadcasts to foreign countries. An inherent civil service obsession with penny-pinching is evident in Walshe's views. He preferred that the diplomats use their own contacts overseas to gain airtime on their resident nations' national radio stations and thus save the Irish state money. Just how they were meant to do this was, as usual, never outlined by Walshe. He simply churned out instructions and recommendations and expected them to be carried out. His basic lack of understanding of how overseas missions were run, or should be run, stemmed from his own professional background—he had never run an overseas mission and had no idea how to do so. He had only been assigned to the Paris mission during the War of Independence before circumstances and events had propelled him rapidly to the most senior position in External Affairs with little practical experience. Another obvious flaw in Walshe's supervision of his department stemmed from his private life. He had never married and had no children. Diplomats who were married, like Kerney, struggled to provide financially for their family and dependents, yet Walshe failed to see their point of view regarding increased allowances. From his perspective it was an honor to be chosen as an "Apostle" of Ireland and to endure hardships to represent their country on the broader international stage.

It is difficult to gauge what contribution Kerney made to the résumé, as it is unsigned, but, given his difficult relationship with Walshe, an experience shared by most of the other diplomats, it is highly likely that he would have been a vocal critic of senior management in the department. All the diplomats agreed that a thirty-minute film titled *A Day in the Life of Catholic Ireland* should be produced to provide a visual image of Ireland abroad. The idea was that it could be shown in parish halls to hundreds of people and could act both as a cultural display and as a tourist attraction to get more visitors to the island. Yet again, however, Walshe vetoed the idea by writing in pen "obvious difficulty" and "public funds" at the margin of the paragraph.[119] The secretary showed little willingness to consider any proposals or to properly assess their feasibility. Like many senior civil servants at this time, Walshe was a firm advocate of the strict fiscal rectitude measures urged by the Department of Finance. He naturally opposed any additional expenses as unnecessary, however minor or trivial these expenses might be, in truth.

It was not until Walshe was posted to the Vatican as ambassador in May 1946—his life's ambition fulfilled—that the full scale of the gross deficiencies in Ireland's efforts to promote the nation abroad became evident to him. He had thought that hard work alone could overcome any obstacle, but now that he was on the front line he began to think differently, did a volte-face, and requested additional supports. De Valera knew that the Irish public would not tolerate large expenditures on overseas missions, but neither would they be happy to learn that their diplomats were surviving on a shoestring. For men like Kerney, idealism could be stretched only so far, and public servants deserved better terms and conditions of employment than what they had been enduring. Historians often credit de Valera for his handling of Irish foreign policy, but for too long he failed to listen to the obvious shortcomings, act on important reports, and pay heed to the distress felt by the diplomatic staff. It was left to Seán MacBride, de Valera's successor, to expand and develop the missions and to aid those who stood on the front lines of Irish foreign policy.

CHAPTER 10

NEW BEGINNINGS,
1946–1948

By 1946 Kerney wanted out of Spain and the diplomatic service entirely. All his children were back living in Ireland, pursuing their education, starting new families, or furthering their careers. Raymonde was also away looking for a new home to purchase and furnish when Kerney reached the statutory retirement age at the end of the year.[1] On his own, he felt lonely, with only the company of his loyal dog, Derry, to make up for the isolation. His mood was not helped by his poor financial position, which meant that he could barely make ends meet, let alone save any money. He was tired of living in a country ruled by a detestable dictator and a brutal regime that had caused such suffering for their own people. He wrote: "The food situation here has gone from bad to worse and it is a mystery to me how the people manage to live; it is the one topic of conversation everywhere and the situation, in that respect at least, is a catastrophic one."[2] Every day was a challenge—electricity was restricted to just three days' use per week, and, when it was on, the voltage was low and of poor quality. Obtaining drinking water was another test of his endurance, with the water collected by Spain's dams depleted by drought. The diplomat counted down the days to when he could finally settle down again and live in some form of normality in Ireland, something he had not done since childhood.

Yet both the Irish government and the Department of External Affairs wanted Kerney to stay on beyond his retirement in December 1946. This was a clear indication that both de Valera and the new department secretary, Frederick Boland, unlike Boland's predecessor, Joseph Walshe, had confidence in Kerney and his abilities. Walshe had been appointed as ambassador to the Holy See, according to his biographer Aengus Nolan, determined to strengthen "international faith, especially in the face of the growing threat of communism."[3] The department's request that Kerney remain in service showed the complete confidence that the Taoiseach maintained, and had always had, in Kerney and in his abilities as a diplomat and representative of his nation abroad. Despite the vote of confidence, Kerney was rather pessimistic about the offer, and he consulted his wife to gauge her opinion. Accepting would mean that he would receive a living salary rather than a pension that yielded less return: "The Taoiseach intends to give the 3 heads of missions who are due to retire this year an opportunity of staying on in their present posts on the usual conditions, if they wish to do so."[4] But for the first time in his life he was inclined to refuse an offer by de Valera: "I can only answer negatively."[5] He had endured much hardship for the republican leader over the years when idealism and a robust constitution drove him on, but now, with recurring health issues and fed up with serving his government on a shoestring, Kerney put his family first. He wrote to his wife that he was "disposed to refuse the offer," and she agreed.[6] He could finally look forward to retirement and being a grandfather.

ADIOS, ESPAÑA

The year 1946 still proved an eventful one for Kerney. His schedule was busy with visits from guests, artists, friends, fellow diplomats, the Loreto sisters, and other callers. He kept in weekly correspondence with Raymonde, informing her about his daily activities and who was asking for her at diplomatic banquets and on other official occasions. In April, Con Cremin stayed for a few days.[7] Cremin, who had already had a varied career in External Affairs, had served on several missions abroad and was a talent for the future: "I consider him a good colleague and a sincere friend," Kerney informed Raymonde.[8] Kerney was already letting Cremin and others know that he longed to be out of the diplomatic service: "I don't hide from them that we are thinking of leaving definitely at the end of the year."[9] Although not religious himself, Kerney kept up some retreats that Raymonde was involved in, which included visiting seven churches and donating money to the poor. On 18 April artist Nelly Harvey finally finished her portrait of the diplomat sitting in a chair holding his habitual cigar. He remarked to Raymonde: "I told Nelly that she had succeeded in reproducing my 'smirk' rather faithfully—'smile' she corrected me, a little indignantly."[10]

He kept up his golf to stay fit and busied himself with planning the move back home. The legation had several staff, including a gardener, a butler, maids, and a chauffeur, all of whom Kerney presented with gifts on the eve of his emotional departure. He searched for a nice present for his long-time typist, Maisie Donnelly: "Ordered another watch for Maisie; I really need to leave her a memento at the end of a collaboration which lasted over 11 years, and I would have liked to do more for her."[11] So close to being a private citizen again, Kerney began to loosen the formal cloak of etiquette and speak his mind on matters both privately to his wife and publicly to his counterparts. He had no doubt that he was right to decline the Taoiseach's offer to stay on in service. As he wrote to Raymonde: "I feel more and more pleased to have made the decision to 'cut the connection' and not to have yielded to the temptation to continue in the service of a gang of civil servants whom I despise. The day of my departure from here will be for me a day of liberation."[12]

Publicly Kerney also set aside the guise of officialdom somewhat by speaking more forthrightly to his Spanish counterparts on what he thought of them and General Franco. In one such meeting, the director general of the Political Section in the Ministry of Foreign Affairs, José Sebastián Erice y O'Shea, expressed, from Spain's perspective, their complete delight with Kerney and with his efforts to promote closer bilateral relations during his many years posted in the country. The Irish diplomat, however, spoke more openly and bluntly. As he described the meeting to his wife: "He told me that I had created a lot of sympathy for myself and for Ireland; grateful for our friendly disposition towards Spain; I explained very frankly to him the attitude of the Irish people—on the one hand, a lot of natural sympathy for religious, historical and other reasons, and on the other little sympathy for dictatorial regimes anywhere, Ireland being for good reason the most democratic country in the world."[13] The two men barely shared a word at the departing banquet for Kerney held in the Palacio de Santa Cruz, where he was presented with the cross of Isabel the Catholic.

Yet the diplomat could also show extraordinary compassion. There were many former diplomats living in Madrid who could not return to their countries because they feared for their lives. Many Eastern European states were now in the communist bloc, and exiles from these states were barely surviving day to day in Spain. Kerney gave them whatever money he could spare: they were among "the many unfortunate exiles who are to be pitied and who cling wherever they can," he confided to his wife.[14] He also showed remarkable kindness to the son of a bitter enemy of his—Michael MacWhite, Ireland's minister to Italy. Kerney and MacWhite had once been friends during the War of Independence in Paris, but the treaty split had seen them take different sides, with neither forgiving the other for what both saw as treachery to the state. MacWhite's son Eóin had won a traveling scholarship from UCD for his first-class MA thesis titled "Some Aspects of the Irish Late Bronze Age, Based on a Study of the Hoards of the Period."[15] Eóin's doctoral thesis was supervised by Professor Julio Martínez Santa Olalla of the University of Madrid. Both men worked in the Sierra Morena, and the young archaeologist began to make a name for himself in the press and on radio. On 14 October 1945, *Arriba* carried the headline "The Illustrious Archaeologist MacWhite in Spain" and declared that "this is the first time that in the field of prehistory, primitive history and archaeology that a foreign university student has arrived here to specialise under the supervision of a Spanish Professor."[16] Despite the publicity, Eóin was rather lonely and homesick. He called at the Madrid legation and stayed there for some time. His spirits improved, and Kerney confided to Raymonde that he felt the boy had been abandoned by his parents and that he was more of a father figure to him than was Michael Mac-White. Although Kerney despised the latter, he did show compassion to his son: "His father and I had not at all times always been the best of friends. I must say that I did my best to rid myself of my prejudices and to be a friend of the son."[17]

Ironically, it was at a farewell banquet for the British ambassador, Sir Victor Mallet, that one could get a glimpse of the changed man that was now departing the diplomatic stage. Never one for getting on with the English, Kerney instantly struck up a rapport with Mallet, something unthinkable only a few years previously, when he had dodged anything English or any English ceremony. Many of the guests enquired after Raymonde, and the evening was a joyous occasion. Kerney remarked to his wife that he owed everything, including the success of his mission, to her: "It represents a feather in our cap and we can mutually congratulate ourselves to have worked together in the fabrication of the feather."[18] On 18 December 1946, Kerney's diplomatic career ended.[19] He left Spain to be reunited with his beloved wife, whom he referred to as "a woman in a million."[20] For the first time in over four decades, he settled back in Ireland at the place he now called home.

RETIREMENT

Now retired, Kerney was back before Christmas to see his extended family, including his grandchildren, who called him "Fafa." He quickly adjusted to retirement by busying himself about his new house in Rathmines, doing odd repair jobs on the house and catching up with old friends. He loved to play chess, bridge, and billiards. His kept up his golf by joining the Grange Golf Club in Rathfarnham, and he enjoyed walking along the banks of the Dodder River. Over the next few years he kept active through walks, sports, and socializing, but despite the exercise, his health was not great. As he wrote to his brother Maurice: "I had my blood pressure tested once more a week or two ago; to my surprise it had come down a bit (171/100) and the Doctor pronounced it to be perfectly normal; on the strength of that report I came home and asked Raymonde to give me 2 bottles of Guinness for my lunch, instead of one, but she didn't quite see it that way."[21] His wife was prudent in this respect, as, by today's standards, a top reading of greater than 140 is considered hypertensive and a cause for concern.

With more time on his hands, Kerney began an extensive correspondence with his brother Maurice in England, particularly after another brother, Mario, passed away: "One by one our numbers are reduced, but that is the natural law."[22] De Valera remained in regular contact with Kerney, and their meetings come to life through his letters to Maurice: "I had half-an hour's cordial chat with de Valera on 13th January; as I was leaving, he thanked me, and also on behalf of the Government, for my services."[23] He also heard a rumor that Seán Lemass had singled out Kerney for a special overseas mission, something the former diplomat was not too enamored with, having just settled into retirement: "It is a bit of a nuisance, of course, that there are so many air crashes these times!"[24]

On other occasions he spoke to the Taoiseach candidly on political matters with respect to England: "I thought he had made a mistake in coining 'Éire' as a name for the 32 counties of Ireland—not realising that it would be made to apply to the 26 counties, just like the hateful words 'Free State'—and that it was a fortunate thing that an amendment to the Constitution had been accepted stating: 'The name of the State is Éire, or, in the English language, Ireland.'"[25] Under the first coalition government, the number of Ireland's overseas missions increased, which Kerney welcomed, as he did not want Ireland to be isolated in the postwar period. The diplomat became something of an attraction to Spanish, South American, and other Latin diplomatic representatives as a point of contact and avenue for direct access to de Valera. Kerney gladly arranged these meetings, as he recorded to Maurice in the case of an Argentine ambassador: "He was anxious to meet de Valera, with whom I arranged an interview; when he asked how we had managed to preserve our neutrality during the war, de Valera smiled and threw his hands up in the air, and then gave him a copy of his famous reply to Churchill at the end of the war."[26] These meeting and recollections delighted Kerney.

The former diplomat also kept a keen eye on domestic politics in the postwar period. He still clung loyally to Fianna Fáil and its leader. His forecasts for the general elections, however, were off the mark, as the 1948 election result showed. He wrote to Maurice:

> Here is my forecast of the election results: Fianna Fáil, 65 to 70, Clann na Poblachta (Seán MacBride) 23 to 28; Fine Gael 22; Labour (both parties) 17; Independents and others 15—total 147. De Valera has plenty of enemies as well as friends; judging by English journalists here, a certain amount of English hatred is coming to the surface, and there appears to be an eager desire on your side for his downfall; I think such people will be disappointed but I do not expect him to get an absolute majority, and this will give rise to an interesting situation. There is no national question at stake and nothing to wax enthusiastic about. A win for de Valera will be the best thing for Ireland; the only alternative would be a coalition Government, which would not last three months.[27]

The formation of the First Inter-Party Government marked a turning point in Irish politics. It broke the stranglehold that Fianna Fáil had had on power since 1932 and ushered in an era of collaborative cross-party coalition governments. On reflection, Kerney felt that the defeat might be a good thing for de Valera: "It might not be a bad thing at all for FF to go into opposition for a few months, when new elections would almost certainly bring them back in greater strength—after their opponents made a hash of things and started squabbling amongst themselves."[28] This pessimistic perception of the Fine Gael–led government was a common one, but as David McCullagh has shown, the coalition government proved itself to be remarkably coherent, despite its diverse composition.[29] In the view of John Horgan, the election defeat for Fianna Fáil was attributable to "the fact that the end of the war did not produce a rapid improvement in living standards for people generally."[30] The former diplomat was heartened by the appointment of Seán MacBride, a well-known republican who had acted as de Valera's baptismal sponsor for Eamon Kerney in Paris, to the portfolio of minister for external affairs. This view was not shared within the diplomatic corps, which was aghast at a perceived "leftist" extremist and former IRA chief of staff holding such a critical post.[31] Kerney backed MacBride to do a good job and wrote to him: "May I take the opportunity to offer you my congratulations on your present appointment, if this leads to the breaking of every connection between this country and England even at the cost of an increase in the cost of living."[32] The next day he wrote a letter to de Valera expressing his hope for his party's "speedy return to power."[33]

It was during Kerney's retirement that he was faced with the first instance, though not the last, of what he considered to be an attack on his reputation. A stream of memoirs by former diplomats or officials who had served in Spain during the war, from Sir Samuel Hoare to Ramon Serrano Súñer, were being published in this postwar period.[34] Some of these publications were written by still-serving officials of the regime who wanted to portray their handling of Spanish foreign policy in the best possible light. One memoir, by the former director general of Political Section in the Ministry of Foreign Affairs—José María Doussinague—angered Kerney because in it Doussinague attributed many statements, which he showed as direct quotes, to the former Irish minister when he recounted Plan D—Spain's proposal to form a neutral bloc and lead that bloc to broker a peace between the Western Allies and Nazi Germany in 1943.[35] Kerney confided to Maurice that Doussinague "is full of himself and of his own importance, puffing himself up for his vain efforts. . . . It [Plan D] was a desperate effort, foredoomed from the start, by men who did not realise how much Spain was hated by the Allies. . . . He misquotes me at length."[36]

The former diplomat lost no time after the book's publication in challenging Doussinague, then the Spanish ambassador to Chile. He wrote a detailed two-page letter in French. It shows the lengths to which Kerney was prepared to go in defense of his name and reputation. Doussinague apologized for the errors in his memoir, but Kerney was stinging in his reply:

In your account of our conversation of the 11th January, you claim that I asserted that I knew the "intimate thoughts" of de Valera. I have never in my life made such an idiotic and absurd assertion. I can only suppose that it is your translation which is at fault here. What is true is that I considered that I had a good idea of how my Chief thought, having closely followed all his political activities for over 24 years, and having read and carefully studied all his political speeches. . . . I could never have expressed myself in the manner described, as such an affirmation would have been manifestly untrue. I first thought of asking you to make a few corrections in the next edition of your book, but, to my great regret, I find that the problem you have created is not capable of being resolved in this way in view of the extent of the necessary corrections. You defend the interests of Doussinague and of Spain; for my part I have to defend those of Ireland and of Kerney.[37]

A MISSION TO SOUTH AMERICA

Despite his own stated commitment not to go back into service, Kerney agreed to head a landmark trade mission on behalf of the Irish government to Argentina in 1947. The primary goal of the mission was to secure substantive grain, fats, and vegetable oil supplies from Argentina to offset the failure of the domestic harvest season caused by prolonged bad weather. The lack of grain for human consumption and of animal feed was causing acute shortages. In his investigations of the weather patterns of 1947, Kevin Kearns has shown how ordinary people were driven by desperation to burn their own furniture just to survive the near-biblical disaster caused by blizzards, freezing temperatures, floods, and hunger.[38] Roads and railways were blocked by snow, canals froze, and electricity pylons were suffocated in the "Big Snow." Although extreme Arctic weather had caused this disaster, some historians contend that the crisis exposed the broader politicoeconomic failings of postwar Ireland, symbolically snowed under by poor economic development, rudimentary health care, poor educational provisions, and mass emigration, for which they used the term "de Valera's Ireland."[39]

The crisis forced the government to reintroduce rationing. The minister for industry and commerce, Seán Lemass, did his best to assuage public concern, but inside the Dáil chamber deputies were already fearful that another famine was possible: "The Taoiseach himself, if necessary, should take a trip to these wheat-producing countries, meet the heads of these countries and explain to them the difficulties of our people here. I should like to remind the Minister that this is 1947, and that 100 years ago, in 1847, our people were afflicted by famine."[40] Opposition deputies such as James Dillon saw the failure of the wheat crop in Ireland as a failure of de Valera's economic policy of self-sufficiency: "I make no apology at all for saying that we behold to-night the Fianna Fáil policy of economic self-sufficiency blowing up in their face, and it is that policy that has us where we are. . . . Go round and proclaim Taoiseach de Valera as the greatest Solomon that ever came to judgement."[41] Kerney did not share Dillon's charge against de Valera as the man responsible for the crisis, but the former diplomat was certainly determined to do something about it.

The snowfalls remained persistent between January and March, and, as they were coming after the failure of the harvest the previous year, the economy ground to a halt and people were already dying. The government needed to take action immediately. Both de Valera and Lemass sufficiently impressed on Kerney the seriousness of the food crisis facing Ireland that he agreed to lead a mission of national importance to secure enough food supplies to stave off famine. The task reawakened Kerney's childhood memories of John Mitchel's warnings that the famine had been caused by British maladministration. Now he would be the one who would have to prevent a repeat food shortage from being blamed on an Irish administration. The mission appealed to his economic outlook of the need to connect Ireland to the world, and he felt morally bound by a sense of national and personal duty to do something. Again, it must be stressed that the Irish government evidently trusted Kerney not only personally but for his abilities to represent and carry out essential work for the state overseas as a competent official. Economic affairs had been a lifelong interest of his, and he had achieved some notable successes in making trade agreements in the past, so naturally appointing an experienced official like Kerney made sense.

Yet when Kerney met the Irish government he was informed that his role in this vital undertaking would extend to political matters as much as economic concerns. De Valera wanted the mission to extend diplomatic ties between Ireland and Argentina in the hope of establishing a legation there and to reach out to the Irish diaspora inside the country. He also gave Kerney precise instructions to raise the injustice of partition at every opportunity. In the contributions he made to the selection of six experts for the delegation alongside the Department of Industry and Commerce, the former diplomat displayed once again just how far he had traveled as a man and as a republican. Three of the delegates were Protestants and three Catholics, two of whom were also English and were chosen for their trade expertise. Kerney hoped the choice of delegates would send the right message abroad. Irish foreign policy would use trade to build relations abroad, this time in South America, as envisioned by Arthur Griffith. For Kerney this had always been a cornerstone of Irish foreign policy, and picking a diverse mission team showed that he was refuting Joseph Walshe's vision of Irish foreign policy as a Catholic-centered one.

The mission landed in Buenos Aires on 27 April and was greeted by a host of well-wishers who ranged from Fr. James Ussher, the "leader or guide of the Argentine-Irish," as Kerney noted, to businessmen, former IRA combatants, and reporters.[42] Fr. Ussher welcomed Kerney with an Irish accent even though he had been "79½ years!" in Argentina.[43] The mood was one of joy at the mission's arrival, as Kerney recalled one member of the diaspora saying, "'I've worn away the brim of my hat by taking it off to de Valera, but I take it off to him again for sending you out here.'"[44] Kerney was struck by the presence of so many Irish-born people and descendants of Irish emigrants in a capital city that had a "Plaza Irlanda" and the tomb of the founder of the Argentine navy, Admiral William Brown. Overall, he liked Buenos Aires, observing in his notes that it was "a splendid city, with majestic buildings, busy streets, intense motor-car traffic, numerous shops with all classes of goods artistically displayed, broad avenues and cleanliness."[45] The delegates busied themselves daily with appointments to see grain exporters and government officials. In the evenings they retired to the Jockey Club and gave interviews to the press. As the weeks went by, Kerney began to get slightly tired of the folksy repetition of "God Save Ireland" and other hyperbolic Irish customs that went on into the early hours of the morning. He disliked hearing criticism of the Protestant delegates on the mission and observing the rabidly anti-English attitude of the diaspora, and he bit his tongue on more than one occasion when guests referred to the Taoiseach as "that b*****d de Valera."[46]

As Kerney noticed, many members of the diaspora were employed in menial jobs. In the mission's residence, the Plaza Hotel, Kerney saw that on every floor Argentine-Irish were employed as maids, many of them educated by the Sisters of Mercy. He visited their headquarters in the Colegio de Santa Brigida and found over 220 boarders there, all cared for with free education and board by ten sisters and six teachers. During his inspection tour he noticed portraits of Padraig Pearse, a 1916 proclamation, and other republican iconography. He also visited San Patricio church and the Passionist Fathers, who were another vital element of the colony. Kerney accompanied them on a trip to Mercedes, sixty miles outside the capital, where he was entertained again by songs and dances. The mission head spoke to over 200 guests about partition and neutrality. He made a favorable impression, bringing the message that the republican homeland still reached out to its diaspora. Many of the Argentine-Irish had traveled far and wide to see him: "A man of 85, named Lalor, who came to the Argentine 65 years ago, travelled 50 miles that morning to be present; he requested me to 'shake hands with de Valera' for him. Another man, 65 years old, told me that he had set out at 5.30 in the morning, with the stars still in the sky, for a 10-mile journey on horseback, to catch a train."[47]

Kerney remarked that on the wider political stage the Irish diaspora's influence in Argentina was not a strong one. Other immigrant communities, such as the Italians and the Germans, had more access to those who pulled the levers of power in Juan Perón's administration. Marriage outside of the colony also diminished the solidity of the diaspora, he noted. Yet he reflected again on the romantic illusions of the Argentine-Irish, who conveyed a nationalism he himself had once exuded as a young man, which had since mellowed with time. He put his best face forward when attending ceremonies where "The Soldiers' Song" was sung again and again and where guests showed up carrying shillelaghs and waving tricolor flags. This romantic nationalism did not appeal to him: "It has to be remembered that men like Fr. Victor, shut off from the outer Irish world, live largely in the past, and allowances must be made. I do not know whether I was the only one to feel a cold shiver down my spine."[48] He noticed, for example, that the members of the diaspora were fervently anti-English, and Kerney had to explain to some English visitors and businessmen who called on him that he could see them only privately and away from the eyes of his hosts. He disliked being put in this position, given the English presence in the trade delegation. As he recorded about his encounter with one Englishman: "I explained to him, and he quite understood, that I could not have Englishmen with me when addressing the descendants of Irish emigrants who had left Ireland often in miserable conditions and who, in many cases, retained some of the feelings inherited from the older generations; that they would never understand or approve such an attitude; that the position was a somewhat delicate one, but meant that I had to meet them alone."[49]

In between more daily meetings with government ministers, trade officials, senior military figures, and the Cardinal-Archbishop of Buenos Aires, Santiago Copello, Kerney visited more of the hinterland around the Argentine capital and remarked on the beauty of the landscape, observing: "All the country round Buenos Aires is extraordinarily flat, with not even the semblance of a mound, and very fertile; I was told no fertilizers were necessary. The road cuts through 'estancias' where we saw plenty of cattle grazing; maize and sunflowers appear to be the chief crops; we seemed to be passing through Irish territory all the way, my companions giving me the names of the owners of different 'estancias'—Kelly, Ryan, Duggan, Deane, Maguire, MacManus."[50] Perhaps the most symbolic event of Kerney's trip was the laying of a wreath on the tomb of Admiral Brown. To many of the Argentine-Irish it was an emotional occasion that transcended time past and present, when Irish emigrants had come to a land so far away and made a lasting contribution to their adopted country. The members of the diaspora were clearly overjoyed that an official representative sent by the Irish government had come to visit them. This reconnection was exactly what de Valera had hoped the mission would fulfil.

On 28 May Kerney made a formal speech in the Plaza Hotel before leading dignitaries of the Argentine-Irish community. He used this opportunity to highlight the injustice of partition and encouraged the members of the diaspora to add their voices to the removal of the last remaining obstacle in Anglo-Irish relations, but he couched this message in a friendly manner toward England rather than adopting doctrinaire anti-partitionist rhetoric: "Our State is recognised internationally and diplomatically as Ireland, not as Éire. If we enter any international organisation (the International Civil Aviation Organisation, for instance) we do so under the name of Ireland. I was till recently Minister of Ireland (not of Éire) in Spain, and it is as a Minister Plenipotentiary of Ireland that I am here amongst you tonight."[51] Kerney argued that partition had been a reason for Ireland's wartime neutrality: "Let it be clearly understood, then, that, so long as Ireland remains partitioned, the most favourable attitude which Ireland can adopt towards England, when the latter is engaged in war, is one of neutrality; and, in this case, we went as far as we could by making that neutrality a benevolent one, so far as the United Nations were concerned."[52]

Ireland's neutrality during World War II had resulted in a cold postwar relationship with the Western powers, while its hyper-Catholicism had encouraged the Soviet Union to bar Irish membership of the United Nations. Kerney used this occasion to argue that de Valera had adopted a benign, neutral policy that had favored the Allies during the war and, therefore, Ireland should not be shunned on the international stage: "We took what steps we could to defend ourselves against any invader. We would have fought tooth and nail against an invasion from either side. . . . But, whether Ireland is judged to have been right or wrong in her policy of neutrality, this policy was the unanimous decision of the Irish people."[53] He also let his audience know that their ancestral home was no longer a colony but a sovereign independent state still emerging from the shadows of England: "Ireland is today a sovereign and absolutely independent nation, recognised as such by every country in the world, and it is this fact that determines our relations with all other countries, including England. England, like other countries, has a diplomatic representative in the Irish capital and we have a diplomatic representative in London."[54]

Kerney also used the occasion to thank the members of the diaspora for helping their mother country out of the current economic impasse with the speedy conclusion of the trade talks, and he assured them that the current economic difficulty was only a short-term crisis. He reassured his audience that his visit was not a one-off. De Valera wanted to foster closer diplomatic ties with Argentina, and the trade mission's trip was therefore the foundation of a lasting legacy: "There is a question on everybody's lips: is Ireland going to have a Legation in Buenos Aires? Well, you have been waiting, patiently or impatiently, for a long time; I would ask you to be patient for a short while longer, in the knowledge that patience is a virtue that does not go unrewarded."[55]

On 3 June the delegation began its departure from Argentina. Countless public ceremonies, speeches, and press interviews had left its members exhausted. The mission achieved all its objectives. Although it was a collective achievement, Kerney, as the head of the mission, must be accorded recognition for swiftly securing a vital trade deal. Argentina agreed to send over 250,000 tons of maize alone to relieve the food crisis in Ireland.[56] The Argentine government agreed to extend bilateral relations, with the establishment of formal diplomatic posts almost immediately, and within a few months, on 17 December 1947, Matthew Murphy was appointed as chargé d'affaires in Buenos Aires. Ireland could look forward to building a substantive diplomatic post in South America at a time when exclusion from the United Nations inhibited Ireland's presence on the international stage. Even in the area of least concern to Kerney, but of maximum concern to de Valera, the mission head had used every opportunity to stress the injustice of partition. Yet he had done this in as benevolent a manner as possible by toning down the anti-English rhetoric normally employed on this topic in public debates.

As well as achieving these successes, Kerney had found time to pay over a week's visit to Santiago in Chile to connect with the Irish diaspora there, further Irish interests in the region, and promote closer bilateral ties. It was his idea to go to Chile, and he had planned for this visit before leaving for South America when he had met the Chilean consul general in Dublin to prepare the groundwork. The Chilean government was receptive to a meeting and so began lengthy preparations that culminated with Kerney's official visit. The plane trip was memorable, as he noted: "We crossed the Andes at an altitude of 15,000 feet; each passenger had an oxygen tube at his disposition; I did not need to use mine; when about half-an-hour from Santiago the drums of my ears began to smart, and continued to pain me for some hours; I noticed other passengers caressing their ears; for several hours after landing I experienced a sensation of peculiar leaden deafness."[57] During the independence struggle Ireland had had some representation in Chile, with Frank Egan carrying out propaganda and other such activities on behalf of the Irish Republic. Egan had since died, but Kerney tried to link up with his associates. The mission head also conferred with the Chilean minister for foreign affairs, Raúl Juliet, who assured Kerney that Chile would stand up for Ireland at aviation and telecommunication conferences that barred its entry. Kerney outlined the positive ties uniting the countries as he commented: "I assured him of our friendly feelings for Chile and pointed out that our common attachment to democratic principles was an additional link between us; I told him that I had already learned with pleasure that Chile was in the forefront in matters of social reform."[58] The speech was notable for its lack of stress on religion as a unifying link. Kerney stressed democracy as a common bond between the states.

On 14 May the Chilean president, Gabriel González Videla, held a personal audience with Kerney during which the president stressed the spiritual ties uniting the countries, while the mission head chose to impart on behalf of his government its good will toward Chile: "I told him that the purpose of my mission was to express to him the goodwill and friendly greetings of the Irish Government."[59] Videla impressed Kerney with his knowledge of Irish contributions to national independence from Spain, as Kerney recorded: "He reminded me that there

New Beginnings, 1946–1948   239

were many other Irishmen as well as O'Higgins who had fought for Chilean independence—[Juan] MacKenna, of course, being the most outstanding after [Bernardo] O'Higgins."[60] This meeting was followed by more serious discussions with high-level officials in the Chilean government, as well as the Trade and Foreign ministries over commercial matters and Kerney's desire that Chile canvass regarding Irish admission into all international conferences that it was excluded from on the grounds of its neutral policy during World War II.

On 17 May, at the main ceremonial event, attended by the Irish colony in Santiago as well as state officials and media, Kerney laid a wreath with a tricolor ribbon at the foot of the statute of General Bernardo O'Higgins—"on horseback trampling on a Spaniard," he noted—the man most Chileans referred to as the "Father of the Nation."[61] Yet again Kerney came away from a foreign engagement with tangible successes for Ireland economically, politically, and diplomatically. He was extending the reach of Ireland onto a continent largely ignored by External Affairs for decades. At a time when the country was quite isolated internationally and excluded from joining the United Nations, it needed to find friendly and receptive states to engage with. Repeatedly during the South American mission, Kerney had demonstrated innate traits he had shown throughout his life, showing that, with minimal resources and free reign, he could achieve significant accomplishments for the state overseas. In this crucial mission he had secured the food imports desperately needed back home and had prepared the groundwork for Ireland's further diplomatic expansion into the republics of Latin America in the postwar period, an area of Irish diplomatic history that has been largely overlooked and underinvestigated.

Despite these achievements, on his return to Dublin Kerney was faced with the all-too-familiar memories of his time as a diplomat in Spain. The Department of Finance put the mission's expenses under a microscope, particularly questioning the rationale for the trip to Chile as well as the increase in the daily subsistence allowance that they had authorized. Owing to this, all reimbursement for expenses incurred as well as payments owed were withheld for some time, even though the allowances were shown to have been miscalculated by

Finance and wholly inadequate to meet the basic accommodation and dietary needs of the delegation. It appears that on this occasion the Taoiseach intervened personally and quickly when he heard of this impasse. He backed Kerney, justifying the political importance of Irish-Chilean links given Ireland's isolation on the international scene. Kerney delighted in writing to his brother Maurice: "It may seem a bit Pecksniffian in its nature, but I am delighted to give the deserved kick to some of the higher officials in Finance—especially as they can't kick back."[62] But this small encounter with the Department of Finance was to prove a mere skirmish in comparison to the biggest battle of his life that Kerney was about to face.

"WHEN SORROWS COME, THEY COME NOT SINGLE SPIES, BUT IN BATTALIONS!"

In notes written nearly a decade after the events he was recalling had taken place, Colonel Dan Bryan recorded: "1940, July 15 [Frank] Ryan delivered to Germans. . . . Early Nov. Veesenaifer [*sic*] talked to Irish diplomat (Kerney). . . . 1942, Aug. Chesmann [*sic*] talks to Kerney."[1] In 1950 Ireland's G2 intelligence chief was still preoccupied with wartime events that concerned Kerney, believing to the very end that the former envoy was hiding something. Bryan's concerns bordered on an obsession; his mind trained in espionage and his lifelong distrust of former anti-treatyites led him to think that a close associate and colleague of Éamon de Valera's had actively and surreptitiously worked to undermine Ireland's neutral policy during its darkest hour, and he still believed his suspicions could be proved right. In the twilight of

Kerney's years, when he should have been enjoying his retirement, he was, instead, confronted with the toughest fight of his life. At stake were his reputation and good name. Arrayed against him were former colleagues, a prominent historian, and, always in the background, Colonel Dan Bryan.

KERNEY AND G2

Bryan's suspicions about Kerney grew during the war from fragmentary information, innuendo, rumor, and guesswork. He formed links and connections that to him formed part of an overall puzzle of collusion with a foreign power. His suspicious and secretive mind found in Joseph Walshe, another pro-treatyite, a receptive ear. Walshe had never supported Kerney's reinstatement from 1932 onward, while Bryan held similar misgivings about the diplomat based on data he had compiled. The role of the Germans in getting Ryan out of Spain, the Clissmanns' association, Mary Mains's trip to Ireland from Spain, Annie Farrelly's talk with the diplomat at the Gresham Hotel—all served, in Bryan's mind, to form links between pro-IRA and pro-German sympathizers and Kerney. The diplomat apparently had either a direct or an indirect hand in these activities, which made Kerney a rogue official who could not be trusted. However, until definitive proof and not mere conjecture could be obtained that Kerney had actively aided Germany and the IRA, neither Walshe nor Bryan could tackle him head-on. Yet the fact that the allegations could not be proven did not assuage the doubts and mistrust they attached to the diplomat. What they knew and when they knew it needs to be examined to explain a long process that would end up in a libel action taken by Kerney in the High Court of Justice in 1954.

G2 had many files on known republicans and acquaintances of Kerney throughout the war. These individuals, because of their political outlook (Seán MacBride), nationality (José Camiña), or religion (Robert Briscoe),[2] were treated as potential dissidents and threats to the state.[3] So paranoid was Bryan and eager to unmask "undesirable" people known to Kerney that he continued house surveillance on individuals such as Ambrose Martin—a businessman and supporter of the Spanish Republic who had helped Basque refugees fleeing Francoist and Nazi persecution to get to Ireland—even after the war in Europe had ended.[4] That many of these people were upright public figures and honorable citizens did not, apparently, concern Bryan. Donal Ó Drisceoil has shown how, in addition to this, the intelligence chief was responsible for many other security and counterintelligence duties, including monitoring telephone and private written correspondence between individuals who were deemed suspicious and put on a blacklist by the censorship authorities.[5] Bryan's mistrust of Kerney grew because of the diplomat's ties to these supposedly suspicious individuals. G2 monitored all of Kerney's private correspondence with family and friends and discovered that he was misusing the diplomatic bag.

Kerney's diplomatic reports to Iveagh House during the war were transported back to Dublin via a diplomatic bag marked with the Irish harp and sealed. The Madrid bag traveled from Spain to Ireland via Britain. The bags of the entire diplomatic corps were exempt from interference or censoring, in theory. Eunan O'Halpin has criticized Kerney's "naïve faith" in the integrity of the diplomatic bag.[6] However, it was common knowledge, even to Kerney, that the diplomatic bag was an insecure method of transferring information. He later referred to it as "the diplomatic bag, which of course was always exposed to violation in the post by the intelligence service of one country or another."[7] Under strict protocol, only documents pertaining to official duties were permitted to be transmitted in the bag. However, External Affairs violated this code itself by frequently sending Kerney provisions (butter and cheese) and allowing the Loreto nuns in Madrid to send letters to and from the Mother General of Loreto Abbey in Rathfarnham.[8] This practice was permitted in other missions, too; for example, the department allowed the Catholic hierarchy to send letters through the Rome diplomatic bag to circumvent the censorship authorities at home and abroad. Despite official misuse of the bag, Joseph Walshe expected all overseas diplomats to conform to protocols. Not one for ever conforming, Kerney broke these protocols repeatedly.

The diplomat broke procedure and instruction mainly on humanitarian grounds. Many Irish people were trapped on the continent without news from their loved ones because of the war and international censorship. One such person was Professor Roger Chauviré, a lecturer in French at UCD who, unable to contact his wife and family in German-occupied France, asked Kerney as a friend to forward his letters on to his relatives.[9] Another correspondent was Charles Bewley, a former diplomatic colleague of Kerney who had been minister to Germany until 1939 but had been subsequently dismissed from the service by de Valera for several reasons, including Bewley's pro-Nazi attitude, anti-Semitism, and failures in performance. Bewley, likewise, wrote to Kerney from Rome pleading for a letter to be passed on to his son in Ireland: "I am sorry to trouble you but I have no other means of communicating with him," he wrote.[10] The controversy of Bewley's past deeds and Chauviré's foreign nationality were indicators to Bryan of the type of "undesirable" people that Kerney allegedly associated with.

More damaging, perhaps, was a note by Bryan's predecessor, Colonel Liam Archer, to Joseph Walshe that established that Kerney had acted as an intermediary between Budge Clissmann and her father, who had passed £50 on to Budge via Kerney. Archer was concerned that due to her "previous associations with the IRA" any correspondence should be routinely searched in case the British censorship authorities discovered it first.[11] Budge had been the one to confirm to Kerney that Frank Ryan was well and in Germany, information that the diplomat passed on to Walshe, who then passed it on to G2.[12] The envoy kept in correspondence with her because she served as a useful backchannel for getting information on Ryan's health to pass on to the Ryan family. As Kerney reported to Ryan's sister Eilís: "He [Ryan] is in excellent health keeping out of mischief and unlikely to embroil himself in any way."[13] The contact also proved beneficial for Irish security reasons, as Ryan's letters, two of which Kerney forwarded to Dublin, confirmed that the chief of staff of the IRA, Seán Russell, had indeed died after Kerney first inquired into the matter through Budge, writing: "It would greatly clear the air to throw some light on the circumstances."[14]

It is extraordinary that Walshe did not immediately pass on G2's misgivings about the Clissmanns to Kerney, which would have prevented him from being held in suspicion at home and cleared up much of this wartime uncertainty, especially as Kerney was largely ignorant of the levels of reservation about him. But this did not suit Walshe's agenda. The secretary played both sides to suit his own purposes. His overriding aim was to build up enough mistrust about Kerney's allegedly shady activities in Spain to discredit the diplomat rather than to do the sensible thing and bring everything out in the open to allay concerns about the diplomat in Irish and British intelligence circles. Believing he was acting out of humanitarian concern, Kerney continued to forward letters for Budge. For Budge, like many other Irish citizens living on the continent, communication with family back home was frustratingly slow, sometimes delayed by "five months."[15] She asked Kerney if he would mind forwarding letters through the Madrid diplomatic bag to speed up correspondence with her family. But she added: "Should such an arrangement cause you any embarrassment please do not hesitate to let me know."[16]

On 21 April 1941 another letter was discovered in the diplomatic bag addressed to a Mrs. Power that was deemed not to pertain to official business. By May Walshe had had enough, and he sanctioned the handing over of the entire Madrid bag to the chief postal censor, who in turn passed it on to G2. With the repeated violations of protocol formally established, the secretary, who opined that both Kerney and Maisie Donnelly knew only to use the bag to send letters to "their relatives and friends," was hoping that military intelligence would do the dirty work and finally uncover something salacious on Kerney.[17] Walshe bided his time. He was well aware that the Taoiseach was a stickler for procedure, and he waited for the opportune moment to reveal to de Valera the extensive breaches of protocol committed by Kerney.

The diplomat began to notice an unusual delay in receiving mail from family and friends back home. On 10 June 1942 Kerney wrote a letter to his long-term friend, Frank Litton, in which he finally forced Walshe to reveal his hand by discussing his ongoing grievance over his salary, a dispute caused by the transfer of his salary from a bank in

Lisbon to Madrid, which had the effect of cutting his income nearly in half: "As for a trip to Ireland, there is not the remotest chance of this before April next year at the earliest, unless, indeed, the Dept. of Finance remains pig-headed, or perhaps just subservient to English finance, and persists in its present attitude, which is to block transfers from my bank in Dublin to Portugal; either they give way or I resign my job here. . . . However, please keep that to yourself; I am sure the censor who opens this letter, in the usual careful manner, will be equally discreet."[18] Furious at this public disclosure and what he saw as Kerney's repeated infractions, Walshe sent a strongly worded note to the diplomat charging him with potentially souring relations with Britain if his continued contraventions of the rules about the diplomatic bag and any ordinary posts addressed to him came to the notice of the British censor, which indeed they had: "You should not allow yourself to be made a channel for transmitting letters of outsiders either from or to Ireland in the bag or through ordinary post. This practice has caused considerable embarrassment with neighbour [Britain] in relation to security matters."[19] Incredibly, Kerney ignored Walshe's protestations. In another letter he wrote: "It is flattering to know that the Irish censor can be interested in the private correspondence of an Irish Minister but it looks as if the Sassenach (Englishman) and the Spaniard trusted me more than some of my own countrymen."[20] Perhaps in defiance to the secretary, whom he loathed, or because of a general dissatisfaction with his position in Spain caused by grievances over his salary, the diplomat continued to contravene Walshe's directive. From the viewpoints of both Walshe and Bryan, Kerney's actions served to confirm his unreliability: he was a loose cannon, indiscreet, in league with suspect individuals, and unsuited to heading a diplomatic mission in a fellow Catholic and neutral state.

In the first half of 1943, both the secretary and Bryan moved against Kerney on two fronts. Walshe wanted to corner the diplomat and put him in disgrace with the Taoiseach. This would provide a just cause for Bryan to send a covert spy to watch Kerney in Madrid and report back on him. If both men could acquire enough evidence to prove Kerney's unreliability and present the proof to the Taoiseach, the diplomat could be dismissed. Yet this was difficult to prove. Loyalty was a critical trait that de Valera respected, and Kerney's loyalty to the Chief had saved his career on many an occasion up until this point. De Valera had shown a remarkable trust in Kerney, so Walshe and Bryan needed substantive confirmation. By his nature Walshe was cautious, yet he was equally manipulative and deadly. Within the confines of External Affairs the secretary gradually ensured that the staff adopted a cautious attitude toward Kerney. He gathered a cloud of disrepute that hung over Kerney's head. When Walshe had enough proof of Kerney's indiscretions, he acted ruthlessly. It was the secretary who was the first to take the diplomat on.

With the active support of Bryan, Walshe presented the Taoiseach with clear evidence of Kerney's misuse of the diplomatic bag, along with a further charge that the diplomat was not being entirely candid in his reports on important matters. The assistant secretary, Frederick Boland, later recalled, at the time of the libel case, the accusations leveled against Kerney by Walshe, which were circulated throughout the department by the secretary: "For some time prior to his return, there had been uneasiness about Kerney on security grounds. He appeared to be in touch with Frank Ryan and others considered dangerous to the State, but there was a feeling that the information he furnished to the Department about these contacts lacked amplitude and candour. Warnings about Kerney's discretion and contacts also reached us from Dan Bryan. We had reason to think that Kerney was misusing the diplomatic bag in a way likely to become obvious to belligerent security services."[21] In February 1943 Kerney was recalled to Ireland for three months, presumably, from his perspective, to have the crisis related to his salary addressed. Boland's recollections show that Walshe used Kerney's financial difficulties as an excuse to recall him for an official reprimand: "Just when these apprehensions were troubling the Department, Kearney [*sic*] wrote a minute complaining bitterly of the inadequacy of his allowances and suggesting that he would not wish to stay in Madrid unless they were improved. The then Secretary spoke to the Taoiseach about this minute, and it was apparently decided to take advantage of it to call Kerney back for consultation."[22]

Kerney's diary records day by day whom he met back in Ireland. On 2 March he went to the censorship authorities to complain that his letters were being scrutinized.[23] On 12 March he met Robert Briscoe, TD.[24] As the Jewish deputy was under close observation by G2, this meeting would not have gone unnoticed by Bryan. On 27 March the diplomat had a forty-five-minute meeting with the Taoiseach at Iveagh House. He had expected the meeting to address his pay, the Spanish proposal of Plan D, and the Veesenmayer report. The last thing he had expected was a reproach. The Taoiseach's bluntness and ire stunned Kerney completely: "Attitude not particularly cordial," he recorded in his diary.[25] De Valera dominated the discussion and turned on his old friend. He refused Kerney's request for a transfer out of Spain. He told Kerney to continue where he was or else "resign" from the service.[26] The Taoiseach, quite agitated, presented evidence from the postal censor claiming that Kerney was "a channel for others" and that he had "accused Finance depending Br. [British] Govt [Government]!!!!"[27] He contended that, but for the vigilance of the censorship authorities, this malpractice would have continued. De Valera then compared Kerney's conduct to that of former anti-treaty diplomat Art Ó Briain, saying that "he too created trouble."[28] Although Kerney was good friends with Ó Briain, he took de Valera's negative statement as a personal insult and an attack on his character. Boland's recollection of this meeting was that the Taoiseach "dealt with this matter himself."[29] Kerney's meeting with de Valera was meant to be a private affair, yet Walshe, who had orchestrated the entire process, spread the word around the department that Kerney had been reprimanded. As Boland wrote: "The then Secretary told me at the time that the Taoiseach had spoken to Kerney very seriously indeed."[30] With Kerney's reputation in External Affairs completely sullied, Walshe and Bryan built on their success and the case against the diplomat by sending a G2 officer to Madrid to spy on Kerney's mission.

Captain Joseph Healy, the former Spanish lecturer at University College Cork and delegate to the Irish Manuscripts Commission in Simancas, was attached to the general headquarters staff during World War II. Using the cover of his attachment to the Irish Red Cross Society mission to distribute the relief aid to refugees in Spain in May 1943, Healy called on the Irish legation in Madrid after initially calling at the British embassy, a fact of which he did not inform Kerney. The

G2 officer relayed everything that he and Kerney had discussed, as well as summary character appraisals of the entire legation staff, in an interim report for Bryan. However, right from the start the spy operation descended into a farce. Healy admitted to Bryan that "adverse circumstances" had prevented him from "following several of your suggestions."[31] Rather than confirming Bryan's innate paranoid notion that Kerney was pro-IRA, pro-fascist, and pro-Axis, Healy found the diplomat to speak "cynically of Spanish Govt." and thought that his friends were all "pro-Ally" and Kerney himself displayed no "evidence of acquaintances in either Axis or British circles."[32] The diplomat was neutral to the core.

The premise of Healy's mission, to gather damning facts on Kerney, particularly his handling of the Frank Ryan case, was also not even raised by the officer: "[Kerney] made no mention of Frank R. (I considered it inadvisable, even if opportunity offered, to open this subject with Miss Donnelly)."[33] Nor did Healy make any mention of other matters Bryan was concerned with, such as Mary Mains and her time in Spain working for the Abwehr or the activities of the legation's lawyer, Champourcin: "I shall do my best to secure information whenever I return to Madrid," he wrote.[34] Healy's cover was also blown, although Kerney "never even hinted at it."[35] Kerney remembered that the officer was present at the meeting on 17 October 1941 at McKee Barracks, where Bryan grilled the diplomat on the whole Ryan case. Kerney understood that Healy worked under Bryan, and so he handled Healy just as he had handled the intelligence director in October 1941. He answered questions sparingly, kept the officer at bay, and gave little away beyond what he was specifically asked.

While Walshe and Bryan thought they were making headway against Kerney after de Valera's reprimand of the diplomat, they were in fact revealing their open opposition to a trusted friend and colleague of the Taoiseach, which the Irish political leader noticed. The day before Kerney had been due to return to Spain, 9 April, de Valera had arranged a private meeting with Kerney alone, away from prying eyes in the department and completely unbeknownst to Joseph Walshe. They met in an office in the Dáil, and the atmosphere was completely different from that of their last meeting, on 27 March at Iveagh House. The Fianna Fáil leader was far more relaxed and "cordial," as Kerney noted in his diary.[36] The Taoiseach's attitude on the whole issue of the diplomatic bag was now rather standoffish. De Valera told Kerney that he was wrong to breach protocol, but he did not admonish or rebuke the diplomat as he had done at the previous meeting. Rather the Taoiseach advised Kerney to "not take letters, not let [himself] be used by 'others,' not report on them but keep them off."[37] Clearly the Taoiseach was disappointed that Kerney had given ammunition to the likes of Walshe to use against him. It appeared that the Taoiseach's sulphurous attack at the last meeting had been all for show, and he was letting the diplomat know that there were officials hell-bent on ruining him. The meeting certainly reassured Kerney that the Chief had continued faith and complete trust in him. There was no question of de Valera's dismissing him now. Rather he noted how they both "laughed" together, and he recorded de Valera's parting words: "Goodbye, good luck."[38] Kerney was still de Valera's man in Madrid.

With de Valera's tacit warning ringing in his ears, Kerney had seen Healy's mission in Madrid as an intelligence-gathering exercise by Colonel Dan Bryan from the start. Yet what is intriguing about Healy's covert activity is the officer's complete failure to raise any questions about the Clissmanns—who should have been at the top of his list of things to inquire into. Bryan made the astonishing claim to Walshe that he made the connection between Helmut Clissmann and the Abwehr only in October 1942: "I have now established beyond doubt that Clissman [*sic*] is an Intelligence Officer in the German Army. . . . I have an idea that I saw on some document in your office a reference to Clissman [*sic*] having been in Madrid at some time and if my recollection is correct I would like to see the relevant context."[39] This seems an incredible declaration by Bryan considering the close liaison and sharing of intelligence between G2 and British intelligence during the war. In addition, it raises serious concerns about Bryan's competence if when he was deputy director of G2 he was singularly unaware of the files the agency had compiled for years on Helmut Clissmann, as well as the correspondence between Bryan's predecessor, Colonel Liam Archer, and Walshe, for example, in December 1940, indicating that the Clissmanns had been flagged as potentially dangerous individuals by G2 for some time: "I am in a position to say that [Helmut] Clissman [*sic*] met Frank Ryan in Dublin in 1936 and was seen occasionally in his company. Furthermore, Clissman's [*sic*] wife was known to have political leanings similar to those of Frank Ryan, consequently it is not at all unlikely that the Clissmans [*sic*] would help Ryan through their German friends."[40]

Administrative ineptitude aside, if one accepts Bryan's claim that he came to the definitive conclusion that Helmut Clissmann was an Abwehr agent only in October 1942, it is astonishing that he did not inform the Taoiseach of this fact, nor did he warn Kerney to break off any further contact with the Clissmanns altogether. This oversight was a dereliction of duty. It would be inconceivable for Bryan not to have instructed Healy to find out something more about Kerney and the Clissmanns. All the evidence and circumstances yet again point to a deliberate effort by Walshe to defuse any further investigations regarding Helmut Clissmann because it impinged on the secretary's past association with the German, something that has never been satisfactorily explained.

It is evident that after de Valera's show of confidence in Kerney, the diplomat began to pay greater heed to the need to act correctly with regard to the diplomatic bag, knowing now, as Kerney did, that G2 was actively reading his postal correspondence and sending agents to spy on him. In one letter he acknowledged: "Confidentially, I have received a short time ago categorical instructions not to forward—by the bag or otherwise—third party letters, and I believe it to be the case that there have been abuses somewhere which have given rise to embarrassing incidents."[41] In another letter to his colleague Seán Murphy in Vichy, France, Kerney wrote: "For your personal information, it appears that considerations of security have made them adopt a severe attitude towards the transmission of letters for third parties, and, if I am not mistaken, my acceptance of letters addressed to me by Chauviré has been the main cause of reproaches levelled at myself; Chauviré understands the position and I am sure he will be able to send his letters by a different channel."[42]

Incredibly, however, Kerney broke protocol again, which he should not have done. Perhaps it was his nature to be unruly, as he once admitted to "the rebellious way which is somewhat after my own heart."[43] Exasperated because his efforts against Kerney had floundered and perhaps angry with de Valera for not sanctioning the envoy, Walshe sent the diplomat a scathing note. It is worth quoting at length:

> The Minister [de Valera] has had before him your minute S.P. 17/5 of the 30th August explaining the circumstances in which you came to forward through the diplomatic bag a cheque for £100 on an English Bank for collection through your son's account.
>
> The Minister can not help feeling that, in this matter, you acted with an extraordinary lack of prudence, and with a surprising disregard of the exhortations to caution so often addressed to you with regard to the use of the [diplomatic] bag. It must surely have occurred to you that any arrangement which involved—however indirectly—the transfer of funds from a London bank account to a person living in territory occupied by Britain's enemies would run counter to British regulations. What the slightest reflection must have suggested to you, too, is that the sending of this cheque bearing your name from an Irish Bank to the Bank in London for collection, would not only have at once drawn the attention of the British authorities to the existence of such an arrangement but would have given them first-hand evidence of your personal complicity in an attempted breach of their finance regulations. What you may perhaps not have realised—although in its consequences, it might have been the most serious and embarrassing aspect of the whole matter—is that it would have been immediately obvious to the British that the cheque had been forwarded to this country through the diplomatic bag.
>
> Only the vigilance of the censorship authorities here averted an incident which could have been very serious for yourself and for the Department alike.
>
> The Minister is pained that you should have been so regardless of what has been so often said to you as to have incurred the risk of such an incident, and he has asked me once again to impress upon you, in the strongest terms, the importance of adhering strictly to the instructions governing the diplomatic bag, and the necessity for restricting its

use to official correspondence and personal letters (without enclosures) between you and the members of your family.[44]

The tone of this rebuke, alternating between anger and exasperation, reflects Walshe's giving up on ousting Kerney. He had tried every possible means available to a senior civil servant to undermine and disgrace a junior colleague—to send the man to a foreign posting and keep him there, to ensure that every conceivable obstacle was placed in his path, to give him no adequate staff or finances, to blacken his name in the confines of his organization, to keep him away from his benefactor, to file away and ignore critical reports, to dismiss any grievances raised and to highlight every infraction in the course of duty. Walshe had even worked with G2 and the censorship authorities against Kerney and put him on a blacklist. As Donal Ó Drisceoil has written: "The Censorship 'Black List' included not only those suspected of being involved in subversion, but also anybody who was known to them or with whom they communicated."[45] Nothing had worked in the end, and, realizing that Kerney was also near retirement, Walshe simply gave up trying to oust him. In addition, it was from this point on that the files show that the secretary stopped passing material to Bryan on Kerney regularly. For example, previously the secretary had passed on to Bryan two letters Kerney had forwarded from Ryan in 1942.[46] In 1945 Walshe suddenly stopped this practice, even after he had requested that Kerney transmit the bulk of Frank Ryan's letters back to Dublin.[47] Bryan had to request to see these Ryan letters from Walshe's successor, Frederick Boland.[48]

As someone who lived and worked in the shadows, Bryan never gave up the hunt on Kerney. On 11 January 1945 he interviewed an informant, Leon Mill Arden (a Breton nationalist), who divulged information to G2 on IRA-German collaboration, particularly by republican Jim O'Donovan.[49] Arden stated that IRA activists like O'Donovan who were in contact with the Abwehr were able to transmit communications to Germany via Madrid. Bryan showed Arden a list of names: "He at once picked no. 4, Champosin [*sic*], as the name of the lawyer in Madrid to whom he sent Jim Donovan's [*sic*] messages written in invisible ink in 1941."[50] Again the intelligence chief could see, in his mind, a link between the Madrid legation, German espionage activities in Ireland, and IRA collusion. He believed that Kerney had to be, at the very least, aware of this, or, worse still, at the center of an IRA-German conspiracy against the state. Even if all this was true, catching a rogue official or traitor was going to be extremely difficult unless the individual was caught in the act or confessed. When Kerney retired from the service in December 1946, it seemed to Bryan that his suspicions might never be proven correct. In fact, a golden opportunity to incriminate and humiliate the former envoy publicly and internationally would arise from the most unlikely of sources.

PROFESSOR THOMAS DESMOND WILLIAMS

After the defeat of the Nazis in 1945, Allied intelligence services had fanned out across Germany to gather material to use as evidence against criminals indicted before the International Military Tribunal at Nuremberg. Some of the documents seized originated from the German Foreign Ministry or the Reich Chancellery and dated as far back as 1867. It was agreed among US, British, and French authorities that all three powers would share custody of the documents. Historians and linguists were employed to help collate and translate the copious archive collection, and the preliminary work for the years pertinent to the Nazis (1933–45) was completed by 1954, by which time all three powers had agreed to release the document collection into the public arena. The series became known as *Documents on German Foreign Policy*. One of the men involved in sifting through the captured archive for the British side was assistant editor Thomas Desmond Williams.

Williams was a rising star on the Irish academic scene. In 1949, at the age of just twenty-eight he had been appointed professor of modern Irish history at University College Dublin, where his father had worked previously as a professor of education. Williams had a long association with the university, where he excelled as an undergraduate, winning scholarships and first-class honors.[51] After graduation he undertook a master's dissertation on the origins of national socialism in Germany. His knowledge of Germany and its language, history, and politics made him a notable authority, and he was approached by British intelligence during the war and by the Foreign Office to edit the captured diplomatic papers from 1919 to 1945. This young, brilliant historian whose research into the captured German archives promised to provide material for a wealth of scholarly publications that would make his name internationally respected was instead to find himself dogged by controversy and his reputation as a historian blighted by the libel case Kerney would take against him. Williams coedited a journal titled the *Leader*, and in 1953 he began to write for that journal a landmark series of articles under the heading "A Study in Neutrality." The series also appeared in the *Irish Press*,[52] the most popular newspaper in the country. In this series he became the first historian to make public an insider's knowledge of Irish neutrality during the war. He was also the first historian to accuse Kerney of collaborating with Nazi Germany based on his archival research into the captured Nazi files.

The initial article in the *Leader* that alluded to an unnamed Irish diplomat was published on 28 March 1953 and alleged that the diplomat's "mysterious" contacts with the Germans had placed Irish neutrality in danger because Berlin viewed the meetings as "giving evidence of a willingness on the part of the Irish Government to co-operate, under changed conditions, with the New Order."[53] This diplomat had met "Ribbentrop's confidential officer, Veesenmayer," in November 1941, and, "in the view of the said diplomat, Mr de Valera saw in a German victory the only possible chance of ending partition; but was unable to take any anti-British step in view of the defenceless-ness of Southern Ireland."[54] This republican dream, however, might be realized, according to the diplomat, if "Germany could only provide Ireland with arms and organise successful assistance, Ireland might no longer, at a critical moment of the war, remain neutral."[55] Williams opined that these secretive meetings between the diplomat and German military intelligence put the Irish government in a "very danger-ous position" and could have had "disastrous consequences for the State's diplomacy," particularly had the British found out at the time.[56] The historian connected the activities of German parachute agents in

Ireland with the diplomat's meetings as part of a single overarching plot to untie the neutral cloak woven by de Valera.

The most damning article in the journal series appeared on 11 April. Before examining this article, it is interesting to note that in a copy of it held in the British National Archives, Williams had scribbled a note in pen at the bottom of the piece acknowledging that he had actually gotten his dates wrong. He had alleged that another meeting between Kerney and Veesenmayer had taken place in October 1942, in addition to the actual one in August: "This is an inaccurate date," he wrote. "The meeting took place in the latter part of August. TDW 1/3/54."[57] Besides this error, he vouched for what he had written. Williams presented the argument that the purpose of the face-to-face meeting between the as-yet-unnamed diplomat and Veesenmayer was to make "arrangements for creating an effective unity between the Irish nationalists and the Germans."[58] A united effort by Germany and the Irish government could have benefited all parties in their collective grievances against Britain if an understanding with the IRA could be achieved also: "The Irishman, in the course of these long and secret conversations, reportedly placed a high value on the importance of the IRA. Although small in numbers they represented an important national tradition, and, therefore, under more suitable circumstances, they would provide a bridge whereby the numerous divided 'National' elements in the country could be united for specific political action directed against the English in the North."[59]

Williams then alleged that the unnamed diplomat had said that Frank Ryan might be a good "liaison officer" between Germany and the Irish government, and the historian reiterated that these secret meetings gave the Nazis a false impression of official Irish attitudes in the war: "He [the unnamed diplomat] felt also that as Irish independence would be assured by a German victory, Mr de Valera would regard Germany as a natural political ally."[60] Williams then stood back from the historic time period and opined that three possible circumstances had given rise to these high-level talks—first, the diplomat had met the Germans without Dublin's knowledge; second, he had been under instruction from the Taoiseach or the Department of External Affairs, and what he said was official opinion; or third, he had been told to meet Veesenmayer and hear him out but make no commitments. The historian, whose articles in the series had hitherto been glowing in their praise of Irish neutral policy under the stewardship of de Valera and Walshe, argued that the diplomat had most likely acted unilaterally and without informing Dublin. The diplomat's actions were judged by Williams to be "dangerous," as they could have impinged on Anglo-Irish relations and did, in fact, accelerate German efforts to draft military plans for Ireland: "He [the diplomat] thought his actions were unobserved by British agents; there is some evidence that the British and the Americans were not entirely unaware of the meeting, although they did not know really anything about the contents of the conversation. The Germans, on the other hand, speedily drew the conclusion that this operation was practical and they proceeded to take steps with the Army and the SS (which was now coming more to the forefront in Irish matters)."[61] Williams finally linked these talks with clandestine missions by German Abwehr agents in Ireland, the clear implication being that the talks gave a green light to espionage operations that violated Irish neutrality: "It was on the basis of these conversations that the ill-fated 'Operation Mainau' was drafted."[62]

Williams concluded the piece by noting what the diplomat's superiors made of his unauthorized approaches to German military intelligence: "It is rumoured, in fact, that he [de Valera] was very angry when he did hear of some of the activities of the Irish diplomat previously mentioned and that subsequently the latter was sharply rebuked for his indiscretion."[63] This last remark by the historian is significant, as up to this point the research materials that had formed the basis for his articles had come from the captured Nazi files that Williams had studied during his tenure with British intelligence and the Foreign Office. The Irish diplomatic files were still under lock and key and subject to the Official Secrets Act in 1953. Williams could not have known that at a particular time and place and on a particular occasion the Taoiseach had privately rebuked this unnamed diplomat within the confines of Iveagh House unless he had had an informant who had been present on the occasion and subsequently chose to pass on this information to Williams. The historian was obviously being fed information by a source or a number of sources who had agendas against this unnamed diplomat. The diplomatic archives in Dublin and London reveal that the historian had a number of personal meetings in Rome with Joseph Walshe (then Ireland's ambassador to the Holy See) and in Dublin with Colonel Dan Bryan (still director of G2) in the lead-up to publication of the series "A Study in Neutrality."

KERNEY'S REACTION

It was obvious from the start that the articles in the *Leader* and the *Irish Press* about this unnamed Irish diplomat in Madrid who had known de Valera for over thirty years could only be Kerney. The former minister to Spain had known for some time, mainly through his colleague Frederick Boland, that a historian wanted to write about him. Boland had spoken to Professor Williams in 1948, and during their conversation the historian revealed that he had copious documents on Kerney regarding Irish-German collaboration and that a series was shortly to be released by the wartime Allies in which Kerney was likely to feature because of his meeting with Edmund Veesenmayer. The former diplomat, on hearing this news, was rather intrigued at the time, writing: "It will interest me to know what I am supposed to have said to some German colleague."[64] Kerney privately believed that this contact with a high-level German could not possibly raise any contention: "In August 1942 I made what I thought was an extremely interesting report—and it was certainly a faithful one—of a long chat I had with a certain German who was high in authority. . . . I place less trust in the 'historians' than in the 'criminal.' I look forward with interest to this publication."[65]

When the articles were made public by Williams, prior to the publication of the *Documents on German Foreign Policy* series, it stunned the former envoy. Kerney had recently suffered a heart attack, and his health was gradually failing. At 71 he admitted in a memorandum that he felt "on the brink of death."[66] What concerned him most was an innate fear that he might die before the accusations made by Williams were found to be untrue. The allegations that Williams had made were truly astonishing. The claim that Kerney had collaborated with Nazi Germany was one of the worst allegations that anyone could make, and the former diplomat could not understand how such a highly respected historian could have written such flagrantly outlandish and bizarre articles based on questionable sources. Williams had never tried to meet Kerney before publishing the series. If he had, he would have quickly realized that Kerney was no militant republican or pro-Nazi sympathizer. He had never been in the IRA, had never had contacts or ties with that organization, and had shown nothing but contempt for fascism as a political ideology. Also, the idea that Kerney, as Williams claimed, would be the go-between for Irish-German cooperation in working for a united Ireland in return for action against Britain was ludicrous. The notion that he, isolated in Spain during the war, with infrequent flights to and telecommunications with Dublin, could have had the ear of the Taoiseach and been his roving ambassador to the Nazis was simply ridiculous. Yet Williams had written his articles as if he was reporting established facts.

Despite his physical decline, the former diplomat found the resolve to confront the accusations made against his reputation head-on. On 13 July he traveled to Iveagh House to personally hand-deliver a letter, compiled after consulting his solicitor, Seán Ó hUadhaigh, for Seán Nunan, then secretary of external affairs.[67] The diplomat wanted the department to make public his report from 24 August 1942, the day he had met Veesenmayer. Its publication would comprehensively refute Williams's claims that Kerney had acted irresponsibly and dangerously. Not only would it "clarify" the whole matter, but Kerney argued that its release into the public domain would "dispense me from the necessity of taking legal proceedings" and would be, he argued, in the interests of himself, of "the Department of External Affairs, of the Government, and of the country."[68] Nunan's attitude was rather reserved. The department, still bound by the Official Secrets Act as Kerney was, was not going to get involved in the dispute. An internal note from Nunan to a colleague is revealing: "The Department is holding aloof from participating in this matter, we are taking the precaution of setting our house in order in case of necessity."[69] The department would not release Kerney's wartime reports and claimed privilege in the whole affair.

A month after the articles appeared in the press, Kerney instructed his solicitor to write to Professor Williams, the *Leader*, and the *Irish Press* strongly refuting the allegations against him and giving each party four days to apologize publicly. No party did. With his former colleagues in External Affairs proving uncooperative and his opponents refusing to withdraw their charges, the former diplomat was left with no choice but to seek legal redress. It seemed that Kerney was being attacked from all sides and getting no help. What he may not have realized at the time was the commotion that his filing a case for libel caused at secretarial and ministerial levels in Dublin and London. At one stage it seemed that External Affairs was going to help Kerney out by releasing a departmental draft on the minister's instruction, but in the end they decided not to. Its publication would have helped their former colleague. It stated:

> [Professor Williams's] allegations in question are not supported by the evidence of his [the minister's] Department's wartime records and reports. The relevant departmental files of the period 1939–1945 indicate that all Irish diplomats then serving abroad loyally represented the Government's policy of unqualified neutrality on which policy the entire people at home were united. All our representatives abroad, without exception, kept the warring Powers and the other neutral States constantly aware of Ireland's determination to remain at peace unless and until she were attacked and, in that case, to resist her attackers, whoever they might be.[70]

In a memorandum Kerney recorded his thoughts about the defendants. On the *Leader* he stated: "It has a Fine Gael outlook, generally speaking, and therefore, in so far as political considerations are concerned, I would not deem it unnatural to be attacked from that quarter."[71] On condition that the journal published an "adequate apology" in a prominent section of the monthly, he was prepared to accept a "relatively small sum" in compensation.[72] The former diplomat was more critical of the historian. He felt that Williams had wronged him, writing defamatory articles without first consulting him to verify or deny the claims, and he noted that Williams had earned good money for the series in the process. Kerney again did not rule out a deliberate political smear campaign as a likely rationale for the attack on him. He was aware that Williams's cousin and solicitor in the libel case was Alexis FitzGerald—son-in-law to former Fine Gael TD and Taoiseach John A. Costello. Kerney had endured political attacks from Fine Gael TDs before, most notably from Desmond FitzGerald, and he no doubt felt that, due to his anti-treaty stance, there were still opponents out to get him. Of the historian he wrote:

> Professor Williams:
>
> From the little I know of him, I understand that, until lately, the circles frequented by him were of a Fine Gael hue. Therefore a political bias against me might not have been unnatural.
>
> I have not a high opinion of him, seeing that he worked for the British Foreign Office, that he must have had some purpose in concealing that fact from his readers, that he made a sudden, malicious and unprovoked attack on me, without giving me any warning whatever, that he stooped very low to do so, and that he earned money by making this attack on me.
>
> I am willing to treat Professor Williams as a natural enemy, from the political point of view, and to be merciful. His youth, recklessness and cocksuredness have placed him in an unfortunate position. He has to be taught a lesson.
>
> An adequate apology, an undertaking to pay all costs and a modest payment in respect of damages is all I demand in his case.[73]

Kerney reserved his deepest resentment for the *Irish Press*. He had been one of the first shareholders to invest in the newspaper in 1931 and had sold copies of the publication in the streets of Paris in its fledgling years. The newspaper was tied to the de Valera family and was associated strongly with Fianna Fáil. It was the best-selling broadsheet in Ireland, with a daily circulation of 170,000 copies at that time. Éamon de Valera acted in an oversight capacity on the board as controlling director, while his oldest son, Vivion, was responsible for the daily editorial management of the newspaper as the managing director. Kerney knew Vivion very well and naturally felt betrayed by the appearance of Williams's articles in the newspaper without his consultation, writing: "The 'Irish Press' could have consulted me before allowing their columns to be used for the purpose of practically branding me as a traitor."[74] The former diplomat felt "stabbed in the back" by his republican colleagues and worried that lifelong friends in the republican movement might interpret his conduct as being treacherous: "It is conceivable that, in the highest quarters, the articles in question may have raised grave doubts concerning my behaviour at a critical moment in our history."[75] For such an attack to come from a perceived friendly source hardened his resolve to seek considerable compensation from the *Irish Press*: "I was 71 years old when they attacked me. They refused to apologise when I gave them an opportunity of doing so. They knew that I might die before any libel action could be heard. They know that 5 or 6 months ago I was on the brink of death. Their attitude is beneath contempt. No matter what the consequence, I repeat that I refuse to make any settlement out of Court."[76]

Proving his innocence, however, was going to be a daunting challenge for Kerney and his legal team. He still had his copy of the Veesenmayer report but was precluded from making this public under the Official Secrets Act. The Irish government and the Department of External Affairs were unwilling to embroil themselves in the case and claimed state privilege in the matter. Without access to critical documents, the plaintiff's case was severely impeded. The only other avenue left open to Kerney was to contact eyewitnesses and authors who could comprehensively refute Williams's allegations. The historian had principally relied on the German accounts of the meetings with the former diplomat as the bases for his articles. Kerney was prepared to contact both Edmund Veesenmayer and Helmut Clissmann to act as witnesses in the case and testify under oath that what the historian had written about their reports was largely inaccurate, outlandish, and skewed to fit a particular interest. This was a difficult choice for Kerney to make, as he had felt betrayed by Clissmann during the war, yet clearing his name superseded all such considerations. Veesenmayer had been released from prison by the Allies, but contacting him was far from easy. Clissmann, on the other hand, had returned to Ireland after serving time in prison, and the former Abwehr agent agreed to give evidence in Kerney's defense.

Clissmann provided Kerney's legal team with two important documents. The first was a signed five-page document that refuted Williams's imputations step by step, finding many of the historian's claims to be "wrong and misleading" and "intentionally suggestive" and stating not only that the historian had repeatedly gotten important facts such as dates and the number of meetings wrong but that his central charge of collusion with a foreign belligerent power was baseless.[77] The former Abwehr agent put it on the record how he had managed to disguise the real nature of his visits to Madrid from Kerney: "I did not mention to Mr Kerney with one word nor insinuated that I held any office in Military Intelligence."[78] Clissmann had used the cover of his former academic work in Ireland as part of the German Academic Exchange Board as a deception, and he told Kerney that the board had "sent me to Madrid to settle some difficulties among the staff of the German Cultural Institute in Madrid. Mr Kerney knew from pre-war days that I had been attached to the German Academic Exchange Board."[79] Clissmann also stated that Kerney had not known the identity of Veesenmayer before the meeting, nor had he known that Veesenmayer was a senior SS official, but rather he had been told that the man was a "high-ranking German economist and personal adviser of Ribbentrop."[80] He also corrected Williams's contention that the meeting had served to make arrangements between "Irish nationalists and the Germans" as "definitely wrong."[81]

Clissmann noted that many statements that Williams had attributed to Kerney, such as that Ireland needed weapons to attack Britain, were, in fact, Clissmann's views: "I, not Mr Kerney, may have suggested this, and I might have reported this view as a conclusion of our discussion."[82] Moreover, at no stage had any "plan" been drawn up, as Williams had contended, for secretive Irish-German collaboration: "The term 'plan' is altogether misleading and suggestive. There was never—neither by Mr Kerney nor by me in my report—any mentioning of a 'plan.' These were informal personal exchanges of views."[83]

Williams had misled readers into thinking otherwise: "Readers must get the idea that Mr Kerney was involved in a sinister pro-German scheme. There was nothing of the kind."[84] Clissmann put it on record that Kerney had met Veesenmayer only once in Madrid, in August 1942, not twice that year, as Williams had claimed: "There was no meeting in October 1942. Dr Veesenmayer and I visited Mr Kerney in August 1942."[85] He also stressed that at no time were these discussions evidence of any "negotiations," and such a loaded term employed by Williams was entirely wrong. He continued: "I can again only stress that there were no 'negotiations.' The term is misleading and intentionally suggestive. It is also without reason—except to create feeling against Mr Kerney—that our talks and the Goertz arrest were related to each other. There could have been no connection whatsoever."[86]

The former Abwehr agent then addressed Williams's inaccurate linking of Kerney to the IRA as part of a wider IRA-German scheme to invade Northern Ireland to counter the Allies ("Operation Mainau"). He found such a suggestion erroneous, as there was no connection between Abwehr agents operating in Ireland and these talks, and, besides, such a suggestion was preposterous given Kerney's lack of enthusiasm for the IRA: "Mr Kerney's views on [the] IRA were always very reserved, also at [the] meeting with Dr Veesenmayer. I remember distinctly that Dr Veesenmayer, after the discussion in a garden Restaurant near the Prado on a Monday morning, came away disappointed, stating that Mr Kerney was not a revolutionary Irishman any longer, but a very careful family man."[87]

The former Abwehr agent denied that Kerney had ever said that Frank Ryan could be a good "liaison officer" between the Germans and the Irish government or that he believed German victory in the war was possible: "Also the statement—'He hoped indeed one day to see him [Frank Ryan] as the liaison officer between Germany and the Irish Government'—is not Mr Kerney's, but reflects the German ideas at the time. The next sentence—'He felt also that, as Irish independence would be assured by a German victory, Mr de Valera would regard Germany as a natural political ally'—is not Mr Kerney's statement, but reflects our German political view of the time."[88] Clissmann further refuted Williams's accusation that the meeting had served as

an "extraordinary exchange of confidences": "Our discussion was not
an exchange of confidences but of views. The initiative came all the
time from Dr Veesenmayer, who expressed his views on Ireland's
situation then and in the event of a German victory in the East in
which he believed. It must not be forgotten that Dr Veesenmayer,
in his expose of the German situation and the development of the
war as he saw it, gave a lot of interesting information about our side
which Mr Kerney could pass on to Dublin."[89] Clissmann also rejected
the notion that Kerney had stated that he knew the Taoiseach's inner
thoughts and could speak on behalf of the Irish political leader: "Mr
Kerney never made such a claim to me or to Dr Veesenmayer. Dr
Veesenmayer or I may have easily mentioned that Mr Kerney knew
Mr de Valera well since the days of the struggle, and in particular when
Mr Kerney refused to hand his documents etc over to the Free State,
also that Mr de Valera was godfather to one of Mr Kerney's sons. This
was probably mentioned to show in Berlin that Mr Kerney was one of
the old Republicans and—apart from being Minister in Spain—also a
friend of Mr de Valera."[90] Again, it appears that the German account
of the meetings was initially exaggerated by Clissmann and then by
Williams, who put a further spin on his source documents in his articles: "As stated before, Operation Mainau and Dr Veesenmayer's
visit to Madrid have no bearing on each other. It is false when Prof.
Williams speaks of 'hopes' which Mr Kerney 'raised.' The last part of
the sentence—'maintained contacts until the end of 1942'—is also
wrong and gives the impression as if Mr Kerney had been the active
part while in reality the initiative all the time came from the German
side."[91]

A final point of contention that Clissmann raised was Williams's
claim, without any reference or quote from a file in his articles, that
British intelligence was well aware of Kerney's meetings with the Germans and that this placed Irish neutrality in danger. We know now
from the British archival evidence that they did not know about these
meetings when they happened, yet Clissmann in 1954 was already
rebutting Williams's supposed sources and claims on this point. None
of the British intelligence files were publicly available to any historian or researcher when Williams wrote his articles, yet the historian

wrote the series in a way that conveyed events and actions as facts despite the absence of any referenced sources. The reader trusted the historian based on his word, his reputation, and his profession at the time, something Clissmann clearly did not believe to be sincere. When Williams had written: "He [Kerney] thought his actions were unobserved by British agents; there is some evidence that the British and the Americans were not entirely unaware of the meeting," Clissmann strongly refuted this:

> What evidence is there? I spent one year in the Interrogation prison of Military Intelligence Five in Bad Nenndorf from October 1945 till October 1946. I was very intensely questioned—even to the extent of maltreatment—up to December 1945 about every aspect of my activities in Ireland up to 1939 and in connection with Ireland during the war. My visits in Madrid were never mentioned until Easter 1946, when translations of my reports to Dr Veesenmayer and of his reports to the 'Führerhauptquartier' were held against me. It was obvious that these documents had only recently been found, and that British Intelligence had no previous knowledge of my visits to Madrid or Dr Veesenmayer's visit in August 1942 before these documents were found.[92]

Clissmann's second document was a signed two-page questionnaire compiled by Kerney's legal team in which he answered, point by point, twenty-four questions put to him, which he was willing to appear in court very soon to swear to under oath.[93] The German was able to refute Williams's claims about the number of meetings he and Kerney had had as being far fewer than those alleged and that at no stage had any "negotiations" been entered into: "Did you, on these occasions or on any other occasions, enter into negotiations of any kind whatsoever with Mr Kerney? *No.*"[94] He admitted that he had never informed Kerney that he worked for the Abwehr:

> Did you at any time inform Mr Kerney that you came to see him as a representative of Dr Veesenmayer or of anyone else, or that you saw him in any official capacity whatsoever? *No.* Is it true that Mr Kerney received you as a friend whom he had known for years, and as the husband of

a lady [Budge] whom he had known for a still longer period? *Yes.* Did you inform Mr Kerney, on the occasion of your first visit, that you had come to Madrid for the purpose of smoothing out some difficulty that had arisen at the German Institute? *Yes.*[95]

Critically, Clissmann confirmed that at no stage had Kerney discussed, entertained, or initiated any secret deals with the Nazis: "Did Mr Kerney at any time furnish you with information of a confidential or secret nature? *No.* Did you make any proposals to him (other than asking him whether he would be willing to meet Dr. Veesenmayer), and did he make any proposals to you? *No.*"[96] These points proved that Kerney had at no stage agreed to act as an intermediary or go-between for the Nazis, the IRA, and the Irish government. What was in the German files was Clissmann's exaggerations to his superiors about what he purported to have been said by the Irishman at the meetings. Clissmann went further and claimed that his Allied interrogators had forced him to attribute to Kerney views and statements that were, in fact, his own and not the diplomat's:

Is it correct that your interrogators sought to make you attribute to Mr Kerney expressions of opinion that were your own? *Yes.* Is it true that Mr Kerney was unaware of the fact that you were making reports based on your conversations with him? *Yes.* Mr Kerney holds that such conversations were as between friend and friend, that they concerned matters of personal interest (e.g. the health of Frank Ryan and that of your own family) in the first place, and dealt, in the second place, with matters of general and all-absorbing interest at the time, such as the state of the war and general conditions, as affected thereby, in Germany, Ireland and elsewhere. Do you consider such an attitude on his part to be justified? *Yes.*[97]

The German verified the ulterior motive behind these visits: "Had your visits any ulterior motive, and, if so, since when? <u>My visits from the beginning i.e. November 1941 onwards had—apart from contacting Mr Kerney as [a] friend of the family and of Frank Ryan—the motive to obtain his views on Ireland's position in the war and on</u>

Irish-German relations. Mr Kerney was one of the few Irishmen in
neutral territory who could be contacted and whose opinion was of
particular interest on account of his Republican record."[98] Clissmann
also confirmed that he had been approached by representatives of the
Irish Press, Vivion de Valera and Brendan Walsh, to serve as a witness
on their behalf. The German had forwarded Veesenmayer's address
to them also: "I informed the two gentlemen that I was already in
contact with Mr Kerney and that I should like to consult him before
replying. A few days later I telephoned Mr Walsh and informed him
that I would be prepared to act as witness on both sides as I regarded
myself as a witness for the truth."[99]

THE LIBEL CASE

On 23 February 1954 Professor Williams wrote to the Foreign Office
to request the release of classified German documents in advance of
the publication of the *Documents on German Foreign Policy* series to assist
him in his defense in court. He believed quite confidently that his
charges against Kerney were legitimate and that the release of this
archival evidence by the Foreign Office would decidedly prove that
this was the case. He informed the British, "I have information 'off
the record,' from certain Irish and English officials," that these documents would prove his argument that Kerney had indeed "(in my
view), co-operated in discussions with German agents on the possibility of bringing about a German invasion of southern Ireland,
directed against the British forces in the north."[100] The news of the
libel case created a furore in Whitehall. This unprecedented case confronted the British Civil Service with a variety of dilemmas. There was
no obvious precedent for papers belonging to a foreign government
to be released in advance for a libel case, even though the series itself
was due for publication shortly, which made claiming privilege very
difficult. They also had to decide whether it was morally right to help a
historian to "attack another [person] with German documents which
we hold for the purpose of objective historical study."[101] The Foreign
Office feared that claiming state privilege might not be possible if the

Irish courts served a *subpoena duces tecum* on the documents. The interests of justice aside, London was also concerned that there might be
a negative impact on "Anglo-Irish relations" if these documents were
released into the public domain.[102]

On 27 February Williams called at the Foreign Office to inquire
into the release of the captured documents. The historian revealed to
the British two of the sources of information for his articles: "Professor Williams explained at some length the sources of his information,
which turned out to be conversations with various Irish officials—
including the Head of the Irish Intelligence Service."[103] This confidential disclosure was, of course, completely unknown to Kerney and his
legal team. The serving head of G2, Colonel Dan Bryan, had actively
conspired to tarnish the reputation of a former colleague. Bryan had
provided Williams with the background information, a trail, a set of
coincidences open to interpretation, circumstantial evidence, and a
correlation of names, dates, and timelines, all of which had helped
sow suspicion and doubt that Kerney was a rogue element. Williams
clearly held the same opinion as Bryan, which is not surprising given
their shared employment in intelligence circles during the war. The
historian had used Bryan's information to help him frame his articles
and present accusations as established facts, without ever naming
Bryan or any other secret source in the publications. A revelation like
that could have ended Bryan's career at a time when he was commandant of the military college, if he had been summoned by Kerney's
legal team for cross-examination in a public court.

Williams claimed in this meeting with the Foreign Office that
"[Helmut] Clissmann, who had been a German Intelligence agent for
some years before 1939," was another confidential source he had used
in preparation for writing the series.[104] This seems quite bizarre considering Clissmann's complete rebuttal of Williams's charges against
Kerney. The British noted in their interviews with Williams that the
historian told them that he would not use Clissmann as a defense
witness in court because he might not be a "reliable witness."[105] Williams seemed to be tying himself in knots. On the one hand, he was
apparently prepared to accept Clissmann's wartime reports on Kerney's alleged liaison with the Germans during the war as facts and to

use such "facts" to compile his articles, and, yet, on the other hand, he quickly discarded the same informant for being untrustworthy as a witness in court. These contradictory opinions of the historian simply did not add up as being credible and raised serious doubts about Williams's entire research for his articles and about the core charges he was alleging against Kerney.

Whitehall's reaction to Williams's articles was scathing. Senior officials such as Richard Sedgwick—the assistant undersecretary of the Constitutions and Political Division of the Commonwealth Relations Office—recorded the shock in Whitehall that Williams had published material obtained from his former employment as a member of the editorial staff researching the captured German archives without prior approval. Sedgwick and his colleagues viewed this conduct as a gross professional violation by Williams: "I asked Mr. Passant if Professor Williams was entitled to publish material obtained in this way. He said certainly not; that Professor Williams had committed a gross breach of trust; and incidentally that in his opinion the documents did not justify the construction placed upon them in the articles, so that Mr Kerney may be expected to win his case."[106]

After reviewing the whole case, and after consulting the other custodians of the captured German archives, particularly the Americans, the Foreign Office, the Commonwealth Relations Office, and the British government made an agreement that, as a special courtesy, the British would not claim privilege if an Irish court requested copies of the documents. Equally, however, London was prepared to grant Kerney "similar treatment" in the interest of justice if his legal team requested documentation as well.[107] Armed with the knowledge that the British were prepared to release what he felt were critical documents in his favor, Williams turned to the Irish authorities for assistance in preparing his defense before the court case. It was from this time onward that his initial confidence in his position began to wane.

Inside Iveagh House a "hands-off" policy was adopted toward the whole case, but this did not stop some younger officials from gathering evidence that strongly contradicted Williams's accusations against Kerney. Conor Cruise O'Brien, then a junior official in the Department of External Affairs, traveled to West Germany, where he met Kurt Haller, a former Abwehr agent who had been heavily involved in Irish matters during the war. O'Brien wrote a detailed report on their conversations in September 1954, and he raised the matter of the extraordinary Kerney-Veesenmayer meeting in August 1942. Haller outlined for O'Brien the German rationale for organizing the meeting. The former agent stated that the Abwehr wanted to "learn more about official Irish thinking and, in particular, the attitude of Mr de Valera through Mr Kerney" on the likelihood of a change in Ireland's neutral policy to a more pro-German foreign policy.[108] The Germans also felt that, given Kerney's close political and familial ties to de Valera, the diplomat was an ideal source of inquiry.[109] However, Haller informed O'Brien that what had seemed at least initially to be a positive initiative soon came to nought. Haller read Veesenmayer's report of the meeting, which, from a German perspective, was very "disappointing" because Kerney had "simply adopted the formally correct attitude of a neutral head of mission and declined to hold out any hope that Ireland would be likely to come in on the German side, or at all."[110] In Haller's view, Kerney had acted appropriately as a head of mission and had listened to Veesenmayer but had given nothing away. O'Brien was himself aware of the libel action, and he informed Dublin that Haller's account ran "contrary" to the one Williams had published in the *Leader* and the *Irish Press*.[111]

After submitting the report of his interview with Haller, O'Brien was eager to publicize the report, as it contradicted not only Williams's allegations against Kerney but also the opinions of others in the department who had been suspicious of Kerney for years, chief among them the former secretary Joseph Walshe. O'Brien was privy to the department's wartime files, which included the correspondence between Joseph Walshe and Colonel Dan Bryan regarding Kerney. Indeed O'Brien was keen to meet Bryan face-to-face and inform him that Kerney had acted entirely appropriately during the war, especially in relation to his meetings with the Germans, noting: "Naturally if Col. Bryan wishes to discuss this report with me I am at his disposition."[112] Within a week the O'Brien report was handed over by the secretary of external affairs, Seán Nunan, to the Department of Defense for Bryan's perusal.[113] The intelligence chief's suspicions about Kerney were now shown, before his own eyes, to have been unfounded and false. Unfortunately O'Brien's report was not known to Kerney or his legal team at the time, but, having passed it on to Bryan, it is likely that the intelligence chief, who had been a confidential informant for Williams in preparing the articles, notified the historian. This would certainly explain Williams's volte-face and his decision to settle the matter outside of court.

There were older colleagues of Kerney, too, who were defending him, though without Kerney's knowledge. Ireland's ambassador to the Court of Saint James, Frederick Boland, called at the Commonwealth Relations Office to meet the Permanent Under-Secretary of State for Commonwealth Relations, Sir Percivale Liesching. Liesching read out a minute from the Foreign Office legal advisor that expressed the opinion that "the papers on the file did not, in his view, justify the criticisms of Mr Kerney which had been made in Professor Williams' articles in the 'Leader' and in the 'Irish Press.'"[114] Importantly, "The legal advisor commented that Mr Kerney's attitude, in the conversations he had had with the emissaries from Germany, seemed to him to have been cautious and perfectly proper in every way."[115] As far as the British were concerned, Kerney had done nothing wrong in meeting the Germans during the war and had acted appropriately as a normal head of mission during these wartime discussions.

This view of the Foreign Office legal advisor showed to be baseless the charges that Walshe and Bryan had made against Kerney that he was held in suspicion as a rogue individual by the British during the war. Presented with the facts, it is clear that Whitehall believed Kerney had acted entirely appropriately and had undertaken due diligence throughout his interactions with the Germans. If there had been some misgivings about him during the war, particularly inside British intelligence circles, it had been the responsibility of Walshe and Bryan to address and clarify those concerns by directly recalling Kerney for interview or to seek answers in writing when the British had first raised any concerns. Yet both men deliberately kept Kerney in the dark, and probably the Taoiseach too, and they worked to collect information against the diplomat rather than airing their suspicions openly to him for clarification.

Boland was then shown four documents by the British that Williams had requested, and he drew the same conclusions as his British counterparts, as he informed Dublin: "If Professor Williams is relying on these four documents to substantiate the suggestions he made in his articles, I doubt whether he will find them of very much use to him."[116] What shocked Boland the most was that the files were completely at variance with Williams's conversations with him back in 1948 when he had alleged that he had damning material on Kerney: "What struck me in reading the four documents, however, was that they bore little or no relation to the account which Professor Williams gave me in 1948 about what he had found in the German Foreign Office archives with regard to Mr Kerney."[117]

Williams himself had been meeting senior officials in External Affairs for assistance once the libel action had been lodged in court. The department's legal advisor, Dr. Michael Rynne, found the historian to be "nonchalant" and "indifferent" to the seriousness of the libel case.[118] Rynne himself had examined all the archival evidence in the department's possession, which included not only Kerney's reports but also correspondence between Walshe and Bryan about Kerney, and he concluded that Williams's articles had made "glaring misinterpretations" about Kerney and other critical matters.[119] Yet another legal advisor found nothing wrong with Kerney's conduct in relation to agreeing to meet the Germans and then in relation to the meeting with Veesenmayer in August 1942. Rynne further argued, like his British counterparts, that Kerney had acted entirely appropriately and within his remit as minister. Yet what mattered as facts to some mattered little to others. There were those who had been lifelong enemies of Kerney and remained hostile toward him. The archival files open a narrow window into the mind of Ireland's then ambassador to the Holy See, Joseph Walshe.

Dermot Keogh examined Joseph Walshe's tenure as secretary of external affairs and made some revealing observations. In his management style Keogh found Walshe to be "autocratic."[120] In his personality Keogh found Walshe to be generally "secretive and mistrustful."[121] Keogh found Walshe's performance in his role as secretary less than adequate, citing "rudimentary diplomatic errors" during his tenure in charge of External Affairs.[122] Walshe's personality and his obsession with "secrecy" created an unusual atmosphere in the department, which was exacerbated under wartime conditions.[123] His successors, Joseph Boland and Seán Nunan, relaxed many of the constraints and formalities Walshe had practiced. At the time of the libel case Seán Nunan struggled to find any correlation in the diplomatic files to make sense of Williams's allegations against Kerney, as well as many other things related to Kerney, such as why he had been recalled to Dublin in 1943. It became apparent to him that a lot had not been recorded, particularly by Walshe, so Nunan wrote to him to get answers. The replies he received from the then ambassador to the Holy See were rather cryptic, yet they reveal a lot about Walshe, his personality, and his attitude toward Kerney that confirm many of Keogh's reflections on Walshe.

In a report marked "Personal and Secret" Walshe confirmed that he had met Williams several times in Rome, most recently on 17 April 1953, a few days after the lead article that attacked Kerney had appeared in public. This proved that Walshe was another unnamed source besides Colonel Dan Bryan who was used by Williams.[124] It was Walshe who had provided the historian with the knowledge that the Taoiseach had firmly rebuked Kerney at Iveagh House on 27 March 1943. De Valera never carried any grudge toward Kerney, so Walshe had to have been the informant for that part of Williams's article. The former secretary outlined his close family acquaintance with Williams: "I had known his mother and his uncles (James and George Murnaghan) very well," he wrote.[125] Both men had similar political outlooks—Williams's close ties to the FitzGeralds and Walshe's pro-treaty stance. Walshe found Williams's articles balanced and fair overall, supported by excellent archival research and in line with "our Departmental conclusions" on many controversial matters.[126] Walshe then went into those controversial matters: "I had, of course, suspected the activities of the individual [Kerney] whose name alone is concealed in the articles, but I found it very hard to believe that he would have gone so far."[127] This was typical of the former secretary's choice use of words—he was using vague and suggestive language to convey suppositions as facts. In the report Walshe did not show any

proof or give an explanation as to why he had found Kerney to be unreliable at the time. In fact, Walshe charged not only Kerney but other
diplomats, such as Michael MacWhite, with failings in the course of
duty: "The men who failed us in the crisis had either been too long
out of Ireland, in their first thirty years, and begun to think themselves
superior to us ordinary Irish, or had already shown a tendency to excessive broadmindedness of the S [Seán] Ó Faoláin type."[128] This last
comment of Walshe comparing Kerney to the acclaimed writer Seán
Ó Faoláin is interesting. According to Donal Ó Drisceoil, Ó Faoláin
"championed the struggle against literary censorship in Ireland."[129]
The writer also challenged the Catholic Church's stranglehold over
Irish society. He was not religious and had many extramarital affairs.
Perhaps Walshe saw in Kerney's lack of devoutness and his conversion to Catholicism similar nonconformist traits that marked him out
in the mind of the former secretary. At no time did Walshe admit
responsibility for his own significant failings over the years to reform
his department, rotate diplomats frequently, or fight to secure a larger
budget from the Department of Finance to provide overseas missions
with adequate financing, which was essential to promote Ireland and
its interests abroad.

On 6 July Walshe wrote another "Very Secret" report to Nunan
that was full of subjective utterances that expressed his disappointment that more shocking material had not been released into the
public domain about Kerney: "The Madrid betrayal, so far, has been
glossed over. It would be a pity to have the whole ugly business
brought on to the tapis just now. Have you spoken to Dan Bryan?
He will remember the recurrence of the name in question in the British black list and the fact that the two chief British agents insisted
on showing it both to him and to me."[130] Just what Walshe meant
by the "Madrid betrayal" is not clear, as Kerney, with the exception
of some of the letters between himself and Frank Ryan, had directly
reported to the secretary all his actions in relation to the Germans at
the time the events were unfolding or shortly thereafter, given wartime conditions.

Walshe was also rather cryptic in relation to the "two chief British
agents." He may have been referring to the brothers Guy and Cecil

Liddell of MI5, who had worked closely with Bryan during the war. Again, it appears that Nunan was completely in the dark about these two men, as Walshe and Bryan guarded their interactions to such an extent that even the Taoiseach might not have been aware that the Liddells might have expressed concerns about Kerney. The former secretary was writing in his usual nebulous way to convey that there had been a cloud of disrepute around Kerney that was murky and ill-defined. He, like Bryan, had hoped that Williams could achieve what neither of them could do during the war—destroy Kerney's reputation and name. Walshe firmly believed that the information in Williams's articles was irrefutable: "For the first time, a qualified historian, trained in England, and, therefore, more likely to be accepted as impartial in this matter, writes what is, on the whole, a serene, impartial, concrete and really splendid account of the policy of neutrality."[131] The Irish High Court would decide if Walshe's assessment was accurate.

Before the High Court of Justice in November 1954 were two cases brought by Kerney—one against Williams and the *Leader*, the other against Williams and the *Irish Press*, for a combined amount of £20,000: "The Plaintiff has been much injured in his credit and reputation and has been brought into public scandal, odium and contempt."[132] Newspapers' interest in the libel action drew widespread public attention. Behind the scenes Williams's legal team had already written to Kerney's solicitor, Seán Ó hUadhaigh, looking to reach an out-of-court settlement.[133] On 28 October 1954 Alexis FitzGerald drafted a letter apologizing for any anguish caused, but it failed to sway Kerney because Williams refused to accept any liability. The case proceeded to court on the appointed day, but moments after a jury was sworn in by Justice Kevin Haugh, the court granted an adjournment for both parties to meet for thirty minutes.[134]

Kerney had written in his own notes that he would not accept any out-of-court settlement, yet, perhaps fearing for his declining health and anxious to secure his reputation as quickly as possible—and completely ignorant of the files held in Iveagh House and Whitehall that disproved Williams's defamation charges entirely—the former diplomat reluctantly agreed to settle the case on condition that the historian admitted liability. In his analysis of the Kerney-Williams libel action, Mark Hull opined that Williams's "contention" against Kerney was accurate and "historically sound."[135] However, such a viewpoint can be challenged by the simple fact that Williams had to admit libel, as both his "evidence" and his core arguments against Kerney were unfounded. Williams's "evidence" was based on assumptions, with little or no proof of the allegations, which could not be upheld in court, and this is why he settled. The archival repositories that have been publicly released since the libel settlement further show that Kerney did not act in any way prejudicial to Irish interests during the war. Kerney's own report of his meeting with Veesenmayer, the opinions of British and Irish legal advisors, Conor Cruise O'Brien's report, and the testimonies of various former Abwehr agents are amongst the documents that show that Williams's core arguments were simply wrong.

It is worth noting that Williams made a full and public declaration of apology to Kerney, and he also admitted that both his sources and his central contentions were incorrect. As his counsel, James McMahon, stated publicly, the historian wished to withdraw "unreservedly" the fallacious allegations he had made in his articles against Kerney and that Mr. Williams "accepted Mr. Kerney's account and regretted the imputations and apologized for them."[136] The apology continued to state that any such imputations were "based on statements now proved to be wrong."[137] Despite Williams's public apology, another historian, Eunan O'Halpin, expressed the view that Williams, not Kerney, had been wronged: "As often happens in Irish libel cases, an undeserving plaintiff won out."[138] Such an opinion runs contrary to the legal settlement and is also at variance with the many archival sources that point to a decidedly different conclusion.

The public declaration that Williams, the top historian in Ireland, had written and made unfounded, uncorroborated statements and baseless claims left a permanent black mark on Williams's reputation as a historian. The public disgrace undoubtedly had a lasting impact on his subsequent career. He produced little in the way of major scholarly publications after this time, and he showed little of his earlier dynamism as a researcher and undergraduate, which had initially marked him out for greatness as a writer. John Duggan, like Hull and O'Halpin, examined the libel case briefly and expressed regret that Williams had been forced to "unjustly" pay damages.[139] This viewpoint, one can argue, ignored the serious defamatory impact that Williams's substandard articles had on Kerney's reputation and his health. Furthermore, if the former diplomat had wanted to be vindictive he could have sought major financial recompense from Williams. Kerney sought instead a token £5 in damages from Williams and the *Leader*, which proved that restoration of his good name and reputation more than monetary reward was what he had wanted all along. If anything, Williams got off very lightly. The *Irish Press* settled out of court for £500 and also apologized publicly for the "untrue statements" and for any "distress and anxiety" caused by the published articles.[140] It was a paltry sum and a large reduction from the £10,000 initially sought against Ireland's best-selling broadsheet.

Andrew Roberts also examined Kerney's interactions with the Germans and chose to overlook Williams's apology and the historian's retraction of his allegations by defending the original thesis that Kerney had colluded with the Nazis. Unsurprisingly, Roberts, like so many other historians, did not cite critical files such as Kerney's wartime reports; the opinions of the Irish and British legal advisors offered in the lead-up to the libel case; the weight of evidence, from the O'Brien report to Clissmann's statements, that showed Kerney had not had any secret negotiated deal with Veesenmayer; and the obvious fact that the Taoiseach retained complete confidence in Kerney both during and after the war. Rather, Roberts, like many subsequent historians who held Williams in high regard, continued to see doubt where the facts showed otherwise.[141]

Another unusual examination of the Kerney-Williams libel case came from Tim Pat Coogan. Coogan was sympathetic to Kerney, citing numerous departmental reports and concluding that the diplomat had acted correctly as head of mission in Spain. However, Coogan made the extraordinary allegation that the Taoiseach, Éamon de Valera, had been the main informant for Williams's articles: "Williams was one of the most brilliant academics of his time: he did not misread documents. I know that he averred privately that his informant about the Veesenmayer-Kearney [*sic*] episode, as about much more in the *Irish Press* series, was none other than the editor-in-chief of the *Irish Press*—Eamon de Valera."[142] Coogan provided no references to substantiate this claim. As godfather to Kerney's youngest son and as a lifelong colleague of Kerney, the Taoiseach had done more than anyone else to help and further Kerney's career, and the two men enjoyed a close friendship. De Valera had no motive for discrediting Kerney, and Coogan perhaps exaggerated de Valera's role in the day-to-day editorship of the *Irish Press*, which was handled at the time by his son Vivion de Valera.

The debunking of Williams's allegations and the legal award did little to aid Kerney either emotionally or financially. That his name had once again been restored and the restoration publicized failed to relieve him from the months of worry and stress caused by the publications, as he still felt bitterly betrayed by the *Irish Press* and held a grievance against Vivion de Valera for what he perceived to be a stab in the back by his republican colleagues. The anxiety contributed to his failing health, and the diplomat suffered repeated strokes. These attacks and poor advice from his doctors that he live a sedentary life-style exacerbated his physical decline. He suffered a massive heart attack in June 1962 and died. At the requiem Mass for Kerney, guests and friends traveled from home and abroad to pay their last respects to him and to his family for their loss. At the ceremony was a man who had shaped, inspired, and transformed Kerney's life over the course of decades; a man whom Kerney had hero-worshipped and stood loyally beside through the dark times and the good; a man who encapsulated Kerney's vision for Ireland, its people, and its political creed. Éamon de Valera paid his last respects to Ireland's revolutionary diplomat.[143]

Introduction

1. McGuire, "T. Desmond Williams."
2. Williams, "A Study in Neutrality."
3. O'Halpin, *Defending Ireland.*
4. Ibid., 194–97.
5. Duggan.
6. Hull, *Irish Secrets: German Espionage in Wartime Ireland, 1939–1945.*
7. Roberts, *A History of the English-Speaking Peoples.*
8. Keogh, *The Vatican, the Bishops and Irish Politics.*
9. Keogh, *Ireland and Europe.*
10. Ó Drisceoil, *Censorship in Ireland.*
11. Coogan, *De Valera.*
12. McLoughlin, *Fighting for Republican Spain.*
13. *Documents on Irish Foreign Policy, 1919–1922*, vol. 1.
14. Kennedy, "Leopold Kerney and the Origin of Irish-Spanish Diplomatic Relations."
15. Kennedy, "Leopold Harding Kerney."
16. Leopold Harding Kerney, Irish Minister to Spain.
17. Russell, *The City in Darkness.*

Chapter 1. From Affluent Sandymount to War-Torn Paris, 1881–1918

1. Incorrectly cited as 23 Sandymount Road in National Archives of Ireland, 1901 census.
2. Kerney is an "Ulster variant spelling" of Kearney. It comes from the Irish surname Ó Cearnaigh (Old Irish, Cearnach, or "victorious"). See MacLysaght, *The Surnames of Ireland,* 177.

3. *Irish Times*, 2 November 1927.

4. Ibid., 15 April 1902.

5. National Archives of Ireland, 1901 census.

6. www://erasmussmithtrustarchives.wordpress.com. Accessed 2 July 2017.

7. Ibid.

8. Trinity College Dublin, "History."

9. Chambers, *T. K. Whitaker*, 16.

10. Coogan, *Ireland in the Twentieth Century*, 15.

11. *Irish Times*, 2 November 1927.

12. Ibid., 10 April 1900.

13. Ibid., 1 March 1902.

14. Ibid., 3 November 1927.

15. Leopold Kerney Private Archive (LKPA), "The First Irish Consul in Paris," memorandum, 1.

16. The Larchets were also Protestant and of Huguenot origin.

17. National Archives of Ireland, 1901 census.

18. Staatsarchive Hamburg, vol. 373-71, viii A1 Band 152, Seite 169, num. K1782, 6 February 1904.

19. UK Census Online, 1911 census.

20. LKPA, letter from the managing director of Lucile Ltd Paris to Leopold Kerney, 26 November 1919.

21. UK Census Online, 1911 census.

22. Ibid.

23. Chadwick, *The Secularisation of the European Mind*, 129.

24. Patricia Craig, *The Oxford Book of Ireland*, x.

25. Ibid.

26. General Register Office, Certificate of Marriage 4880882-1, no. 126.

27. Kedward, *La Vie en Bleu*, 63.

28. See Johnstone, *Orange, Green and Khaki*.

29. Hastings, *Catastrophe*, 288.

30. Ibid., 289.

31. Kedward, *La Vie en Bleu*, 73.

32. Regan, *Famous British Battles*, 151.

33. Ibid.

34. LKPA, letter from Leopold Kerney to John Redmond, 1 December 1917.

Chapter 2. The First Irish Consul in Paris, 1919–1921

1. Manning, *Irish Political Parties*, 1.

2. Ferriter, *The Transformation of Ireland*, 184.

3. *Dáil Éireann Debates* (DÉD), vol. f, no. 6, 10 April 1919.

4. Ibid.

5. Ibid.

6. Ibid., 18 June 1919.

7. LKPA, "The First Irish Consul in Paris, 31st July 1925," memorandum, 1.

8. Ibid.

9. Ibid.

10. Ibid.

11. Bureau of Military History (BMH), Military Archives of Ireland (MAI), WS 825, "Statement of Leopold H. Kerney Former Consul of the Irish Republic in France, July 1919–December 1922," 30 March 1953, 1.

12. DÉD, vol. f, no. 7, 11 April 1919.

13. LKPA, "The First Irish Consul in Paris, 31st July 1925," memorandum, 1.

14. Ibid.

15. Ibid.

16. Ibid., 2.

17. Ibid.

18. Ibid.

19. Ibid., 1.

20. Maillot, *New Sinn Féin*, 8.

21. Keown, *First of the Small Nations*, 15.

22. BMH, MAI, WS 825, 1.

23. Ibid., 3.

24. Maguire, *The Civil Service and the Revolution in Ireland*, 100.

25. Ibid., 103.

26. BMH, MAI, WS 825, 4.

27. Ibid.

28. University College Dublin Archives (UCDA), George Gavan Duffy papers, P152/100.

29. Gerard Keown, *First of the Small Nations*, 66.

30. UCDA, George Gavan Duffy papers, P152/114, Ernest Blythe to George Gavan Duffy, 22 March 1920.

31. Ibid., P152/116.

32. Ibid., P152/124, Ernest Blythe to George Gavan Duffy, 2 July 1920.

33. Ibid., P152/126, George Gavan Duffy to Michael Collins, 3 July 1920.

34. Martin Gilbert, *History of the Twentieth Century*, 126.

35. This was soon after Duffy was expelled from France and moved to Brussels. See DÉD, vol. f, no. 17, 17 September 1920.

36. Keogh, 127.

37. BMH, MAI, WS 825, 5.

38. Ibid.

39. Ibid.

40. Aldcroft and Morewood, *The European Economy since 1914*, 37.

41. *Irish Times*, 19 August 1921.

42. BMH, MAI, WS 825, 7.

43. Ibid.

44. Diarmaid Ferriter, *The Transformation of Ireland*, 236–37.

45. Gerard Keown, *First of the Small Nations*, 46.

46. LKPA, "The First Irish Consul in Paris, 31st July 1925," memorandum, 1.

Chapter 3. The Treaty and the Irish Civil War, 1921–1922

1. George Plunkett, 22 January 1919–26 August 1921; Arthur Griffith, 26 August 1921–9 January 1922; George Gavan Duffy, 10 January 1922–25 July 1922.

2. LKPA, "The First Irish Consul in Paris, 31st July 1925," memorandum, 2.

3. Ibid., "An Officer of the Republican Government," 12 June 1923, memorandum, 1.

4. Ibid.

5. Ibid.

6. Ibid.

7. Keown, *First of the Small Nations*, 94.

8. UCDA, Michael MacWhite papers, P194/213, letter from George Gavan Duffy to Michael MacWhite, 11 January 1922.

9. Ibid., P194/270, Michael MacWhite to Seán Mulroy, 11 February 1923.

10. National Archives of Ireland (NAI), Dáil Éireann, 2/206, Irish Race Congress.

11. DÉD, vol. s2, no. 3, 2 March 1922.

12. Ibid.

13. Keown, *First of the Small Nations*, 18.

14. UCDA, Éamon de Valera private papers, Irish Race Congress in Paris, P150/1590–1605.

15. Ibid.

16. Bureau of Military History (BMH), MAI, WS 825, 5.

17. Ryan, *Liam Lynch*, 133.

18. LKPA, "The First Irish Consul in Paris, 31st July 1925," memorandum, 3.

19. BMH, MAI, WS 825, 6.

20. Ibid.

21. Ibid.

22. DÉD, vol. s2, no. 3, 2 March 1922.

23. See Ryan, *Liam Lynch*.

24. Coogan, *Ireland in the Twentieth Century*, 113.

25. Ferriter, *The Transformation of Ireland*, 254.

26. Maguire, *The Civil Service and the Revolution in Ireland*, 137.

27. LKPA, "The First Irish Consul in Paris, 31st July 1925," memorandum, 3.

28. BMH, MAI, WS 825, 7.

29. Until 1938, the British retained control of two other ports, known as the Treaty ports: Lough Swilly and Berehaven.

30. BMH, MAI, WS 825, 8.

31. *Irish Independent*, 3 October 1922.

32. Maguire, *The Civil Service and the Revolution in Ireland*, 159.

33. LKPA, "The First Irish Consul in Paris, 31st July 1925," memorandum, 3.

34. Maguire, *The Civil Service and the Revolution in Ireland*, 158.

35. LKPA, "An Officer of the Republican Government," memorandum, 12 June 1923, 1.

36. UCDA, P80/395 (1), report by George Gavan Duffy to Desmond FitzGerald, 20 June 1922.

37. LKPA, "The First Irish Consul in Paris, 31st July 1925," memorandum, 3.

38. Ibid. In the Second Provisional Government (9 September 1922–

6 December 1922) McGrath was appointed minister for industry and commerce, while Blythe moved to local government.

39. Ibid.

40. UCDA, Éamon de Valera papers, P150/1647, Éamon de Valera to Professor Culverwell, 13 October 1922.

41. LKPA, "The First Irish Consul in Paris, 31st July 1925," memorandum, 3.

42. Ibid., 4.

43. Ibid.

44. Ibid., 3–4.

45. UCDA, Éamon de Valera papers, P150/1771, Éamon de Valera to Leopold Kerney, 22 November 1922.

46. LKPA, "The First Irish Consul in Paris, 31st July 1925," memorandum, 4.

47. NAI, DFA, ES Paris, Joseph Walshe to Vaughan Dempsey, 26 January 1923.

48. LKPA, "The First Irish Consul in Paris, 31st July 1925," memorandum, 5.

49. DÉD, vol. 2, no. 22, 30 January 1923.

50. LKPA, "The First Irish Consul in Paris, 31st July 1925," memorandum, 4.

51. Ibid., 5.

Chapter 4. The Consular and Diplomatic Envoy of the Irish Republic, 1922–1926

1. UCDA, Éamon de Valera papers, P150/1695, official communiqué, 5 January 1923.

2. Ibid., 5 November 1922.

3. LKPA, "The First Irish Consul in Paris, 31st July 1925," memorandum, 4.

4. UCDA, Desmond FitzGerald papers, P80/384(16), Desmond FitzGerald to Diarmuid Ó hÉigeartaigh, 5 March 1923.

5. Donal Hales was the republican consul in Genoa.

6. Keown, *First of the Small Nations*, 114.

7. Keatinge, *The Formulation of Irish Foreign Policy*, 76.

8. Nolan, *Joseph Walshe*, 21.

9. Keogh, *The Vatican, the Bishops and Irish Politics*, 126.

10. UCDA, Michael MacWhite papers, P194/270, Michael MacWhite to Seán Mulroy, 11 February 1923.

11. NAI, DFA, ES Paris 1922–23, Vaughan Dempsey to Desmond FitzGerald, 31 January 1923.

12. Ibid., 142, Vaughan Dempsey to Desmond FitzGerald, 3 February 1923.

13. Ibid., 147, Seán Murphy to Desmond FitzGerald, 4 April 1923.

14. Ibid.

15. UCDA, Éamon de Valera papers, P150/1771, Éamon de Valera to Leopold Kerney, 23 May 1923.

16. Ibid., Éamon de Valera to Leopold Kerney, 20 June 1923.

17. Keown, *First of the Small Nations*, 90.

18. UCDA, P150/1771, Éamon de Valera to Thomas Hughes Kelly, 26 July 1923.

19. National Library of Ireland (NLI), Máire O'Brien papers, MS 43/245, "Documents Relating to the Red Cross and the Treatment of the Irish Republican Prisoners in Free State Prisons, Aug.–Sep. 1923," statement by Joseph Clark, 15 November 1922.

20. O'Halpin, *Defending Ireland*, 13.

21. NLI, Máire O'Brien papers, MS 43/245, "Documents Relating to the Red Cross and the Treatment of the Irish Republican Prisoners in Free State Prisons, Aug.–Sep. 1923," female delegation's praise of Kerney's work.

22. *Éire*, 4 August 1923.

23. See Matthews, *Dissidents*.

24. UCDA, P150/1771, "Analysis of the Report on the British Prisons in Ireland Published by the International Committee of the Red Cross," by Leopold Kerney, 12 July 1923.

25. Ibid., letter from Leopold Kerney to Éamon de Valera, 12 July 1923.

26. Ibid., P150/1744, Mary MacSwiney to Commandant D IRA HQ, 5 December 1923.

27. Kennedy, "The Irish Free State and the League of Nations," 11.

28. UCDA, P150/1771, Leopold Kerney to the minister for foreign affairs, 16 February 1924.

29. Ibid.

30. Michael Colivet replaced Austin Stack, who had been arrested by the Free State authorities.

31. UCDA, P150/1771, minister of finance to the minister of foreign affairs, 27 February 1924.

32. NAI, DFA, 147, departmental records of Kerney's publications in France, 14 March 1924.

33. Ibid., Vaughan Dempsey to Joseph Walshe, 19 March 1924.

34. Ibid.

35. Ibid., Joseph Walshe to Vaughan Dempsey, 24 March 1924.

36. UCDA, Mary MacSwiney papers, P48A/35, Leopold Kerney to Sinn Féin Headquarters, 29 March 1924.

37. Ibid., P150/1771, Leopold Kerney to the minister for foreign affairs, 15 May 1924.

38. LKPA, letter from Éamon de Valera to Leopold Kerney, 20 October 1924.

39. Ibid., Leopold Kerney to Éamon de Valera, 7 November 1924.

40. Ibid., Éamon de Valera to Leopold Kerney, 19 December 1924.

41. Military Archives of Ireland (MAI), Contemporary Document 260/4/1-6, Leopold H. Kerney collection, undersecretary of foreign affairs to Leopold Kerney, 26 March 1925.

42. Ibid., Leopold Kerney to the undersecretary of foreign affairs, 24 June 1925.

43. *Inis Fáil: Bulletin de la Ligue pour l'indépendance de l'Irlande*, no. 1, April 1925, 5.

44. MAI, Contemporary Document 260/4/1-6, Leopold H. Kerney collection, undersecretary of foreign affairs to director of economic affairs, 6 May 1925.

45. Ibid., undersecretary of foreign affairs to Leopold Kerney, 26 June 1925.

46. Keogh, *The Vatican, the Bishops and Irish Politics*, 47.

47. MAI, Contemporary Document 260/4/1-6, Leopold H. Kerney collection, undersecretary of foreign affairs to Leopold Kerney, 3 June 1925.

48. Ibid., minister for finance to the minister for foreign affairs, 3 June 1925.

49. Ibid., Leopold Kerney to the undersecretary for foreign affairs, 19 June 1925.

50. UCDA, Desmond FitzGerald papers, P80/867 (19), the republican minister for finance to Mary MacSwiney, 20 October 1925.

51. Ibid.

52. Ibid.

53. Ibid., P80/867 (23), Leopold Kerney to the undersecretary for foreign affairs, 23 October 1925.

54. Ibid., P80/867 (32), Leopold Kerney to the undersecretary for foreign affairs, 23 December 1925.

55. Ferriter, *Judging Dev*, 102.

56. LKPA, handwritten letter from Éamon de Valera to Leopold Kerney, 23 April 1926.

57. Ibid., signed copy of Pamphlet No. 1, "Fianna Fáil: A National Policy Outlined by Éamon de Valera," Dublin, May 1926.

58. Ibid., letter from Art O'Connor to Leopold Kerney, 25 April 1926.

59. Ibid., handwritten letter from Éamon de Valera to Raymonde Kerney, 28 June 1926.

60. Ibid., handwritten letter from Éamon de Valera to Leopold Kerney, 23 April 1926.

61. Ibid., Art O'Connor to Leopold Kerney, 31 August 1926.

62. Ibid., 12 October 1926.

63. Ibid., Leopold Kerney to Art O'Connor, 20 October 1926.

Chapter 5. *The Wilderness Years, 1926–1932*

1. Aldcroft and Morewood, *The European Economy since 1914*, 66.

2. LKPA, typed letter from Leopold Kerney to Henry Kerney, 31 December 1920.

3. Ibid., handwritten letter from Henry Kerney to Leopold Kerney, 21 December 1920.

4. Ibid.

5. Ibid.

6. Ibid.

7. LKPA, Leopold Kerney to Henry Kerney, 31 December 1920.

8. Ibid.

9. LKPA, Philip Kerney to Leopold Kerney, 29 December 1926.

10. Ibid.

11. For a detailed account of these acts, see Lee, *Ireland, 1912–1985*.

12. For a good biography of Hanna Sheehy Skeffington, see Margaret Ward, *Hanna Sheehy Skeffington*.

13. NLI, Hanna Sheehy Skeffington papers, MS 41/178/51, Leopold Kerney to Hanna Sheehy Skeffington, 18 August 1927.

14. Cronin, *The McGarrity Papers*, 149.

15. NAI, JUS/8/675, police report, 15 December 1927.

16. NLI, Hanna Sheehy Skeffington papers, MS 41/178/51, Leopold Kerney to Hanna Sheehy Skeffington, 18 August 1927.

17. Ibid., MS 41/178/69, undated letter from Leopold Kerney to Hanna Sheehy Skeffington, circa April 1929.

18. Ibid.

19. Ibid., 5 March 1931.

20. Ibid. Lord Ashbourne also went under the name Mac Giolla Bhríde.

21. Erskine Childers was the future minister for posts and telegraphs and president of Ireland.

22. NLI, Hanna Sheehy Skeffington papers, MS 41/178/71, Leopold Kerney to Hanna Sheehy Skeffington, 5 March 1931.

23. LKPA, file titled "Saint Patrick's Day—1931–32 (Classified)." The file contains photographs of the celebrations, menus, speeches, poems, and lyrics. Some files relating to Kerney's reinstatement are also present.

24. NAI, DFA, ES Paris, Joseph Walshe to Vaughan Dempsey, 26 January 1923.

25. Keown, *First of the Small Nations*, 203.

26. LKPA, file titled "Saint Patrick's Day—1931–32 (Classified)," typed letter from Count Gerald O'Kelly to Leopold Kerney, 25 February 1931.

27. Ibid., typed letter from Leopold Kerney to Count Gerald O'Kelly, 28 February 1931.

28. Ibid., typed letter from Count Gerald O'Kelly to Leopold Kerney, 4 March 1931.

29. Ibid., Éamon de Valera to Leopold Kerney, 5 February 1931.

30. Ibid.

31. Horgan, *Seán Lemass*, 62.

32. NLI, Hanna Sheehy Skeffington papers, MS 41/178/77, Rose Gartland to Hanna Sheehy Skeffington, 20 March 1932.

33. Ibid., Raymonde Kerney to Hanna Sheehy Skeffington, 15 January 1932.

34. Cronin, *The McGarrity Papers*, 151.

35. LKPA, file titled "Saint Patrick's Day—1931–32 (Classified)," telegram from Leopold Kerney to Éamon de Valera, 23 February 1932.

36. See Feeney, *Seán MacEntee*.

37. LKPA, file titled "Saint Patrick's Day—1931–32 (Classified)," letter from Frank Litton to Leopold Kerney, 14 March 1932.

38. Ibid., letter from Seán T. O'Kelly to Leopold Kerney, 1 March 1932.

39. Nolan, *Joseph Walshe*, 59.

40. Keogh, *The Vatican, the Bishops and Irish Politics*, 187.

41. Andrews, *Man of No Property*, 119.

42. Dermot Keogh, *The Vatican, the Bishops and Irish Politics*, 123.

43. LKPA, file titled "Saint Patrick's Day—1931–32 (Classified)," Leopold Kerney to Máire O'Brien, 16 March 1932.

44. Ibid.

45. Ibid.

46. Ibid.

47. Ibid., letter from Leopold Kerney to Frank Litton, 3 April 1932.

48. NAI, JUS 8/675, Fianna Fáil Ard Fheis resolution no. 11.

49. LKPA, file titled "Saint Patrick's Day—1931–32 (Classified)," Fianna Fáil resolution, 20 January 1928.

50. NAI, Department of the Taoiseach (DT), S/2350.

51. LKPA, file titled "Reinstatement as Commercial Secretary, 7 April 1932–8 October 1935," telegram from Robert Brennan to Leopold Kerney, 18 March 1932.

52. Ibid., 23 March 1932.

53. LKPA, file titled "Reinstatement as Commercial Secretary, 7 April 1932–8 October 1935," letter from Leopold Kerney to Robert Brennan, 24 March 1932.

54. Ibid., typed letter from Leopold Kerney to Éamon de Valera, 26 March 1932.

55. Ibid.

56. Ibid.

57. LKPA, file titled "Reinstatement as Commercial Secretary, 7 April 1932–8 October 1935," typed letter from Leopold Kerney to Frank Litton, 3 April 1932.

58. Ibid., report of the committee of inquiry concerning Leopold Kerney's reinstatement as commercial secretary, 7 April 1932.

59. O'Halpin, *Defending Ireland*, 194.

60. Maguire, *The Civil Service and the Revolution in Ireland*, 207.

61. LKPA, file titled "Reinstatement as Commercial Secretary, 7 April 1932—8 October 1935," report of the committee of inquiry concerning Leopold Kerney's reinstatement as commercial secretary, 7 April 1932.

62. Ibid., letter from Leopold Kerney to Éamon de Valera, 13 April 1932.

63. Ibid.

64. LKPA, file titled "Reinstatement as Commercial Secretary, 7 April 1932—8 October 1935," Leopold Kerney to Robert Brennan, 9 April 1932.

Chapter 6. From France to Spain, 1932–1939

1. Nolan, *Joseph Walshe*, 56.

2. Ibid., 57.

3. Ferriter, *The Transformation of Ireland*, 408.

4. Garvin, *The Lives of Daniel Binchy*, 40.

5. Keown, *First of the Small Nations*, 249.

6. Ibid., 230.

7. Keogh, *The Vatican, the Bishops and Irish Politics*, 192.

8. Ibid., 127.

9. Chambers, *T. K. Whitaker*, 39.

10. NAI, DT, S2303, Joseph Walshe to the secretary of the executive council, 25 April 1932.

11. Ibid.

12. Garvin, *The Lives of Daniel Binchy*, 40–41.

13. Keogh, *The Vatican, the Bishops and Irish Politics*, 127.

14. NAI, DT, S2303, minutes of the executive council meeting, 12 August 1932.

15. Kennedy, "Leopold Harding Kerney."

16. Ferriter, *The Transformation of Ireland*, 368.

17. O'Rourke, "Burn Everything British but Their Coal," 357.

18. NAI, DT, S2303, Department of External Affairs minutes, 25 April 1932.

19. LKPA, file titled "Reinstatement as Commercial Secretary, 7 April 1932–8 October 1935," letter from Joseph Walshe to Leopold Kerney, 18 June 1934.

20. Keogh, *The Vatican, the Bishops and Irish Politics*, 127.

21. NAI, DFA S3, statistics on Irish-Belgian trade relations, 1933–34.

22. Dáil Éireann Debates (DÉD), vol. 48, no. 16, 11 July 1933.

23. Ibid.

24. Ibid. Relations between Ireland and the USSR stretched back to the 1920s. In April 1920 de Valera, as president of the Dáil and one of its trustees, loaned $20,000 to a Bolshevik envoy named Ludwig Martens in New York. See Barry Whelan, "Éamon de Valera: A Republican Loan and the Secret of the Lost Russian Jewels," *Scoláire Staire* 3, no. 1 (2013): 24–28. Shortly after this preliminary encounter, on 29 June 1920, the Dáil unanimously moved to "dispatch a Diplomatic Mission to the Government of the Russian Socialist Federal Soviet Republic with a view to establishing

diplomatic relations with that Government." Patrick McCartan was sent as Ireland's envoy to Moscow. Even the Irish Free State, of which Desmond FitzGerald was a serving minister, approved contact with the communist state. See NAI, DFA, P135.

25. Ibid.

26. Ibid.

27. Ibid.

28. Ibid.

29. NAI, DT S2303, details on Kerney's reinstatement, salary, and allowances.

30. LKPA, "Personal File—L.H. Kerney—9 May 1932–29 June 1936," letter from Leopold Kerney to the secretary of the Revenue Commissioners, 20 January 1933.

31. Ibid., letter from Leopold Kerney to Joseph Walshe, 9 May 1932.

32. Ibid., 16 June 1933.

33. Ibid., 2 July 1932.

34. Ibid., 16 June 1933.

35. Ibid., 9 June 1934.

36. NLI, Hanna Sheehy Skeffington papers, MS 41/178/82, Leopold Kerney to Hanna Sheehy Skeffington, 28 January 1934.

37. LKPA, "Personal File—L.H. Kerney—9 May 1932–29 June 1936," Leopold Kerney to Éamon de Valera, 20 March 1934.

38. NAI, S31, Daniel Twomey to Joseph Walshe, 3 July 1934.

39. Ibid., Joseph Walshe to Daniel Twomey, 16 November 1934.

40. Eunan O'Halpin, *Defending Ireland*, 194.

41. NAI, DFA, 19/7A, Count Gerald O'Kelly to Joseph Walshe, 4 June 1932.

42. LKPA, "Personal File—L.H. Kerney—9 May 1932–29 June 1936," letter from Leopold Kerney to Kathleen O'Connell, 18 March 1935.

43. Ibid.

44. Ibid.

45. Ibid.

46. Ibid.

47. Ibid., letter from Art Ó Briain to Leopold Kerney, 23 September 1935.

48. Ibid., letter from Leopold Kerney to Art Ó Briain, 16 September 1935.

49. Keogh, *Con Cremin*, 13.

50. LKPA, "Personal File—L.H. Kerney—9 May 1932–29 June 1936," letter from Art Ó Briain to Leopold Kerney, 23 September 1935.

51. Keogh, *Con Cremin*, 15.

52. One of Kerney's nephews worked for several years in banking in Barcelona, and Kerney frequently traveled there to see him.

53. See NLI, Máire O'Brien papers, MS 43242/3.

54. NAI, S791/A, approval by the executive council for an Irish representative in Spain, 28 June 1935.

55. NAI, DFA, 1935 Madrid letter boxes, Joseph Walshe to Leopold Kerney, 3 August 1935.

56. LKPA, "Personal File—L.H. Kerney—9 May 1932–29 June 1936," Leopold Kerney to Joseph Walshe, 29 July 1935.

57. Ibid., letter from Leopold Kerney to Art Ó Briain, 16 September 1935.

58. Ibid., Leopold Kerney to Joseph Walshe, 1 July 1935.

59. NAI, DFA, 246/109, letter from Olive Byrne to Joseph Walshe, 8 July 1940.

60. Ibid., 1935 Madrid letter boxes, Joseph Walshe to Leopold Kerney, 6 August 1935.

61. Ibid., 13 September 1935.

62. LKPA, "Letters to Maurice file, 1937–50," Leopold Kerney to Maurice Kerney, 12 December 1948.

63. NAI, DFA, 1935 Madrid letter boxes, Joseph Walshe to Leopold Kerney, 14 September 1935.

64. Ibid.

65. Ibid., 16 September 1935.

66. NAI, DFA, 1936 Madrid letter boxes, Seán Murphy to Leopold Kerney, 20 January 1936.

67. NAI, DFA, 19/93, Leopold Kerney to Joseph Walshe, 17 April 1936.

68. Vincent, *Spain 1833–2002*, 139.

69. NAI, DFA, 19/93, Leopold Kerney to Joseph Walshe, 23 November 1935.

70. Ibid., 18 February 1936.

71. Ibid., 11 May 1936.

72. Ibid., 13 March 1936.

73. Ibid., 30 March 1936.

74. Ibid., 11 May 1936.

75. Ibid., 17 April 1936.

76. *ABC* (a Spanish newspaper), 17 April 1936.

77. NAI, DFA, 17/4, Leopold Kerney to Joseph Walshe, 8 June 1936.

78. *Irish Press*, 21 August 1936.

79. Ibid.

80. NAI, DFA, 1936 Madrid letter boxes, Joseph Walshe to Leopold Kerney, 4 June 1936.

81. *Irish Press*, 21 August 1936.

82. See Beevor, *The Battle for Spain*.

83. NAI, DFA, 1937 Madrid letter boxes, departmental note to Leopold Kerney, 18 March 1937.

84. Ibid., departmental note authorizing reimbursement of 3,700 francs for the typewriter expense, 24 June 1937.

85. McLoughlin, *Fighting for Republican Spain*, 20.

86. For an account of the Irish involvement in the Spanish Civil War, see McGarry, *Irish Politics and the Spanish Civil War*.

87. Franco was voted by his fellow generals to be head of state of nationalist Spain and generalissimo of the armed forces in Burgos. The Republican Government had transferred to Valencia.

88. DÉD, vol. 64, no. 8, 27 November 1936.

89. Ibid., vol. 65, no. 3, 17 February 1937.

90. Ibid., vol. 65, no. 4, 18 February 1937.

91. Ibid., speech by James Dillon TD, vol. 65, no. 5, 19 February 1937.

92. Kennedy, "Leopold Harding Kerney."

93. NAI, DFA, 119/17A, Leopold Kerney to Joseph Walshe, 6 March 1937.

94. Ibid.

95. LKPA, "Letters to Maurice file, 1937–50," letter from Leopold Kerney to Maurice Kerney, 25 November 1937.

96. Ibid., 26 August 1938.

97. For a roll of honor of British and Irish soldiers of the 25th International Brigade killed in action or executed after surrendering, see Rust, *Britons in Spain*, 189–99.

98. NAI, DFA, 1937 Madrid letter boxes, Joseph Walshe to Leopold Kerney, 6 March 1937.

99. LKPA, "Letters to Maurice file, 1937–50," letter from Leopold Kerney to Maurice Kerney, 12 December 1937.

100. Ibid., 25 April 1938.

101. Ibid., 30 February 1939.

Chapter 7. Franco's Most Famous Foreign Prisoner and Escapee—Frank Ryan

1. See McGarry, *Irish Politics and the Spanish Civil War*.
2. O'Halpin, *Defending Ireland*, 197.
3. Kennedy, "Leopold Harding Kerney."
4. McLoughlin, *Fighting for Republican Spain*, 94.
5. For a biography of Ryan, see Cronin, *Frank Ryan*.
6. *Irish Press*, 23 September 1936.
7. Rust, *Britons in Spain*, 8.
8. Ibid., 51–54.
9. NAI, DFA, A20/3, document titled "Condensed Translation of Procedure Relating to Frank Ryan's Death Sentence with Precise Translation of Actual Sentence."
10. Ibid.
11. Ibid., note from the juridical assessor to the headquarters of General Franco commuting Ryan's death sentence, 12 November 1939.
12. These were Andrew O'Toole and John Madden. Both were subsequently repatriated by the minister.
13. Archivo del Ministerio de Asuntos Exteriores (AMAE), leg. R—1056/E10, Juan Garcia Ontiveros to the Ministry of Foreign Affairs, 25 May 1939.
14. Ibid.
15. *Irish Workers' Weekly*, 27 May 1939.
16. Archivo General de Administración (AGA) (10) 3954/11731, Juan Garcia Ontiveros to the Ministry of Foreign Affairs, 14 June 1939.
17. Ibid.
18. *Evening Mail*, 4 July 1939, letter to the editor from "R.E."
19. Included in the files in the AGA Alcalá de Henares are processed visa applications issued by Ontiveros. The vast majority of the applicants were priests and nuns.
20. AGA (10) 3954/11732, letter from Father James Cleary to Juan Garcia Ontiveros, 28 January 1940.
21. Ibid.
22. Ibid., (10) 3954/11730, Juan Garcia Ontiveros to the Ministry of Foreign Affairs, 2 July 1939.

23. Ibid., letter from an unknown correspondent to Juan Garcia Ontiveros, 15 July 1939.

24. Among the Dáil signatories were P. J. Little, parliamentary secretary to the Taoiseach; Dr. Ward, parliamentary secretary to the minister for public health and local government; Seán Moylan, parliamentary secretary to the minister for industry and commerce; and William Norton, leader of the Labour Party.

25. AGA (10) 3954/11730, letter from an unknown correspondent to Juan Garcia Ontiveros, 15 July 1939.

26. Ibid., Juan Garcia Ontiveros to the Ministry of Foreign Affairs, 28 July 1939.

27. Ibid.

28. NAI, DFA, A20/1, Leopold Kerney to Joseph Walshe, 30 May 1939.

29. Ibid.

30. The Spanish ambassador in London, the Duke of Alba, was, like Ontiveros, under severe pressure from republican sympathizers to intercede in the Ryan case and speed up his release. See Communist Party of Ireland Archive (CPIA), "Frank Ryan," no. 16 (since relocated to the Dublin City Library and Archive).

31. AMAE, leg. R—1051/E75, "Prisioneros de guerra de Irlanda en la guerra civil española," written note, 29 May 1939.

32. NAI, DFA, A20/2, Leopold Kerney to the Department of External Affairs, 17 June 1939.

33. Ibid., Leopold Kerney to Frederick Boland, 17 June 1939.

34. Ibid., Leopold Kerney to the Department of External Affairs, 6 July 1939.

35. Ibid., 5 July 1939.

36. Ibid., 14 September 1939.

37. NAI, DFA, A20/3, Leopold Kerney to Joseph Walshe, 17 October 1939.

38. Ibid., letter from Leopold Kerney to Eilís Ryan, 16 October 1939.

39. Ibid., Leopold Kerney to Joseph Walshe, 21 November 1939.

40. Ibid.

41. Ibid., 27 November 1939.

42. Ibid., 16 December 1939.

43. Preston, *The Spanish Civil War*, 310.

44. NAI, DFA, A20/3, Leopold Kerney to Joseph Walshe, 2 February 1940.

45. Ibid.

46. Ibid., Joseph Walshe to Juan Garcia Ontiveros, 23 February 1940.

47. Ibid., Joseph Walshe to Leopold Kerney, 26 March 1940.

48. Ibid., 5/4, Joseph Walshe to Leopold Kerney, 12 April 1940.

49. Ibid., Leopold Kerney to Joseph Walshe, 23 April 1940.

50. Ibid., resolution passed by Chichester Trades Council and forwarded to the Taoiseach, 15 April 1940.

51. CPIA, "Frank Ryan," no. 17, letter from Tom Jones to Seán Nunan, 1 May 1940.

52. NAI, DFA, A20/3, Leopold Kerney to Joseph Walshe, 7 May 1940.

53. Ibid., telegram from Leopold Kerney to Joseph Walshe, 10 May 1940.

54. Ibid., 23 May 1940.

55. DÉD, vol. 80, no. 13, 6 June 1940.

56. For a full account of the infighting among the various Nazi intelligence agencies, see Höhne, *The Order of the Death's Head.*

57. Paine, *The Abwehr,* 11.

58. File no. 198, 19 October 1940, in *Documents on German Foreign Policy, 1918–1945,* Series D, vol. 11, 329.

59. Whealey, *Hitler and Spain,* 67.

60. For a full account of clandestine Abwehr activities, see Tusell, *Franco, España y la Segunda Guerra Mundial.*

61. Paine, *The Abwehr,* 72.

62. Also known as the SIS (Secret Intelligence Service).

63. British National Archives, Kew (BNAK), KV—Records of the Security Service files, KV 2/101, "Friedrich Knappe" file.

64. Ibid., note from the British embassy to the Spanish Ministry of Foreign Affairs, 14 December 1944.

65. Ibid., KV 2/2863, "George Helmut Lang" file, note by MI6, 22 January 1946.

66. Ibid., KV 2/102, undated note on Karl Eric Kuehlenthal.

67. See Andrew, *The Defence of the Realm,* 259–62.

68. NAI, DFA, CON 4/7/22, no. 3, 30 April 1940.

69. Ibid., A20/4, report from Leopold Kerney to Joseph Walshe, 26 August 1940.

70. Ibid.

71. Hull, *Irish Secrets,* 191.

72. BNAK, KV 2/1291, "Frank Ryan" file, intercepted telegram from the International Brigade Association, 26 September 1940.

73. Ibid., Valentine Vivian to Cecil Liddell, 10 March 1941.

74. Ibid., KV 5/130, "Frank Ryan" file, note on general history of his movements.

75. O'Halpin, *Defending Ireland*, 196.

76. Ibid., 109.

77. BNAK, KV 2/1976, "Friedrich Wolfgang Blaum" file, report by US Forces European Theater Military Intelligence Service Center, 12 January 1946.

78. NAI, DFA, A20/4, Leopold Kerney to Joseph Walshe, 26 August 1940.

79. For a biography of Clissmann, see Clarke, "Helmut Clissmann."

80. NLI, Hanna Sheehy Skeffington papers, MS 41/178/82, Leopold Kerney to Hanna Sheehy Skeffington, 28 January 1934. As with all other efforts to learn Irish, Kerney failed.

81. Hinsley and Simkins, *British Intelligence*, 17.

82. Jupp Hoven was another of the Abwehr circle in Ireland before the war. BNAK, KV 6/79, "Jupp Hoven" file.

83. NAI, DFA, A20/4.

84. See Eunan O'Halpin, *Defending Ireland*.

85. MAI, G2/X/0093.

86. BNAK, KV 6/80, "Helmut Clissmann" file, report by Colonel Liam Archer to Harker of the British War Office, 5 December 1938. See also MAI, G2/X/0093.

87. Ibid., FO 940/49, "Helmut Clissmann" file.

88. Ibid., KV 6/80, "Helmut Clissmann" file, Special Branch report, 9 September 1939.

89. The name Brandenburgers was chosen because the unit's training and supply facility was at Brandenburg, forty miles west of Berlin.

90. BNAK, KV 2/769, "Kurt Haller" file.

91. Ibid., KV 2/1292, "Frank Ryan" file, final interrogation of Kurt Haller, 7 August 1946.

92. NAI, DFA, CON 4/7/22, no. 4, Leopold Kerney to Joseph Walshe, 29 July 1940.

93. Ibid.

94. Ibid., A20/4, Leopold Kerney to Joseph Walshe, 26 August 1940.

95. Ibid., A20 annex, letter from Frank Ryan to Leopold Kerney, 20 August 1940.

96. Ibid.

97. Ibid., A20/4, letter from Budge Clissmann to Leopold Kerney, 21 November 1940.

98. Ibid., 10/11, part 4, telegram from Leopold Kerney to Joseph Walshe, 5 December 1940.

99. Ibid., A8, Colonel Liam Archer to Joseph Walshe, 7 March 1941.

100. Ibid., A20/4, 12 December 1940.

101. Hinsley and Simkins, *British Intelligence*, 17.

102. LKPA, libel case file, Kerney pocket diary entry, 15 December 1940. The entry notes only the meeting with Budge in the Palace Hotel. Kerney did not record what was discussed.

103. NAI, DFA, A20 annex, letter from Frank Ryan to Leopold Kerney, 11 December 1940.

104. Ibid.

105. Ibid., A20/4, Leopold Kerney to Joseph Walshe, 26 August 1940.

106. Ibid., note by Frederick Boland to Colonel Dan Bryan, 8 June 1946.

107. Ibid., Leopold Kerney to Frederick Boland, 22 January 1945.

108. Bryan's report of this meeting is dated 20 October 1941. Kerney's diary records the meeting as taking place on 17 October at McKee Barracks. Kerney also noted that Captain Joseph Healy, who was later used by Bryan to spy on Kerney in Madrid in 1943, was also in attendance. Bryan did not record Healy's attendance at this meeting in his report. LKPA, "Jan. 1941– Apr. 43 Personal LHK," diary entry, 17 October 1941.

109. NAI, DFA, A20/4, memorandum written by Colonel Dan Bryan on the Ryan case for Joseph Walshe, 20 October 1941.

110. Ibid.

111. Ibid.

112. Ibid.

113. Ibid., A47, cipher wire from the Madrid legation to the Department of External Affairs sent 24 November 1941.

114. MAI, G2/X/0093, secret report from Colonel Dan Bryan to Joseph Walshe, 16 January 1946.

Chapter 8. Inside the Viper's Nest

1. Years later, Eilís Ryan still felt grateful to Kerney for all he had done to try to free her brother: "He [Kerney] did everything possible," she said. See Ó Canainn, "Oral History," 138.

2. Lemass was the minister for Industry and Commerce and minister for Supplies, Little the minister for Posts and Telegraphs, and Ryan the minister for Agriculture; Leydon was the secretary of Industry and Commerce; Briscoe was a Fianna Fáil politician who served as TD and was the first Jewish deputy elected to the Dáil; MacBride was a republican lawyer; Gallagher was director of the Government Information Bureau; and Camiña was a Basque exile living in Ireland who had been sentenced in absentia by a Francoist court.

3. LKPA, "Jan. 41–Apr. 43 Personal LHK," diary records.

4. O'Kelly was the minister for finance, Aiken the minister for the coordination of defensive measures.

5. LKPA, "Jan. 41–Apr. 43 Personal LHK," speech by Leopold Kerney on the occasion of Micheline Kerney's marriage, 30 September 1941.

6. Ferriter, *Judging Dev*, 189.

7. The opinions of writers such as Francis Stuart were also sought by the Germans.

8. NAI, DFA, A51, Frederick Boland to Leopold Kerney, 6 May 1940.

9. Ibid., Leopold Kerney to Joseph Walshe, 22 May 1940.

10. BNAK, KV 2/1976, "Friedrich Wolfgang Blaum" file, report by US Forces European Theater Military Intelligence Service Center, 12 January 1946.

11. Ibid., KV 2/769, "Kurt Haller" file.

12. Ibid.

13. BNAK, KV 6/81, "Helmut Clissmann" file, notes concerning conversations with L. H. Kerney, Irish minister in Spain, 4 April 1946.

14. NAI, DFA, A51, Chief Superintendant Patrick Carroll to Joseph Walshe, 4 May 1943.

15. Ibid., secret report from Colonel Dan Bryan to Joseph Walshe, 7 October 1943.

16. BNAK, Constitutional Department, Con 386/9/1, Dr Edmund Veesenmayer to Under State Secretary and Director of the Political Department, German Foreign Ministry, Ernst Woermann, 21 June 1941.

17. Ibid., 18 May 1941.

18. Höhne, *The Order of the Death's Head*, 281.

19. *Documents on German Foreign Policy, 1918–1945*, 365.

20. "Operation Taube II" was Veesenmayer's sequel to the failed landing of Russell and Ryan by submarine. It, too, failed to materialize. See BNAK, KV 2/1292, "Frank Ryan" file.

21. BNAK, Constitutional Department, Con 386/9/1, request issued by Under State Secretary Ernst Woermann to Hofrat Reimke, 3 November 1941.

22. NAI, DFA, A20 annex, letter from Frank Ryan to Leopold Kerney, 6 November 1941.

23. Ibid.

24. Kerney's record of the second meeting states that it took place on 10 November.

25. BNAK, Constitutional Department, Con 386/9/1, report signed by Helmut Clissmann and forwarded for submission to Under State Secretary and Director of the Political Department, German Foreign Ministry, Ernst Woermann, 5 December 1941.

26. Ibid.

27. Ibid.

28. Ibid.

29. Ibid.

30. Ibid.

31. Ibid.

32. BNAK, Constitutional Department, Con 386/9/1, Dr Edmund Veesenmayer to Under State Secretary and Director of the Political Department, German Foreign Ministry, Ernst Woermann, 24 November 1941.

33. Ibid.

34. Ibid.

35. Ibid.

36. Ibid.

37. Ibid.

38. BNAK, 6/81, "Helmut Clissmann" file, secret interview with Helmut Clissmann concerning conversations with L. H. Kerney, Irish minister to Spain, 4 April 1946.

39. Ibid.

40. NAI, DFA, A47, extract from the decoding of a cipher wire from the Madrid legation, 24 November 1941.

41. BNAK, HS 9/834/7595916, "Michael Kerney" file.

42. Ibid.

43. Ibid., HS 9/834/7595916, commandant's report, 30 June 1942.

44. Ibid., finishing report, 20 July 1942.

45. Ibid., note from D/R to D/F, 25 September 1942.

46. Ibid., letter from H. Trevor Jones, 4 September 1942.

47. LKPA, memorandum, "Ireland in Relation to the War of 1939 to 19??," 20 September 1940, 2.

48. Ibid.

49. Ibid., 3.

50. Ibid., 4.

51. Ibid., 4–5.

52. Ibid., 5.

53. Ibid.

54. Ibid.

55. Ibid., 5–6.

56. Ibid., 6.

57. Ibid.

58. LKPA, letter from Leopold Kerney to Frank Ryan, 20 January 1942.

59. BNAK, Constitutional Department, Con 386/9/1, Dr Edmund Veesenmayer to Under State Secretary and Director of the Political Department, German Foreign Ministry, Ernst Woermann, 29 January 1942.

60. O'Halpin, *Defending Ireland*, 197.

61. Mark Hull, *Irish Secrets*, 191.

62. Kennedy, "Leopold Harding Kerney."

63. BNAK, KV 2/769, "Kurt Haller" file.

64. Paine, *The Abwehr*, 57.

65. NAI, DFA, A47, report by Frederick Boland to Seán Nunan, 23 March 1954.

66. West, *The Guy Liddell Diaries*, vol. 2, 5.

67. NAI, DFA, A20 annex, letter from Frank Ryan to Leopold Kerney, 14 January 1942.

68. BNAK, Constitutional Department, Con 386/9/1, Dr Edmund Veesenmayer to Under State Secretary and Director of the Political Department, German Foreign Ministry, Ernst Woermann, 29 January 1942.

69. Ibid., KV 2/769, "Kurt Haller" file.

70. LKPA, "Libel Case" file, memorandum, 23 July 1953, 1.

71. NAI, DFA, A20 annex, letter from Frank Ryan to Leopold Kerney, 14 May 1942.

72. Ibid.

73. LKPA, "Libel Case" file, memorandum, 23 July 1953, 2.

74. NAI, DFA, A20 annex, letter from Frank Ryan to Leopold Kerney, 13 August 1942.

75. *Documents on German Foreign Policy*, 365.

76. LKPA, "Libel Case" file, memorandum, 23 July 1953, 2.

77. Hull, *Irish Secrets*, 192–93.

78. Ibid., 193.

79. Beevor, *Stalingrad*, 129.

80. BNAK, Constitutional Department, Con 386/9/1, synopsis of report by Dr Edmund Veesenmayer on his meeting with Leopold Kerney, 5 October 1942.

81. Ibid.

82. Ibid.

83. Ibid.

84. O'Halpin, *Defending Ireland*, 196–97.

85. Kennedy, "Leopold Harding Kerney."

86. NAI, DFA, A47, Leopold Kerney to Joseph Walshe, 24 August 1942.

87. Ibid.

88. Ibid.

89. Ibid.

90. Ibid.

91. Ibid.

92. Ibid. In the document Kerney typed "England" when he probably meant "Britain." He always equated Ireland's troubles with just the English.

93. Ibid., Leopold Kerney to Joseph Walshe, 24 August 1942.

94. Ibid.

95. Ibid.

96. Ibid.

97. Ibid.

98. Ibid.

99. Ibid.

100. Ibid.

101. Ibid.

102. Ibid.

103. Ibid.

104. Ibid.

105. Ibid.

106. Ibid.

107. Keogh, *Ireland and Europe*, 169.

108. AMAE, leg. R—987/E30, records of a private meeting between Juan Garcia Ontiveros and the Taoiseach, 6 January 1941.

109. NAI, DT S12622, incidences of meetings during Emergency, 1941–1944, 13 February 1943.

110. West, *The Guy Liddell Diaries*, vol. 1, 190.

111. MAI, G2/X/0040A, file titled "Masonic Studies," G2/4001–3 files on Basque exiles, G2/X/0923 file on Catalan exile Federico Sabater Cid, G2/0267 file on Ambrose Martin, etc.

112. TCD, Frederick Boland Papers, 10470/62.

113. Keogh, *Ireland and Europe*, 36.

114. NAI, DFA, A47, decode of cipher wire from Madrid legation to External Affairs, 24 November 1941.

115. BNAK, KV 6/81 "Helmut Clissmann" file, secret interview with Helmut Clissmann concerning conversations with L. H. Kerney, Irish minister in Spain, 2 February 1946.

116. Ibid., 4 April 1946.

117. Ibid., Constitutional Department, Con 386/9/1, Dr Edmund Veesenmayer to Under State Secretary and Director of the Political Department German Foreign Ministry Ernst Woermann, 23 January 1943.

118. Ibid.

119. Ibid.

120. Ibid.

121. LKPA, "Letters to Maurice file, 1937–50," letter from Leopold Kerney to Maurice Kerney, 28 August 1943.

122. Ibid., "Jan 41–Apr 43 Personal LHK," diary records, 27 March 1943.

123. Ibid.

124. NAI, DFA, A47, report by Frederick Boland to Seán Nunan, 3 March 1954.

125. LKPA, "Jan. 41–Apr. 43 Personal LHK," diary records, 8 April 1943.

126. Ibid., "Libel Case" file, memorandum, 23 July 1953, 2.

127. Ibid.

128. Ibid.

Chapter 9. Confidential Reports from Fascist Spain, 1939–1945

1. Garvin, *Preventing the Future*, 44.

2. Bartlett, *Ireland*, 352.

3. LKPA, letter from Leopold Kerney to Maurice Kerney, 30 August 1941.

4. NAI, DFA, 119/17A, trade statistics between Ireland and Spain for the years 1935 and 1936.

5. LKPA, "Organisation and Activities of the Irish Legation in Spain for the Year Ended 31st March 1940," annual report compiled by Leopold Kerney for the Department of External Affairs, 4 April 1940.

6. Ibid.

7. Ibid.

8. Ibid.

9. Ibid.

10. AMAE, leg. R—2073/E14, report titled "Memorandum of Reply to the Irish Legation," 11 June 1940, 3.

11. LKPA, "Organisation and Activities of the Irish Legation in Spain for the Year Ended 31st March 1940."

12. NAI, DFA, 235/24, telegram from the Catholic Boy Scouts of Ireland for General Franco, 14 April 1939.

13. LKPA, letter from Leopold Kerney to Maurice Kerney, 20 March 1939.

14. Ibid., "Organisation and Activities of the Irish Legation in Spain for the Year Ended 31st March 1940."

15. NAI, DFA, 219/2, Kerney to the Department of External Affairs, 7 July 1939.

16. Ibid.

17. AMAE, leg. R—1467/E14, BOE, 4 September 1939.

18. Whealey, *Hitler and Spain*, 67.

19. NAI, DFA, 219/2, Kerney to the Department of External Affairs, 1 October 1939.

20. For a good account of the National Tribunal for Political Responsibilities, see Ruiz, *Franco's Justice*.

21. Vincent, *Spain 1833–2002*, 157.

22. NAI, DFA, 219/2, Kerney to the Department of External Affairs, 9 October 1939.

23. Ibid., 2 November 1939.

24. Ibid.

25. Ibid.

26. Ibid., 9 November 1939.

27. Ibid., 17 November 1939.

28. Ibid.

29. Ibid.

30. Ibid.

31. Ibid., 202/482, Leopold Kerney to the Department of External Affairs, 9 July 1940.

32. Ibid., Leopold Kerney to Joseph Walshe, 17 January 1941.

33. Ibid., Joseph Walshe to Leopold Kerney, 28 January 1941.

34. Ibid., Leopold Kerney to Joseph Walshe, 14 February 1941.

35. Ibid., 219/2A, 25 March 1940.

36. Ibid., 11 March 1940.

37. *Irish Independent*, 22 January 1940.

38. AMAE, leg. R—4006/E7, letter from *Irish Independent* editor Frank Geary to the Spanish minister in Dublin, Juan Garcia Ontiveros, 30 January 1940.

39. *Irish Independent*, 5 June 1940.

40. Preston, *The Spanish Civil War*, 302.

41. NAI, DFA, 219/2A, private meeting between Leopold Kerney and Ramón Serrano Súñer, 3 December 1940.

42. Ibid.

43. *Documents on German Foreign Policy, 1918–1945*, Series D, vol. 11, 788.

44. LKPA, Leopold Kerney to the Department of External Affairs, 8 June 1943.

45. Ibid.

46. Ibid.

47. Ibid.

48. Ibid.

49. Ibid., 17 June 1943.

50. Ibid.

51. Ibid.

52. Ibid., 23 September 1943.

53. Ibid.

54. Ibid.

55. Ibid.

56. Ibid., 6 October 1943.

57. Ibid.

58. NAI, DFA, 219/2B, Leopold Kerney to the Department of External Affairs, 29 January 1945.

59. Ibid., 313/9, Leopold Kerney to the Department of External Affairs, 13 June 1945.

60. Preston, *The Spanish Civil War*, 313.

61. Bartlett, *Ireland*, 463.

62. Kennedy, "Leopold Harding Kerney."

63. UCDA, Éamon de Valera papers, P150/2676, Éamon de Valera to Robert Brennan, 21 May 1945.

64. Ibid.

65. NAI, DFA, 219/2B, report of the private meeting between Leopold Kerney and General Jordana, 10 September 1942.

66. Ibid.

67. Ibid.

68. 17 March 1939—"Treaty of Friendship and Non-Aggression," and 29 July 1940—Additional Protocol, both in Whealey, *Hitler and Spain.*

69. Gómez-Jordana Souza, *Milicia y diplomacia*, 192.

70. Doussinague, *España tenía razón*, 144.

71. NAI, DFA, 205/120, Leopold Kerney to the Department of External Affairs, 7 January 1943.

72. Doussinague, *España tenía razón*, 151.

73. AMAE, leg. R—1375/E11, file titled "Foreign Policy: Information of or about Ireland."

74. Ibid., report from J. M. Doussinague to General Jordana, 9 February 1943.

75. Ibid.

76. Ibid.

77. Ibid.

78. Ibid.

79. Ibid., leg. R—1370/E7, J. M. Doussinague to General Jordana, 11 January 1943.

80. NAI, DFA, 205/120, Joseph Walshe to Leopold Kerney, 29 January 1943.

81. Ibid., 243/895, letter from the IRCS to Joseph Walshe, 20 January 1943.

82. For an account of Spain's relationship with the Jewish community, see Chillida, *El antisemitismo en España.*

83. NAI, DFA, 243/895, John Dulanty to Joseph Walshe, 12 February 1943.

84. Ibid., John Belton to Joseph Walshe, 18 February 1943.

85. Ibid., 19 February 1943.

86. AMAE, leg. R—1371/E9, Duke of Alba to General Jordana, 25 February 1943.

87. Ibid.

88. Ibid.

89. Ibid.

90. Ibid., General Jordana's instructions to the Spanish embassy, 25 February 1943.

91. NAI, DFA, 243/895, permission granted by the Dominions Office for the transport of relief aid on Irish ships, 24 February 1943.

92. Ibid., notes on a private meeting between Juan Garcia Ontiveros and Joseph Walshe, 25 February 1943.

93. Ibid.

94. Ibid., Leopold Kerney to Joseph Walshe, 9 February 1943.

95. Ibid.

96. Ibid., letter from Reverend Allen to Joseph Walshe, 4 March 1943.

97. *Irish Press*, 30 March 1943.

98. Irish Red Cross Society (IRCS), *Report of the Chairman of the Irish Red Cross Society*, 1943, 212.

99. AMAE, leg. R—2149/E21, letter from Joseph Walshe to Juan Garcia Ontiveros, 18 November 1943.

100. Ibid., General Jordana to Juan Garcia Ontiveros, 14 August 1943.

101. NAI, DFA, 243/895, Leopold Kerney to Joseph Walshe, 9 August 1943.

102. Ibid.

103. Ibid.

104. Ibid., P. J. O'Byrne to the Department of External Affairs, 1 October 1943.

105. Ibid., Leopold Kerney to Joseph Walshe, 11 February 1944.

106. Ibid.

107. Ibid., 31 December 1943.

108. Ibid., 15 February 1944.

109. Ibid., Joseph Walshe to Leopold Kerney, 3 July 1944.

110. Ibid.

111. Ibid., 219/2B, speech delivered by General Franco in Almería, 9 May 1943.

112. Ibid., speech delivered by General Jordana, 16 April 1943.

113. Nolan, *Joseph Walshe*, 300.

114. NAI, DFA, P100, meeting of Irish diplomats in Iveagh House, 11 September 1945.

115. Ibid.

116. Ibid.

117. For an account of Walshe's character, see Dermot Keogh, "Profile of Joseph Walshe."

118. NAI, DFA, P100, meeting of Irish diplomats at Iveagh House, 11 September 1945.

119. Ibid.

Chapter 10. New Beginnings, 1946–1948

1. The couple purchased 5 Merton Road, Rathmines, which became Kerney's home until he died in 1962.

2. LKPA, "Letters to Maurice file, 1937–50," letter from Leopold Kerney to Maurice Kerney, 27 October 1946.

3. Nolan, *Joseph Walshe*, 313.

4. LKPA, "Letters to Raymonde File, 15 Nov. 1945–15 Dec. 1946," letter from Leopold Kerney to Raymonde Kerney, 6 February 1946.

5. Ibid., 26 February 1946.

6. Ibid.

7. For a biography of Con Cremin, see Keogh, *Con Cremin*.

8. LKPA, "Letters to Raymonde File, 15 Nov. 1945–15 Dec. 1946," letter from Leopold Kerney to Raymonde Kerney, 14 April 1946.

9. Ibid.

10. Ibid., 21 April 1946.

11. Ibid., 16 November 1946.

12. Ibid.

13. Ibid., 15 December 1946.

14. Ibid.

15. UCDA, Michael MacWhite papers, P194/707.

16. *Arriba*, 14 October 1945.

17. LKPA, "Letters to Raymonde File, 15 Nov. 1945–15 Dec. 1946," letter from Leopold Kerney to Raymonde Kerney, 15 December 1946.

18. Ibid.

19. NAI, DT, S7911B, report on Kerney's retirement and proposal for his successor, John Belton.

20. LKPA, "Letters to Raymonde File, 15 Nov. 1945–15 Dec. 1946," letter from Leopold Kerney to Raymonde Kerney, 15 December 1946.

21. Ibid., "Letters to Maurice file, 1937–50," letter from Leopold Kerney to Maurice Kerney, 12 September 1948.

22. Ibid., 3 February 1947.

23. Ibid.

24. Ibid.

25. Ibid., 1 August 1948.

26. Ibid., 11 December 1949.

27. Ibid., 29 January 1948.

28. Ibid., 15 February 1948.

29. See McCullagh, *A Makeshift Majority*.

30. Horgan, *Seán Lemass*, 131.

31. AGA, 10/3954/11736, Marquess Miraflores to the Ministry of Foreign Affairs, 31 October 1947.

32. LKPA, letter from Leopold Kerney to Seán MacBride, 19 February 1948.

33. Ibid., letter from Leopold Kerney to Éamon de Valera, 20 February 1948.

34. Hoare, *Ambassador on Special Mission*; Súñer, *Entre Hendaya y Gibraltar*.

35. Doussinague, *España tenía razón*.

36. LKPA, "Letters to Maurice file, 1937–50," letter from Leopold Kerney to Maurice Kerney, 19 March 1950.

37. Ibid., letter from Leopold Kerney to José María Doussinague, 1 April 1950.

38. Kearns, *Ireland's Arctic Siege*.

39. Doherty and Keogh, *De Valera's Irelands*.

40. DÉD, vol. 104, no. 4, 29 January 1947.

41. Ibid.

42. LKPA, memorandum titled "Political Side of Mr. Kerney's Mission to Argentina," 22 June 1947, 1.

43. Ibid.

44. Ibid., 2.

45. Ibid., 3.

46. Ibid., 5.

47. Ibid., 12.

48. Ibid., 17.

49. Ibid., 13.

50. Ibid., 16.

51. Ibid., speech delivered by Leopold Kerney to the Argentine-Irish community in Buenos Aires, 28 May 1947.

52. Ibid.

53. Ibid.

54. Ibid.

55. Ibid.

56. *Irish Times*, 5 June 1947.

57. LKPA, memorandum titled "Mr. Kerney's Visit to Chile 10th–19th May, 1947," 22 June 1947, 1.

58. Ibid., 2.

59. Ibid., 3.

60. Ibid.

61. Ibid., 5.

62. Ibid., "Letters to Maurice file, 1937–50," letter from Leopold Kerney to Maurice Kerney, 20 August 1948.

Chapter 11. "When sorrows come, they come not single spies, but in battalions!"

1. UCDA, Dan Bryan papers, P71/142, Dan Bryan's written notes recollecting events for the years 1940, 1950.

2. MacBride was a prominent republican, Camiña a Basque refugee in Ireland during World War II, and Briscoe a Jewish TD.

3. NAI, DFA, A8.

4. MAI, G2/0267, "Ambrose Martin" file, Colonel Dan Bryan to Joseph Walshe, 6 December 1945.

5. Ó Drisceoil, *Censorship in Ireland*, 83–84.

6. O'Halpin, *Defending Ireland*, 194.

7. LKPA, libel case file, typed memorandum by Leopold Kerney, 23 July 1953.

8. NAI, DFA, 202/984, correspondence related to the Loreto nuns in Spain and the mother general, Loreto Abbey, Rathfarnham, 9 September 1940.

9. Ibid., A8.

10. MAI, G2/3666, letter from Charles Bewley to Leopold Kerney, 30 January 1942.

11. NAI, DFA, A8, Colonel Liam Archer to Joseph Walshe, 7 March 1941.

12. Ibid., A20/4, departmental note from Joseph Walshe to Colonel Dan Bryan related to copies of "letters received from Frank Ryan," 10 January 1942.

13. LKPA, libel case file, letter from Leopold Kerney to Eilís Ryan, 18 December 1940.

14. Ibid., letter from Leopold Kerney to Frank Ryan, 10 November 1941.

15. Ibid., letter from Budge Clissmann to Leopold Kerney, 17 July 1941.

16. Ibid.

17. NAI, DFA, A8, Joseph Walshe to Colonel Liam Archer, 10 May 1941.

18. Ibid., P71, letter from Leopold Kerney to Frank Litton, 10 June 1942.

19. Ibid., Joseph Walshe to Leopold Kerney, 15 June 1942.

20. Ibid., letter from Leopold Kerney dated 5 December 1942 and opened by the Irish censor.

21. Ibid., A47, report by Frederick Boland to Seán Nunan, 3 March 1954.

22. Ibid.

23. LKPA, "Jan. 41–Apr. 43 Personal LHK," diary records, 2 March 1943.

24. Ibid., 12 March 1943.

25. Ibid., 27 March 1943.

26. Ibid.

27. Ibid.

28. Ibid.

29. NAI, DFA, A47, report by Frederick Boland to Seán Nunan, 3 March 1954.

30. Ibid.

31. Ibid., A8, report by Captain Joseph Healy to Colonel Dan Bryan, 24 May 1943.

32. Ibid.

33. Ibid.

34. Ibid.

35. Ibid.

36. LKPA, "Jan. 41–Apr. 43 Personal LHK," diary records, 8 April 1943.

37. Ibid.

38. Ibid.

39. NAI, DFA, A20/4, Colonel Dan Bryan to Joseph Walshe, 29 October 1942.

40. Ibid., Colonel Liam Archer to Joseph Walshe, 12 December 1940.

41. LKPA, letter from Leopold Kerney to Mrs Chauviré, 13 July 1942.

42. Ibid., letter from Leopold Kerney to Seán Murphy, 21 May 1942.

43. Ibid., letter from Leopold Kerney to Mrs Chauviré, 24 July 1942.

44. NAI, DFA, P71 (II), note by Joseph Walshe to Leopold Kerney, 19 December 1944.

45. Donal Ó Drisceoil, *Censorship in Ireland*, 290.

46. NAI, DFA, P71 (II). On 10 January 1942 and 18 March 1942 Walshe sent Bryan two copies of Frank Ryan's letters that Kerney had forwarded to Dublin.

47. Ibid., A20/4, telegram from Joseph Walshe to Leopold Kerney, 31 August 1945.

48. Ibid., request from Colonel Dan Bryan to Frederick Boland for copies of Frank Ryan's letters to Leopold Kerney, 17 August 1945.

49. Ibid., note by Colonel Dan Bryan and Major Guilfoyle on interview with L. V. Mill Arden, 11 January 1945.

50. Ibid.

51. McGuire, "T. Desmond Williams," 3.

52. The most damning articles by Williams in the *Irish Press* were published on 10 and 11 July 1953.

53. Williams, "A Study in Neutrality," 19.

54. Ibid., 19–20.

55. Ibid., 20.

56. Ibid.

57. Handwritten note by Professor Thomas Desmond Williams, 1 March 1954, in ibid., vol. 53, no. 7 (11 April 1953).

58. Williams, "A Study in Neutrality," 21.

59. Ibid.

60. Ibid.

61. Ibid.

62. Ibid.

63. Ibid., 21–22.

64. LKPA, "Letters to Maurice file, 1937–50," letter from Leopold Kerney to Maurice Kerney, 11 December 1949.

65. Ibid., 19 March 1950.

66. LKPA, libel case file, memorandum by Leopold Kerney, 29 October 1954.

67. NAI, DFA A47, letter from Leopold Kerney to Seán Nunan, 13 July 1953.

68. Ibid.

69. Ibid., note from Seán Nunan to Leo McCauley, 10 March 1954.

70. Ibid., undated department draft.

71. LKPA, memorandum, "Mr Kerney's attitude towards defendants," 29 October 1954.

72. Ibid.

73. Ibid.

74. Ibid.

75. Ibid.

76. Ibid.

77. LPKA, signed memorandum by Helmut Clissmann, 23 April 1954.

78. Ibid.

79. Ibid.

80. Ibid.

81. Ibid.

82. Ibid.

83. Ibid.

84. Ibid.

85. Ibid.

86. Ibid.

87. Ibid.

88. Ibid.

89. Ibid.

90. Ibid.

91. Ibid.

92. Ibid.

93. LPKA, signed questionnaire by Helmut Clissmann submitted to Leopold Kerney and his solicitor, Seán Ó hUadhaigh, 8 October 1954.

94. Ibid.

95. Ibid.

96. Ibid.

97. Ibid.

98. Ibid.

99. Ibid.

100. BNAK, FO 370/2380, copy of a letter from Professor Thomas Desmond Williams to Ernest Passant, 23 February 1954.

101. Ibid., handwritten notes by Margaret Lambert, 24 February 1954.

102. Ibid., handwritten notes by Ian Sinclair, 25 February 1954.

103. Ibid., handwritten minutes of a meeting between Professor Thomas Desmond Williams and Ernest Passant, 27 February 1954.

104. Ibid.

105. Ibid.

106. Ibid., Constitutional Department, Con 386/9/1, letter from Richard Sedgwick to Sir Percivale Liesching, 8 March 1954.

107. Ibid., FO 370/238, letter from Ernest Passant to Professor Thomas Desmond Williams, 19 March 1954.

108. NAI, DFA, A47, report by Conor Cruise O'Brien, 29 September 1954.

109. Ibid.

110. Ibid.

111. Ibid.

112. NAI, DFA, P168, notes by Conor Cruise O'Brien, 13 October 1954.

113. Ibid., departmental record of transfer of a copy of the Haller interview by O'Brien to the Department of Defense, 19 October 1954.

114. Ibid., A47, report by Frederick Boland to Seán Nunan, 23 March 1954.

115. Ibid.

116. Ibid.

117. Ibid.

118. Ibid., Dr. Michael Rynne to Seán Nunan, 22 October 1953.

119. Ibid., note by Seán Nunan to Joseph Walshe on Dr. Michael Rynne's viewpoints, 6 October 1953.

120. Keogh, *The Vatican, the Bishops and Irish Politics*, 127.

121. Ibid.

122. Ibid., 150.

123. Ibid., 127.

124. NAI, DFA, A47, report by Joseph Walshe to Seán Nunan, 21 May 1953.

125. Ibid.

126. Ibid.

127. Ibid.

128. Ibid.

129. Ó Drisceoil, *Censorship in Ireland*, 185.

130. NAI, DFA, A47, report by Joseph Walshe to Seán Nunan, 6 July 1953.

131. Ibid., 9 July 1953.

132. LKPA, libel case file, cases lodged with the High Court of Justice, nos. 1283P and 1284P, December 1953.

133. Ibid., letter from Alexis FitzGerald of McCann, White & FitzGerald to Seán Ó hUadhaigh, 28 October 1954.

134. *Irish Times*, 5 November 1954.
135. Hull, *Irish Secrets*, 193.
136. *Irish Times*, 5 November 1954.
137. Ibid.
138. O'Halpin, *Spying on Ireland*, 292.
139. Duggan, *Herr Hempel at the German Legation in Dublin*, 211.
140. *Irish Times*, 5 November 1954.
141. Roberts, *A History of the English-Speaking Peoples*.
142. Coogan, *De Valera*, 619.
143. *Irish Times*, 11 June 1962.

Aldcroft, Derek, and Steven Morewood. *The European Economy since 1914*. 5th ed. London: Routledge, 2013.

Andrew, Christopher. *The Defence of the Realm: The Authorized History of MI5*. London: Allen Lane, 2009.

Andrews, C. S. *Man of No Property*. Dublin: Lilliput Press, 1982.

Bartlett, Thomas. *Ireland: A History*. Cambridge: Cambridge University Press, 2010.

Beevor, Antony. *The Battle for Spain: The Spanish Civil War, 1936–1939*. London: Penguin Books, 2006.

———. *Stalingrad*. London: Penguin Books, 1999.

Bewley, Charles. *Memoirs of a Wild Goose*. Dublin: Lilliput, 1989.

Chadwick, Owen. *The Secularisation of the European Mind in the Nineteenth Century*. Cambridge: Cambridge University Press, 1990.

Chambers, Anne. *T. K. Whitaker: Portrait of a Patriot*. London: Doubleday Ireland, 2014.

Chillida, G. Á. *El antisemitismo en España: La imagen del Judío*. Madrid: Marcial Pons, 2002.

Clarke, Frances, "Helmut Clissmann." Entry in the *Dictionary of Irish Biography*. www.dib.cambridge.org. Accessed 15 September 2016.

Coogan, Tim Pat. *De Valera: Long Fellow, Long Shadow*. London: Arrow Books, 1994.

———. *Ireland in the Twentieth Century*. London: Arrow Books, 2004.

Craig, Patricia. *The Oxford Book of Ireland*. Oxford: Oxford University Press, 1999.

Cronin, Seán. *Frank Ryan: The Search for the Republic*. Dublin: Repsol, 1980.

———. *The McGarrity Papers: Revelations of the Irish Revolutionary Movement in Ireland and America, 1900–1940*. Tralee: Anvil Books, 1972.

Crowley, John, Mike Murphy, Donal Ó Drisceoil, and John Borgonovo. *Atlas of the Irish Revolution*. Cork: Cork University Press, 2017.

Documents on German Foreign Policy, 1918–1945. Series D, vol. 11: *The War Years, 1 September 1940–31 January 1941*. London: H. M. Stationery Office, 1961.

Documents on German Foreign Policy, 1918–1945. Series D, vol. 13: *The War Years, 23 June 1941–11 December 1941*. London: H. M. Stationery Office, 1964.

Documents on Irish Foreign Policy, 1919–1922. Vol. 1. Dublin: Royal Irish Academy, 1998.

Doherty, Gabriel, and Dermot Keogh. *De Valera's Irelands*. Cork: Mercier Press, 2003.

Doussinague, J. M. *España tenía razón, 1939–1945*. Madrid: Espasa Calpe, 1949.

Duggan, J. P. *Herr Hempel at the German Legation in Dublin, 1937–1945*. Dublin: Irish Academic Press, 2003.

English, Richard. *Armed Struggle: The History of the IRA*. London: Pan Books, 2004.

———. *Irish Freedom: The History of Nationalism in Ireland*. London: Pan Books, 2007.

Feeney, Tom. *Seán MacEntee: A Political Life*. Dublin: Irish Academic Press, 2009.

Ferriter, Diarmaid. *Judging Dev: A Reassessment of the Life and Legacy of Eamon de Valera*. Dublin: Royal Irish Academy, 2007.

———. *The Transformation of Ireland, 1900–2000*. London: Profile Books, 2005.

Garvin, Tom. *The Lives of Daniel Binchy: Irish Scholar, Diplomat, Public Intellectual*. Kildare: Irish Academic Press, 2016.

———. *Preventing the Future: Why Was Ireland So Poor for So Long?* Dublin: Gill and MacMillan, 2004.

Gilbert, Martin. *History of the Twentieth Century*. London: Harper Collins, 2002.

Girvin, Brian. *The Emergency: Neutral Ireland, 1939–45*. London: Pan Books, 2007.

Gómez-Jordana Souza, Francisco. *Milicia y diplomacia: Los diarios del Conde de Jordana, 1936–1944*. Burgos: Dossoles, 2002.

Harmon, Maurice. *Seán Ó Faolain*. London: Constable, 1994.

Hastings, Max. *Catastrophe: Europe Goes to War, 1914*. London: William Collins, 2013.

Hinsley, F. H., and C.A.G. Simkins, eds. *British Intelligence in the Second World War: Security and Counter Intelligence*. 4 vols. London: H. M. Stationery Office, 1990.

Hoare, Sir Samuel. *Ambassador on Special Mission*. London: Collins, 1946.

Höhne, Heinz. *The Order of the Death's Head: The Story of Hitler's SS*. London: Penguin Books, 2000.

Horgan, John. *Seán Lemass: The Enigmatic Patriot.* Dublin: Gill and MacMillan 1999.

Hull, Mark. *Irish Secrets: German Espionage in Wartime Ireland, 1939–1945.* Dublin: Irish Academic Press, 2003.

Jeffery, Keith. *MI6: The History of the Secret Intelligence Service, 1909–1949.* London: Bloomsbury, 2010.

Johnstone, Tom. *Orange, Green and Khaki: The Story of the Irish Regiments in the Great War, 1914–18.* Dublin: Gill and MacMillan, 1992.

Kearns, Kevin. *Ireland's Arctic Siege: The Big Freeze of 1947.* Dublin: Gill and MacMillan, 2011.

Keatinge, Patrick. *The Formulation of Irish Foreign Policy.* Dublin: Institute of Public Administration, 1973.

Kedward, Rod. *La Vie en Bleu: France and the French since 1900.* London: Penguin Books, 2006.

Kennedy, Michael. "The Irish Free State and the League of Nations, 1922–32: The Wider Implications." *Irish Studies in International Affairs* 3, no. 4 (1992).

———. "Leopold Harding Kerney." Entry in the *Dictionary of Irish Biography.* www.dib.cambridge.org. Accessed 3 September 2016.

———. "Leopold Kerney and the Origin of Irish-Spanish Diplomatic Relations: 1935–36." In *Spanish-Irish Relations through the Ages,* ed. Declan Downey and J. C. MacLennan. Dublin: Four Courts Press, 2008.

Keogh, Dermot. *Ireland and Europe, 1919–1948.* Dublin: Gill and MacMillan, 1988.

———. "Profile of Joseph Walshe, Secretary, Department of Foreign Affairs, 1922–46." *Irish Studies in International Affairs* 3 (1990): 59–80.

———. *The Vatican, the Bishops and Irish Politics, 1919–39.* Cambridge: Cambridge University Press, 1986.

Keogh, Niall. *Con Cremin: Ireland's Wartime Diplomat.* Cork: Mercier Press, 2006.

Keown, Gerard. *First of the Small Nations: The Beginnings of Irish Foreign Policy in the Interwar Years, 1919–1932.* Oxford: Oxford University Press, 2016.

Laffan, Michael. *The Resurrection of Ireland: The Sinn Féin Party, 1916–1923.* Cambridge: Cambridge University Press, 1999.

Lee, J. J. *Ireland, 1912–1985: Politics and Society.* Cambridge: Cambridge University Press, 1989.

Leitz, Christian. *Nazi Foreign Policy, 1933–1941: The Road to Global War.* London: Routledge. 2004.

———. *Nazi Germany and Neutral Europe during the Second World War.* Manchester: Manchester University Press, 2000.

Leopold Harding Kerney, Irish Minister to Spain, 1935–1946. Website. http://www.leopoldhkerney.com. Accessed 15 October 2016.

MacLysaght, Edward. *The Surnames of Ireland*. Dublin: Irish Academic Press, 1985.

Maguire, Martin. *The Civil Service and the Revolution in Ireland, 1912–38: "Shaking the Blood-Stained Hand of Mr Collins."* Manchester: Manchester University Press, 2008.

Maillot, Agnès. *New Sinn Féin: Irish Republicanism in the Twenty-First Century*. London: Routledge, 2005.

Manning, Maurice. *Irish Political Parties: An Introduction*. Dublin: Gill and MacMillan, 1972.

Matthews, Ann. *Dissidents: Irish Republican Women, 1923–1941*. Cork: Mercier Press, 2012.

McCullagh, David. *A Makeshift Majority: The First Inter-Party Government, 1948–51*. Dublin: Institute of Public Administration, 1998.

McGarry, Fearghal. *Irish Politics and the Spanish Civil War*. Cork: Cork University Press, 1999.

McGuire, James. "T. Desmond Williams (1921–87)." *Irish Historical Studies* 26, no. 101 (1988): 3–7.

McLoughlin, Barry. *Fighting for Republican Spain, 1936–38: Frank Ryan and the Volunteers from Limerick in the International Brigades*. Cork: Lettertec Ireland, 2014.

National Archives of Ireland. 1901 Census. www.census.nationalarchives.ie/pages/1901/Dublin/PembrokeEast_Donnybrook/Sandymount_Road/1285884. Accessed 18 May 2015.

Nolan, Aengus. *Joseph Walshe: Irish Foreign Policy, 1922–1946*. Cork: Mercier Press, 2008.

O'Brien, Máire Cruise. *The Same Age as the State*. Dublin: O'Brien Press, 2003.

Ó Canainn, Aodh. "Oral History: Eilís Ryan in Her Own Words." *Saothar: Journal of the Irish Labour History Society* 21 (1996).

Ó Drisceoil, Donal. *Censorship in Ireland, 1939–45: Neutrality, Politics and Society*. Cork: Cork University Press, 1996.

O'Halpin, Eunan. *Defending Ireland: The Irish Free State and Its Enemies since 1922*. Oxford: Oxford University Press, 1999.

———. *MI5 and Ireland, 1939–1945: The Official History*. Dublin: Irish Academic Press, 2002.

———. *Spying on Ireland: British Intelligence and Irish Neutrality during the Second World War*. Oxford: Oxford University Press, 2008.

O'Rourke, Kevin. "Burn Everything British but Their Coal: The Anglo-Irish Economic War of the 1930s." *Journal of Economic History* 51, no. 2 (1991): 357.

Paine, Lauran. *The Abwehr: German Military Intelligence in World War Two*. London: Robert Hale, 1984.

Patterson, Henry. *Ireland since 1939: The Persistence of Conflict*. Dublin: Penguin Books, 2006.

Preston, Paul. *Franco: A Biography*. London: Harper Collins, 2003.

———. *The Spanish Civil War: Reaction, Revolution and Revenge*. London: Harper Perennial, 2006.

Regan, Geoffrey. *Famous British Battles*. London: O'Mara Books, 1997.

Roberts, Andrew. *A History of the English-Speaking Peoples since 1900*. London: Weidenfeld and Nicolson, 2007.

Roth, Andreas. *Mr. Bewley in Berlin*. Dublin: Four Courts Press, 2000.

Ruiz, Julius. *Franco's Justice: Repression in Madrid after the Spanish Civil War*. Oxford: Oxford University Press, 2005.

Russell, Michael. *The City in Darkness*. London: Constable, 2016.

Rust, William. *Britons in Spain: The History of the British Battalion of the XVth International Brigade*. London: Lawrence and Wishart, 1939.

Ryan, Meda. *Liam Lynch: The Real Chief*. Cork: Mercier Press, 2012.

Shakespeare, William. *The Complete Works of William Shakespeare Comprising His Plays and Poems*. London: Spring Books, 1958.

Súñer, R. S. *Entre Hendaya y Gibraltar*. Madrid: Planeta, 1947.

Trinity College Dublin. "History." https://www.tcd.ie/about/history. Accessed 2 July 2017.

Tusell, Javier. *Franco, España y la Segunda Guerra Mundial: Entre el eje y la neutralidad*. Madrid: Temas de Hoy, 1995.

UK Census Online, 1911 census. https://www.ukcensusonline.com/search/index.php?fn=leopold&sn=kerney&phonetic_mode=1&event=1911. Accessed 18 May 2015.

Vincent, Mary. *Spain, 1833–2002: People and State*. Oxford: Oxford University Press, 2007.

Ward, Margaret. *Hanna Sheehy Skeffington: A Life*. Cork: Cork University Press, 1997.

West, Nigel. *The Guy Liddell Diaries*. Vol. 1: *1939–1942*. London: Routledge, 2005.

———. *The Guy Liddell Diaries*. Vol. 2: *1942–1945*. London: Routledge, 2009.

Whealey, R. H. *Hitler and Spain: The Nazi Role in the Spanish Civil War, 1936–1939.* Lexington: University Press of Kentucky, 1989.

Whelan, Barry. "Éamon de Valera: A Republican Loan and the Secret of the Lost Russian Jewels." *Scoláire Staire* 3, no. 1 (2013): 24–28.

Williams, Thomas Desmond. "A Study in Neutrality." *Leader* 53, no. 6 (28 March 1953).

Wills, Clair. *That Neutral Island: A Cultural History of Ireland during the Second World War.* London: Faber and Faber, 2008.

BARRY WHELAN

is a lecturer of Irish and European history

at Dublin City University.

CPSIA information can be obtained
at www.ICGtesting.com
Printed in the USA
LVHW081120090121
675796LV00032B/300